THE EXTRAORDINARY JOURNEY OF DAVID INGRAM

AN ELIZABETHAN SAILOR IN NATIVE NORTH AMERICA

DEAN SNOW

OXFORD
UNIVERSITY PRESS

OXFORD
UNIVERSITY PRESS

Oxford University Press is a department of the University of Oxford. It furthers
the University's objective of excellence in research, scholarship, and education
by publishing worldwide. Oxford is a registered trade mark of Oxford University
Press in the UK and certain other countries.

Published in the United States of America by Oxford University Press
198 Madison Avenue, New York, NY 10016, United States of America.

CIP data is on file at the Library of Congress

ISBN 978-0-19-764800-1

DOI: 10.1093/oso/9780197648001.001.0001

1 3 5 7 9 8 6 4 2

Printed by Sheridan Books, Inc., United States of America

To Janet Charlene Snow

Contents

Preface

An Elizabethan sailor named David Ingram was cast away by the queen's slaver in 1568. In 1690 he was cast away again by his first editor, Richard Hakluyt. As a consequence, Ingram was repeatedly cast away as a liar by modern historians. Fortunately, a trio of key archival sources have survived, and their evidence shows that Ingram's remarkable story was a true account of one man's journey in the age of European discovery.

David Ingram was an ordinary man who lived an extraordinary life. Unfortunately, he has been vilified and condemned as a fraud and a liar by generations of historians for over four centuries. Once a reputation has been disgraced, it is easy for any number of others to follow the lead set by precedent and endlessly repeat the verdict. The loss of reputation, and sometimes freedom, can be swift, and its restoration can take a very long time. Here are just two examples of many condemnations in the Ingram case. "There are shreds of truth in what Ingram said, but most of his story was fantasy." "Verrazzano labeled the Penobscot River 'Norumbega' and David Ingram concocted an elaborate fantasy about the place 60 years later. Ingram's imaginary fairyland never existed, but it helped stimulate interest in English colonization." I wrote those lines in 1978, as a young scholar following the views established and maintained by leading scholars. I was wrong, not once but twice. Scholars should admit their mistakes, especially when they are repeated.

David Quinn, with whom I had brief correspondence in 1978–1980, was an exception to the traditional casual dismissal of Ingram's testimony. The redoubtable Quinn was apparently the only one who really studied the manuscripts that recorded Ingram's 1582 interrogation. Over the centuries, almost everyone else depended on Richard Hakluyt's badly flawed but more legible published version. However, even Quinn did not notice that the first 18 of the 84 entries in the most original manuscript all pertain to Ingram's time in Africa. He did not notice that Ingram had started his story with Africa in his 1582 interrogation. This might be because Quinn was not familiar enough with African ethnology to detect this important feature of the manuscript. Nevertheless, Quinn sensed that there might be more there than was generally appreciated in Ingram's testimony. In 1979 he wrote, "Ingram lied in things greater or smaller, but his tales of North America in the 1580s may have just sufficient substance to repay some further research by scholars with time on their hands." That observation has lingered in the back of my mind for over 40 years. Quinn died in 2002, not knowing how right he was about Ingram.

The primary reason that dismissal of Ingram has continued is that historians, like archaeologists and other practitioners of the historical disciplines, find that they must depend upon each other for reliable examinations and evaluations of primary evidence. There is simply too much of it to allow scholars to become intimately familiar with all the primary evidence underlying their generalizations and conclusions. Conclusions about historical events are sometimes contested, but this more often takes the form of critical exchanges of opinion rather than as attempts to reproduce results using the same evidence. The same problem burdens the sciences, except that in science one more frequently finds repeated testing of fundamental observations and conclusions, rigorous peer review of reported findings, attempts to reproduce results, and explicit retraction of flawed studies. In the long term, science has proven to be self-correcting in ways that too often historiography is not.

It is possible that young historians have seen Quinn's observation and have contemplated pursuing a reevaluation of David Ingram's story. They have been wise to avoid it, partly because there was always a good chance that the evidence would show that Ingram truly was a liar or that the evidence would be insufficient to show much of anything at all. This is also the kind of project that should only be taken on by an established scholar old enough to safely ignore such risks. Some of what is written in this book will not be well received by academics who have already invested in a negative view of Ingram, as I did in the 1970s. However, the evidence refuting that generally accepted view is all laid out in the chapters that follow. If I fail to persuade, the fault will not be with the evidence.

To the extent that I have succeeded in rescuing the valuable words of a long-dead explorer, I owe a huge debt to family and friends who have encouraged my decision to avoid living an unproductive retirement. Jan Snow, Kate Snow, and Mary Snow all read and helped make multiple versions of the manuscript clearer and more accessible. Three anonymous reviewers and my editor, Stefan Vranka, also saw multiple versions, and without them I would not have been able to produce an acceptable manuscript. Chris Breault, Barb Snow, Matt Vannelli, Josh Snow, Adrienne Costa Snow, Doug Gonzales, Barb Peterson, and Julie Whitney have all helped me to stay focused on David Ingram's story. They did so with unassuming generosity. My seven grandchildren have inspired me constantly, mainly by asking pointed questions and by simply being the unique people they already are.

To the extent that I have been able to avoid error here I owe my sincere thanks to the able critics in my family and in my circle of friends. Many of my friends are also professional colleagues. I am especially grateful to Jerald Milanich, Stanley Bond, David Guldenzopf, James Herbstritt, William Starna, Marianne Mithun, Ives Goddard, Micah Pawling, Philip Jenkins, Henry Miller, Julia King, Lorena Walsh, Joanne Bowen, Heather Lapham, Melinda Zeder, Susan Moore, Kaitlyn Krieg, George Chaplin, and Matthew McKnight for help that each of them probably regard as minor assistance but without which I would have been vulnerable to blunder. I have also had the help of many anonymous people working in museums, libraries, archives, and the media, people who love their work, do it well, and rarely receive the credit they deserve.

I am mindful that good authors invariably need excellent editors. David Ingram was incapable of writing his own account, and he was ill served by his editor, Richard Hakluyt. I have been much luckier. Stefan Vranka has been unfailingly supportive and highly skilled in coaching me through this and my previous book project with Oxford University Press. Tamsin Ballard, Jeremy Toynbee, Sean Decker, Patterson Lamb, Bob Land, and their able colleagues at OUP all made critical contributions, earning my profound thanks and my enduring admiration.

I

Introduction

In autumn 1567, a small fleet commanded by John Hawkins had sailed from Plymouth, England, with just over 400 men. Hawkins, who would come to be known as the queen's slaver, was launching his third slaving expedition, which he hoped would be as lucrative as the previous ones. David Ingram was one of the mostly anonymous able-bodied seamen manning the ships. Ingram, called Davy by his friends, had left the world of Elizabethan England as an ordinary seaman on a slaving expedition that took him from his familiar world, across the Tropic of Cancer to West Africa, then across the Atlantic to the Caribbean Sea. This second destination was what Columbus had called *El Otro Mundo*, the other world.

Almost a year after leaving Plymouth, a hurricane forced all but one of the ships to seek refuge in a hostile Spanish harbor on the Mexican Gulf Coast. After a furious battle, only two of the English ships escaped destruction, and half of the fleet's 400 men were either killed or captured. The larger of the two surviving ships was overloaded with most of the surviving half, but it had too little food for them all to endure a difficult voyage back to England. One hundred of them elected to be put ashore. Of those, half soon decided to turn themselves over to Spanish authorities and take their chances in captivity while the other half tried to escape northward. Half of those who initially went north soon turned back to join the others headed for captivity. Of the 26 who continued northward, only Ingram and two other men survived their walk of more than 3,600 miles to eventually be rescued 11 months later.

In the years that followed his return, no one doubted that David Ingram had been put ashore near Tampico, Mexico, in October 1568. No one doubted that Ingram was rescued by a French ship on the Bay of Fundy about a year later. Those facts were and are still certain. But the period between landing and rescue has generated considerable curiosity, controversy, and uncertainty. It has been an enigma for more than four centuries.

After returning to England in 1570, Ingram and the other two sailors, Richard Browne and Richard Twide, had gone back to work. Once the surprise of seeing them return alive wore off, their celebrity faded. Over a decade went by. During that time, Twide left sailing and found less dangerous work ashore at Ratcliff, in what is now the Limehouse section of London. He died there in about 1579. Browne went back to sea but was killed aboard the *Elizabeth* in 1578.[1] That left David Ingram as the only surviving veteran of the long walk from Tampico to New Brunswick, the only living Englishman with any substantial experience in the interior of eastern North America. But Ingram's knowledge of America was of little interest in England for as long as official interest in colonization there was left to the Portuguese, Spanish, and French.

English interest in the colonization of North America was ripening by 1582. A dozen years after Ingram's return, officials of Queen Elizabeth's administration and some leading investors finally sought him out for his unique insights into this foreign continent.

Leading explorers and investors approached Queen Elizabeth for permission and for support of a proposed venture. No one was certain about what resources, costs, perils, or opportunities faced the enthusiastic but poorly informed gentlemen of Elizabeth's court. An effort was launched to acquire as much information as possible for the planning of what would certainly be a costly and dangerous colonizing venture. David Ingram turned out to be a key source in that effort.

Ingram's story, his long walk through eastern North America at its core, plays out through the chapters that follow. However, that story is embedded in the wider history of the Age of Discovery. The threads of that wider history seriously corrupted Ingram's story in multiple ways, rendering it almost fatally incoherent. As a consequence, in telling Ingram's story it is necessary to disentangle those threads. The story, after all, was not independent of the context of Ingram's times. In that sense, it all began with an interrogation.

The Interrogation

On a day in late August 1582, Ingram found himself seated before a panel of distinguished gentlemen. They were a mix of officials from the court of

Elizabeth, some promoters of colonization in America, and a few less prominent men who had some firsthand knowledge of the things that were to be the subjects of Ingram's interrogation.

Ingram was facing Francis Walsingham, the queen's intimidating secretary of state, arguably the second most powerful figure in England, and a panel of other leading men. Walsingham had learned that Ingram purportedly knew much about the people and the resources of the east coast of North America. The interrogation was scheduled for late August and early September 1582.[2]

George Peckham, a wealthy Catholic investor, was the second man certain to have been in attendance at Ingram's interrogation. He reappears repeatedly in Ingram's story. The adventurer and would-be colonist Humphrey Gilbert and his employee John Walker were probably present for at least part of the interrogation. Richard Hakluyt, or his agent, was also there. Miles Phillips, another survivor of John Hawkins's third voyage who had recently escaped from the Spanish, was probably present at the interrogation. Phillips was educated and able to vouch for what Ingram said so far as what had happened before they parted company in October 1568. For what happened after that, Phillips was as dependent on Ingram's testimony as anyone else present.

Walsingham had brought a list of seven questions to Ingram's interrogation:

Certain questions to be demanded of Davy Ingram, sailor, dwelling at Barking in the county of Essex—what he observed in his travel on the North side of the River of May, where he remained three months or thereabouts.

1. Imprimis: how long the said Ingram traveled on the north side of the River of May.
2. Item: whether that country be fruitful, and what kind of fruits there be.
3. Item: what kinds of beasts and cattle he saw there.
4. Item: what kinds of people there be and how they be appareled.
5. Item: what kinds of buildings and houses they have.
6. Item: whether there is any quantity of gold, silver and pearl and of other jewels in that country.
7. Item whether he saw a beast far exceeding an ox in bigness.[3]

The interrogators were intelligent, but they were also largely ignorant of both relevant background evidence and what they would hear from Ingram. It is often the case in such situations that the less people know, the more certain they are of their limited knowledge. Charles Darwin said it well three centuries later: "Ignorance more frequently begets confidence than does knowledge."[4] It is a shortcoming of all human beings, but it is one that can be overcome by an appreciation for new information.

The assembled gentlemen hoped to have their sketchy knowledge filled out by Ingram's testimony.[5] The panelists expected that Ingram would be able to confirm what they thought they already knew and then help them expand upon that knowledge. What they thought they knew was colored by bias and misperception, but at least some of them were prepared to test their own assumptions and be receptive to unexpected new evidence. Others on the panel were more inclined to ask leading questions and to construe what they heard to serve their own political agendas.

They were also wary of the possibility that Ingram was just another travel liar, a man who profited from inventing, or at least embellishing, experiences beyond the horizon of their ordinary world. The Age of Discovery produced some notable travel liars, as has every century since. Even Amerigo Vespucci, for whom two continents were later named, has been accused of deception. Percy Adams included Ingram in his 1962 rogue's gallery of travel liars.[6] While most of Adams's condemnations are probably deserved, a few amount to nothing more than undeserved character assassination. Ingram is the most notable among the undeserving. It turns out that the confusion about Ingram's description of his travels was the fault of those who recorded and edited his testimony, not Ingram himself.

Ingram was a common sailor, and most likely functionally illiterate. Walsingham and other questioners were literate and well educated by the standards of the day. The tone and confusion of the manuscript records suggest that the interrogators did not bother to adequately explain what they were seeking from Ingram. To them he was only an informant, and it is likely that in their estimation, the purpose of the interrogation was beyond his need, and probably beyond his capacity, to know and understand. They had little prior knowledge, some of it wrong, and this was made worse by the social distance between Ingram and his gentlemen interrogators. Understanding who David Ingram was, who the formidable gentlemen he now faced were, and why they were so interested in his story requires a brief excursion into English history prior to 1582.

1582 Background

David Ingram was born in 1542, when the future Queen Elizabeth was nine years old. Ingram was a commoner, destined for little or no education and a career as an ordinary sailor. When he was born, England was ruled by Henry VIII (1491–1547), the second Tudor king, about whom much has been written. Henry famously had six wives, more or less one after the other, and Elizabeth was the daughter of Anne Boleyn, the second of them. Elizabeth had an older half-sister, Mary, the daughter of Henry's first wife, Katherine of Aragon, whom Henry had divorced. Ingram grew up in these tumultuous years, reaching manhood by 1558, when Elizabeth became queen of England. By 1582, at the age of 40 and his long walk in North America a dozen years behind him, Ingram found himself seated before a panel of powerful men, some of whom served the queen and some of whom sought her favor.

The cultural and political circumstances that surrounded David Ingram in 1582 were largely the consequence of events during the reigns of King Henry VIII and his successors (Figure 1.1).[7] Henry had quickly married Katherine of Aragon, his first wife and his brother Arthur's widow, when he had become king in 1509. This kept the alliance between English and Spanish royalty alive. Katherine was 23 years old when the two set about the task of producing a new heir to the throne, which did not go well. Katherine gave birth to a stillborn girl in 1510. A boy, promptly named Henry, was born the next year, but he too died seven weeks later. These disasters were followed by two stillborn sons, until finally their daughter, Mary, was born in 1516. As a girl, Mary was not an entirely satisfactory heir, but she had the advantage of being a survivor.

Henry VIII and Katherine were practicing Catholics. For the time being the reciprocal mechanisms by which church and state reinforced each other in European countries continued to function for them, while monarchs engaged in various political and military competitions. Katherine's failure to produce a viable male heir helped lead Henry to become enamored with the much younger Anne Boleyn, the queen's lady-in-waiting. Anne's sister Mary had been one of Henry's mistresses, but Anne was made of tougher stuff and refused to follow her sister's example. She held out for a legitimate role. Beginning in 1527, Henry undertook to divorce Katherine. He sought a papal annulment on the curious grounds that his marriage to his brother's

Figure 1.1. Henry VIII. Public Domain via
Wikimedia Commons. Hans Holbein, the
Younger, around 1497–1543—Portrait of Henry
VIII of England.

widow had been against biblical law in the first place. Pope Clement VII
balked for a variety of political considerations that were concealed behind
pious arcane reasons.

The political rise of Thomas Cromwell in 1532 provided Henry with the
ally he needed in Parliament, and Henry formally separated the Church of
England from the Catholic Church in Rome.[8] Henry thus became the head
of a new independent Church of England. As the new master, he could now
marry Anne Boleyn, which he hurriedly did in January 1533. His marriage
to Katherine was officially annulled after the fact a few months later. Anne
gave birth to daughter Elizabeth in September. The timing explains why
Henry was in such a rush to marry Anne before his divorce from Katherine
was finalized. The dodges and trickery that surrounded both of Henry's first
two marriages would eventually lead to claims that neither of his daughters,

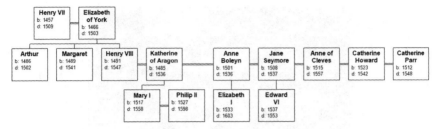

Figure 1.2. The Tudor line from Henry VII to Elizabeth I. Figure by author.

Mary or Elizabeth, was legitimate and thus was not eligible to inherit the throne. But these problems would not be fully deployed by English politicians until another two decades had passed (Figure 1.2).

Henry soon tired of Anne Boleyn, who, like his first wife, failed to produce a male heir. Anne was executed in 1536 for alleged adultery, along with several other members of the court. In that year, Thomas Cromwell began dissolving monasteries across Henry's realm, a program of confiscation that brought huge new wealth into the king's coffers. Henry's greed trumped his piety, and heads rolled as Henry presided over the elimination of leading Catholics.

Henry married Jane Seymour soon after Anne's execution. Jane at last produced the male heir, Edward, whom Henry so keenly desired. She died in childbirth, thus escaping whatever awful fate Henry might have later concocted for her. Henry went on to marry and divorce Anne of Cleves, to marry and execute Catherine Howard, and to marry Catherine Parr. The last Catherine, the most durable of his wives, had been twice widowed before marrying Henry, and she married again after his death in 1547.

It was into this context that David Ingram was born in Barking, Essex, in 1542, near the end of Henry VIII's reign. Barking, now a suburb of eastern London, afforded employment opportunities for people of the lower classes even in the sixteenth century. Nothing is known of Ingram's early years, but he grew up during the chaotic politics that followed the death of King Henry, his life conditioned by the politics of the remote Tudor monarchs of his time. Ingram might never have come in contact with any of them or their peers if not for the events of his career at sea.

Henry was succeeded by his son from his third marriage, Edward VI, but Edward lived only a few years as king. Edward's older half-sister, Queen Mary I (1517–1558) succeeded him and ruled from 1553 to 1558, during which time she earned the epithet "Bloody Mary" (Figure 1.3). Like her

Figure 1.3. Mary I. Public domain via Wikimedia Commons. Antonis Mot, Museo del Prado.

mother, Katherine of Aragon, Mary was a devout Catholic, and she attempted to roll back the religious reforms made by her father, Henry, and her half-brother Edward. The year following her accession she married King Philip II (Felipe) of Spain. While this was a powerful union that revived the English-Spanish alliance, Mary made sure she ruled England in her own right, the first woman to do so. This was facilitated partly by the age difference between the two: Mary was 37 and Philip 26.

Mary's marriage to Philip triggered a Protestant insurrection in England led by a man named Thomas Wyatt. This was suppressed and Wyatt was executed. Subsequently Mary persecuted Protestants more generally in an attempt to restore Catholicism as the state religion, burning hundreds at the stake in the process. She was soon widely detested. Her prospects did not improve when she undertook an unpopular and unsuccessful war with France. The war resulted in England's loss of Calais, its last toehold on the continent. Mary died in 1558, possibly of cancer and largely unlamented.

Elizabeth I (1533–1603) ascended to the throne upon the death of her half-sister (Figure 1.4). Thus began the Elizabethan age. Elizabeth was a confirmed Protestant, so Mary's attempts to restore Catholicism during her short five-year reign came to naught. Elizabeth was intelligent, attractive, and 25, a striking contrast with her middle-aged half-sister. She used these qualities to establish admiration and loyalty among those in government as well as among her subjects generally. During the first 12 years of her reign, she enforced Protestantism while also tolerating Catholicism, policies that did not diminish her popularity. Unfortunately, Pope Pius V dismissively declared Elizabeth as "the Pretended Queen of England," and later dispatched Jesuit missionaries to England. These acts led to new penal laws to suppress Catholicism in young Elizabeth's domain.

Figure 1.4. The Darnley Portrait of Elizabeth I, ca. 1575 when Elizabeth was 42. This youthful face was standardized on all her authorized portraits for many years. Public Domain via Wikimedia Commons. The "Darnley Portrait" of Elizabeth I of England.

David Ingram was a teenager during Mary's reign, and it is not entirely clear where, if anywhere, he stood in the Catholic/Protestant disputes. Later evidence suggests that Ingram chose to avoid Spanish captivity at least in part because he feared the likely consequences of Protestant heresy. Most people like David Ingram lived near the bottom of the social scale, doing the best they could with a small set of skills that probably did not include functional literacy.[9]

Despite their often-lethal differences, the contending variants of Christianity in sixteenth-century England all derived their fundamental ideology from medieval roots. Christianity, of whatever stripe, provided its adherents with simple explanations of life and creation. It protected them from evil and promised them a pleasant afterlife in exchange for unquestioning devotion to orthodoxy. Faith comforted the ill, the bereaved, the dispossessed, and the merely unfortunate. It also explained the way things were in simple comprehensible terms. Such things included the rigid hierarchical nature of the prevailing social pyramid. However, all of this was put at risk by the many unexpected and unexplained discoveries of the sixteenth century.

De facto race-based slavery was well established by the beginning of Elizabeth's reign. The notion of "race" as a contest of speed or as a fast-flowing stretch of water was well established in English before 1300, but its alternative definition as a recognizable group of people of common origin did not appear in English vocabulary until 1570.[10] Thus the coincidence of the appearance of the idea of race as a biological category and the initial exploits of English slavers is telling.

The smug belief of most English, most Europeans, by that time was that white people were the epitome of all things civilized, while black people were condemned by birth to permanent servitude. Elizabeth was said to epitomize the white ideal personally, her complexion, as lily-white as the many pearls that decorated her, and her virginal purity being an example to all.[11]

David Ingram became a low-level participant in the slave trade, and because of that employment he became a source of information that would baffle many of those who heard it. His story generated a reactionary denial even among the open-minded of the day. Once established, that denial has persisted even until today. David Ingram's story illustrates how easy it was for rationality to be thwarted in the sixteenth century, even in a time and place that was, compared to earlier centuries, relatively accepting of it. It also illustrates the ease with which error can persist for centuries. That outcome was conditioned not just by Elizabeth's forebears but also by the people who surrounded her at court.

The Rise of Walsingham

Francis Walsingham was born in the midst of Henry VIII's tumultuous courtship of Anne Boleyn. Part of that courtship, of course, was Henry's assertion that England's centuries-old allegiance to the papacy in Rome had been an illusion from the beginning. The 1533 Act of Appeals officially settled the matter by putting the Church of England under the sovereign, namely, Henry VIII. Walsingham grew up knowing no viable alternative. He went to King's College, Cambridge, early in his youth, and he was there for at least two years. When young King Edward died in 1553, Walsingham found himself subject to Catholic Queen Mary and at the same time living in the political hotbed of the Protestant insurrection. In these risky circumstances, Walsingham decided to pursue his education abroad (Figure 1.5).[12]

Francis probably went to Padua, Italy, with other young Englishmen in 1554, moving on to Basel, Switzerland, a year later. These stays exposed him to both the evidence-based thinking of the Renaissance and to the German Reformation. This also led him to an appreciation for the examination of evidence in the practical matter of solving problems. Walsingham learned to use his persistence and intelligence to find the evidence necessary to solve many practical problems. He consistently ignored the surpassing ideological orthodoxies that most people then used as shortcuts to easy but often false conclusions. People like Walsingham followed Leonardo da Vinci's example, quietly practicing scientific reasoning and getting results that would change the course of history (Figure 1.6).[13]

The English students in exile were politically active, and Walsingham was both well educated and politically astute when he returned to England in 1559. The throne was by that time occupied by the Protestant Elizabeth I. Walsingham, like his queen, was nearing 30 years of age, and also like her, he was ambitious.

Walsingham rose from obscurity by his own merits to become a savvy nominal Protestant who worked his way up in government. He gained the support of William Cecil, then still the queen's secretary of state. Cecil,

Figure 1.5. Francis Walsingham. Alamy 2C51WYJ.
Francis Walsingham.

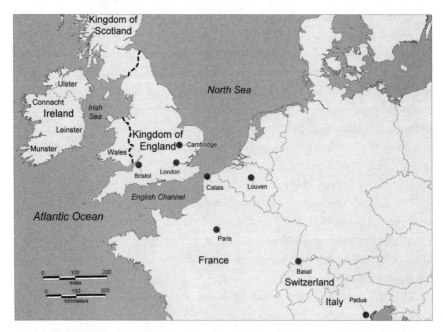

Figure 1.6. Places mentioned in Chapter 1. National boundaries are modern.
Figure by author.

himself an accomplished schemer, put Walsingham in charge of intelligence gathering. It was a job for which he proved to have unusual aptitude.

In 1568, Walsingham's intelligence organization uncovered evidence that the kings of France and Spain were conspiring to remove Elizabeth from her throne and replace her with Mary, Queen of Scots, a Catholic alternative. This was the same year that David Ingram had sailed for the second time with Captain John Hawkins, on a slaving expedition supported by Elizabeth.

As part of her response to the plot, Elizabeth appointed Walsingham ambassador to France in 1570. There he was well placed to further develop his intelligence network. Walsingham was skilled at gathering and evaluating evidence. He let it take him wherever it led him, but he was understandably circumspect when it led him into the area of religious heresy. He was also skilled at the recruitment, interrogation, evaluation, and turning of agents. His native abilities and real experience flourished during his service in France.

A million French Calvinists, Protestants referred to as Huguenots, were struggling for survival amid religious persecution. The persecution reached a bloody climax in the St. Bartholomew's Day Massacre, in which tens of thousands of them were killed. Walsingham and his family witnessed the massacre, and Walsingham used its outraged survivors to good effect. The Huguenots and their supporters stood out among those whom he recruited as French operatives. His talents eventually led historians to refer to him as Elizabeth's spymaster. "Knowledge is never too dear" was Walsingham's motto. In recent years he has had a place of honor in the International Spy Museum in Washington, DC.

Walsingham returned from France to London in 1573 and was appointed to the Privy Council, where he served as joint principal secretary to the queen with Thomas Smith. The two of them jointly replaced Baron Burghley (William Cecil's new title) in that role. Smith retired in 1576, leaving Walsingham as sole secretary of state. He was in his early 40s, holding a powerful position, as well as controlling the Privy Seal. In his new position he uncovered foreign spies and new plots initiated on behalf of Mary, Queen of Scots. He would, with Burghley's cooperation, eventually arrange Mary's beheading in 1587.

By 1582, English pirates had been marauding Spanish outposts in the Caribbean for years, but English sea power had reached a point where Elizabeth could consider supporting an effort to colonize America with permanent settlements, preferably in the temperate coastal zone north of Spanish Florida and south of French interests on the St. Lawrence River. There were venture capitalists like Humphrey Gilbert, Gilbert's younger half-brother Walter Ralegh, and Martin Frobisher interested in doing it, but they needed royal backing.

To advise his queen, Walsingham needed evidence to support the proposition that colonizing could be a successful effort. He had the reports of adventurers like John Hawkins and young Francis Drake, but such men often employed self-serving exaggeration. He needed evidence from knowledgeable sources less inclined to exaggerate, or at least transparent enough to allow Walsingham to detect and compensate for their lies and exaggerations.

The interrogation of David Ingram was the kind of effort that bright young men like Galileo and Francis Bacon, both of them scientists still in their middle 20s, would have appreciated. Walsingham and the other men present had only the most limited prior knowledge of America on which to base their evaluation of the new evidence they were hoping to elicit from their unlikely source. That sketchy background, for the moment, had to pass for what a modern scientist would call "theory," an internally consistent and well-substantiated explanation of some aspect of the world that is capable of producing testable hypotheses.

The Interrogation Gone Awry

Walsingham had his personal objectives in the interrogation, but others present also had their own agendas. As a consequence, the questioning of Ingram was sometimes at cross purposes, and the organization of his testimony could not be maintained by its recorders.

George Peckham, a Catholic, was primarily interested not in the quest to verify evidence but to find a destination for Catholic colonists searching a place to get away from persecution. Walsingham's efforts to learn more about North America thus drew Peckham's interest because of that practical goal.

Humphrey Gilbert was probably present for at least part of the interrogation. His interest was in steering the conversation toward colonies on the American coast to provide naval bases from which to prey on Spanish shipping. Gilbert's employee John Walker appears to have been present for most or all of it.

Richard Hakluyt, or his agent, was also there most of the time. He was busy compiling accounts of English exploration. Hakluyt was three decades younger than Francis Walsingham, but they had known each other for several years by 1580. Around then, Hakluyt wrote a pamphlet recommending English seizure of the Strait of Magellan. He wrote it either at Walsingham's request or as a means to get the man's attention. Hakluyt was also collecting and assembling accounts of English explorations with the intent of editing and publishing them all, which he eventually did seven years later. Meanwhile, he published his more preliminary *Divers Voyages touching the Discoverie of America* in 1582. Around the same time, Hakluyt was paying attention to Humphrey Gilbert's efforts and those of others interested in North America. The 1580 report of John Walker on the River of Norumbega, today Maine's Penobscot River, was particularly interesting to Hakluyt. He used the available sources to compile his notes on colonization, which included lists of plants, animals, minerals, and other resources. That list, and probably Hakluyt himself, were present at David Ingram's interrogation.[14]

The evidence in the three manuscripts shows that Ingram thought he was there to tell his whole story regarding Hawkins's third slaving voyage. That is probably what Ingram thought Walsingham asked him for as the proceedings began. It appears that only as his narrative dragged on did the gentlemen begin interrupting to ask Ingram specific questions or get him to expand the seven topics on Walsingham's agenda. Ingram's responses to questioning were mostly the kinds of brief stories people tell about their past experiences. There was no extended narrative, just anecdotes from Ingram's memory, the kind of accounts one would expect from a nonliterate ordinary sailor of his time. Apart from the seven questions stated in the agenda, what was specifically asked and how the questions were framed is unknown.

The interrogation thus got off to a confused start. The agenda clearly called for the interrogation to focus on "what he observed in his travel on the North side of the River of May." The River of May was what we now know as the St. Johns River of northeastern Florida. The State Papers Domestic manuscript says that Ingram spent three months north of the river. However, that estimate is contradicted in the Tanner manuscript, where Ingram is reported to have said he traveled north of the River of May for a more believable seven months.[15] The contradiction is an early indication that despite Walsingham's talents as an interrogator, the proceedings were at least occasionally chaotic, and the records were thus sometimes contradictory.

Ingram apparently thought that what he was being asked initially was how much time he spent in West Africa. Other sources make clear that Ingram and other crew members were in West Africa or just off its coast for three months during November, December, and January of 1567–1568. He probably was asked separately about how long he spent north of the River of May, which led to the Tanner manuscript entry. The two statements were later confused by the recorder of the State Papers Domestic manuscript. Later historians have noted the contradiction and have often concluded that it was evidence that Ingram was at best unreliable and at worst a classic travel liar. However, the confusion was not only with Ingram but with his recorders and his editor as well.[16]

Richard Hakluyt was the editor who published what he called "The Relation of David Ingram" as part of a much larger *Principall Navigations* project in 1589, having used the records of Ingram's interrogation as his sources.[17] Hakluyt introduced his version of Ingram's testimony by specifying that it described what Ingram and his companions had seen on their long walk through eastern North America. However, Hakluyt badly misunderstood what Ingram had told his questioners, and he made things worse with his editing.

A Legacy of Doubt

Nearly all later historians have preferred to use Hakluyt's 1589 publication as the authoritative version of Ingram's testimony. Even though it was published in now unfamiliar Gothic font, and it contains many exotic spellings and punctuation, it is much easier to acquire, read, and quote than are the original manuscripts from the 1582 interrogation. Later historians also have tended to accept Samuel Purchas's 1625 condemnation of Ingram at face value. Few have looked at the original manuscripts, and there is no evidence that any of them have done so critically enough. The truth is that Hakluyt bungled his task and that historians have subsequently faulted Ingram rather than Hakluyt. This is despite evidence that Hakluyt also embellished or misrepresented some other accounts by changing, adding, subtracting, and rearranging narratives written by their authors, all of them firsthand observers.[18] Because Ingram apparently could not write or correct it himself, Hakluyt's inept compilation of Ingram's story had all these problems and more. The Ingram enigma was of Hakluyt's making.

Richard Hakluyt would leave Ingram out of a 1598–1600 second edition of his magnum opus. Hakluyt died in 1616, and Samuel Purchas took over the editing of the *Principall Navigations*. Purchas did not publish his explanation for Hakluyt's decision to cut Ingram out of the 1598–1600 second edition until 1625. He wrote, "As for David Ingram's perambulation to the north parts, Master Hakluyt published the same but it seemeth some incredibilities of his reports caused him to leave him out in the next impression, the reward of lying not to be believed in truths."[19] This statement condemned Ingram as a travel liar, and this has been the lead followed by a majority of historians for nearly four centuries.

For a start, the distance Ingram and his companions must have traveled has seemed too great for many historians to believe.[20] The landmarks mentioned in his testimony have seemed too few to reconstruct his route. The details of what he said he had seen often seemed too ridiculous to be believed. If he was telling the truth, Ingram's account of his long walk in eastern North America was vitally important then for the anticipated English colonization, just as they are important now to our understanding of the history of the Age of Discovery. But if his accounts could not be trusted, they were worse than useless, both to officials then, and to historians now.

Few have looked at the manuscript evidence, and scholars are reluctant to impugn the work of Richard Hakluyt, in whose honor the Hakluyt Society was founded in 1846. To carry out its mission, the society has published over 350 edited volumes of primary historical documents as its main activity over many years. A dozen of those excellent sources have been cited in the bibliography of this book. However, the sources of the "incredibilities" mentioned by Purchas turn out to have included the court recorders and Hakluyt, but not Ingram.

The Three Surviving Manuscripts

It is rare for the words of an ordinary person to have survived since the sixteenth century. More typically, they endure only in modified secondhand form, reworked by chroniclers, journalists, and politicians for their own purposes. The historical documents that have survived to the present were usually written by just a few people, who had their own agendas. Worse, they were often writing so many years after the facts they reported had occurred that their subjects had already been at least partially mythologized through the course of oral repetition. For example, much of what is known about early Anglo-Saxon history comes from a single book that was completed by the Venerable Bede in AD 731, long after many of the events he described. In a case like that, source criticism based on a knowledge of the culture of the time and how oral tradition tends to change content over the passage of time are important tools for improving our understanding. The situation improves further if there are additional sources that can be compared. If literary or philosophical appreciation is the goal, then comparison is an end in itself. However, if there are enough alternative versions and enough complementary documentation of context, then a modern, evidence-based investigation is possible. There were three recorders of Ingram's testimony and multiple observations by his contemporaries. Ingram's story has survived because those elements exist, but the primary sources have long been largely ignored.

New research based on the long-neglected manuscripts that were written during and just after Ingram's interrogation has shed new light on Ingram's testimony. Confirming evidence from contemporary and later observations has provided fresh and illuminating context. It has revealed three different kinds of historical evidence. The first is the primary evidence the interrogators heard and recorded from Ingram's testimony. This is found in the three contemporary manuscripts. The second kind is the evidence relating to how the interrogators and others subsequently compiled and rearranged what Ingram had said. This is preserved in the manuscripts and in Richard Hakluyt's defective 1589 published version of Ingram's story. The third line of evidence is made up of the long history of misled commentary by historians who have depended on Hakluyt's flawed published version. The surviving three sets of evidence relating to Ingram's case provide a rare opportunity to detect what truly happened to an ordinary man who lived an extraordinary life, and then how his story was subsequently corrupted by those who made use of it.[21]

Their handwriting shows that three anonymous people each recorded parts of what Ingram said in 1582.[22] This constitutes all the surviving primary evidence of the Ingram case. The first of them, the State

Papers Domestic manuscript, contains the interrogation agenda that has already been quoted. There are two more primary manuscripts that are more lengthy and consequently more important for an understanding of Ingram's long journey. One is the State Papers Colonial manuscript and the other is the Tanner manuscript. Updated transcripts of all three manuscripts are provided on this book's Companion Website (https://global.oup.com/us/companion.websites/9780197648001/). There are two more early manuscripts known, the Calthorpe and the Sloane manuscripts, but these have proven to be copies of the State Papers Colonial and the Tanner manuscripts, respectively, and they are not included here.[23]

Manuscripts handwritten in Elizabethan English are typically very difficult for modern eyes to read. Formal government and business documents like these were mostly written in secretary hand, a script that is variably flamboyant and cryptic to the point of illegibility. This form of handwriting was established by 1525, and it was esoteric enough to provide secretaries with employment security. Secretary hand would gradually go extinct over the next hundred years as literacy expanded and a more attractive and readable Italian hand came to replace it. The confusingly variable spellings and punctuation of Elizabethan documents also later came to be much more standardized, probably at the insistence of frustrated printers.[24]

The printed versions derived from Elizabethan manuscript versions, such as Hakluyt's 1589 publication, are more easily read today, but they still feature many alternative spellings and punctuation that is often either arbitrary or missing altogether. It should not be surprising that modern readers, including most historians, have preferred to use printed documents, Hakluyt's 1589 version and other later ones, over the handwritten manuscripts from which they were derived.

The State Papers Domestic Manuscript

The title of this short manuscript is *Examination of David Ingram*. It is a single-sheet document, on which the seven-question agenda of Walsingham and his committee was written.[25] The writer left margins and spaces between the questions for insertion of some of Ingram's answers. This manuscript was unquestionably written at the time of the 1582 interrogation.

The recorder's combination of separate statements made by Ingram into only seven brief entries, each pertaining to one or another of the seven questions, has confused the efforts of nearly all later historians. For example, the recorder did not realize that Ingram's separate statements on the subject of animals pertained to the whole range of animals he had seen in Africa, the Caribbean, and North America.

In addition to notes on Ingram's testimony, there are also two marginal notes that appear to have been postscripts added at the end of the proceedings. They are supplementary comments made by Humphrey Gilbert's employee John Walker, who was present at the interrogation. The two notes appear at first glance to provide useful corroborating evidence produced by Walker, but it was just one of many instances of the confusion displayed by all three recorders. In both cases, Walker agreed that Ingram was correct about specific things (houses and hides) that Walker assumed Ingram had seen in America, even though the evidence shows that in the case of hides Ingram was talking about Africa.

The seventh and last entry on Walsingham's agenda is very specific compared to the first six topics. This too was probably added at the prompting of Walker or Gilbert. Walker had stolen a large number of moose hides from the people living along the Penobscot River in Maine in 1580, just about the only thing he had to show for the exploratory voyage Gilbert had sent him on. In answering the question, Ingram told the panel all about the buffalos he had seen in Africa, and no one present realized they were talking past one another.

State Papers Colonial Manuscript

The second primary manuscript is titled *Reports of the country Sir Humphrey Gilbert goes to discover*.[26] The importance of this manuscript is that although it is shorter than the Tanner manuscript discussed later, it preserves the chronological order in which Ingram responded to early questioning. This unique and crucially important feature of the manuscript shows that Ingram started his story with Africa. It also shows that the manuscript was written at the time of the 1582 interrogation.

The facts they contain show that all of the first 18 entries in the manuscript pertain to Africa. The odds are vanishingly small that all of the first 18 of 84 entries would cluster at the beginning by chance alone. That near impossibility indicates that Ingram was telling his story in chronological order, beginning, logically enough, with Africa. Walsingham and his panel were interested only in the North American part of Ingram's long story, but they lacked the background knowledge to evaluate what they were hearing.

Under questioning by various people Ingram later abandoned the chronological order of his narrative, and the recorders began rearranging Ingram's statements by topics: plants, animals, houses, and so forth. None of them realized that Ingram was drawing on his memories of the entire voyage. Any effort he made to reference where he saw the things he reported in answers to their questions was overlooked. All three recorders neglected to include any such information much of the time.[27]

The Tanner Manuscript

The Tanner is the third primary manuscript deriving from Ingram's testimony. Titled "The Relation of David Ingram," it is the longest of the three manuscripts, containing 99 entries.[28] The Tanner manuscript is made up of seven leaves written on both sides, a total of 14 pages. Richard Hakluyt published this manuscript in *The Principall Navigations, Voiages and Discoveries of the English nation* in 1589. The published version is what most scholars have used to evaluate Ingram's testimony. The publication is, with a few additional edits, a faithful typeset version of the Tanner manuscript. The Tanner might be the very manuscript version that Hakluyt gave to his printer.[29] This indicates that the manuscript could have been completed anytime up to six years after the 1582 interrogation.

Comparison of the State Papers Colonial and Tanner manuscripts reveals that a total of 60 entries are shared between them, sometimes almost word for word. Thus, it is likely that the Tanner recorder copied entries from the State Papers Colonial manuscript and combined them with other entries of his own. Hakluyt might have acquired these additional observations from Ingram in 1582 or later, or he might have lifted some of them from other sources he acquired before submitting the Tanner version for publication in 1598. These possibilities have had to be examined case by case.

Seven years passed between the interrogation and Hakluyt's publication of "The Relation of David Ingram of Barking" in his *Principall Navigations*. A portion of his 107-word extended title of the relation reads, "things which he with others did see, in traveling by land from the most northerly part of the Bay of Mexico . . . through a great part of America."[30] By 1589, Hakluyt either never understood or did not remember that Ingram's testimony covered topics regarding his experiences on both sides of the Atlantic. Ingram's secondhand relation was published together with firsthand reports by John Hawkins, Miles Phillips, and many others that Hakluyt and his readers assumed to be generally accurate and truthful, if occasionally incomplete and self-serving.

A New Transcript of David Ingram's Testimony (Appendix)

To combine and collate the contents of the three primary documents, one must undertake a process analogous to reconstructing recipes by examining the resulting meals, a kind of reverse engineering. Thoroughly mixed ingredients cannot always be convincingly unmixed, but in Ingram's case it has been almost entirely achievable.

Analysis of the short-term consequences of Ingram's interrogation is also analogous to a modern criminal investigation. There are many puzzles, many unknowns, much noise to obscure small amounts of useful evidence, the inadvertent loss of information over time, and sometimes deliberate omissions or misleading statements. Yet despite these several limitations, a new coherent version of Ingram's recorded testimony has been possible to re-create.

The complete new modern English transcript is provided in the Appendix. Updated transcripts of the three primary manuscript sources and a reproduction of Hakluyt's 1589 publication are provided on the Companion Website hosted by Oxford University Press. All entries in the new transcript are linked to their sources in the three manuscripts. Anyone wishing to check updated transcripts or the ways in which they were unscrambled and reordered in the new edition can do so by consulting the online documents.

After four centuries, this is the first version of Ingram's story that can be read as a true, albeit brief, relation. It is true to what Ingram told his interrogators, and it lays out what Ingram observed and remembered, in proper chronological order. His story is also shown to be largely true in the context of what is now known about the peoples of Africa, the Caribbean, and North America and their environments in the sixteenth century.

Even now, David Ingram's story is briefly told and incomplete, but it is no longer an enigma. It is a remarkable story, particularly as it was told by an uneducated English sailor who had to rely on only his memory of the many strange experiences that he had encountered a dozen years before his interrogation. Because of David Ingram, historians and anthropologists now have access to a more complete understanding of the Age of Discovery. In some instances, the evidence that Ingram provided is unique and would otherwise be unknown today.

2

Ingram in the 1560s

David Ingram was 18 years old at the beginning of this decade. He grew up in Barking, just a few miles east of central London, a place from which young sailors were regularly recruited to serve in England's growing maritime enterprises. Ships came up the Thames, past Barking to the Tower of London, where they were fitted out and equipped with guns, crews, and much else needed for long voyages. From there they often moved downstream again, past Barking and the Royal Observatory at Greenwich, to the natural harbor on the lower Medway River near the mouth of the Thames. There they typically continued preparations and waited for orders to sail (Figure 2.1).

The American hemisphere had been explored and colonized since the days of Columbus, but those efforts had been limited, spotty, and often haphazard. Spanish and Portuguese exploration often included the east coast fringe of North America, but their colonization efforts concentrated in the tropics, which had been neatly (if imprecisely) divided between them by the 1494 Treaty of Tordesillas. Neatly because it was a simple north-south meridian line, but imprecisely because its exact longitude was only vaguely defined. The westernmost of several sixteenth-century approximations for the north-south line had it striking South America on the equator, at the mouth of the Amazon. Consequently, for the time being, Portugal focused on coastal Brazil, which lies east of the line (Figure 2.2).

Spain mainly colonized well west of the Tordesillas line from Cuba southward through the Caribbean. The north coasts of Colombia and Venezuela became the Spanish Main. Their efforts in Florida and northward would prove to be too expensive to maintain for long. The gap between Spanish and Portuguese interests in South America eventually allowed for the establishment of the three Guianas by English, Dutch, and French colonists.

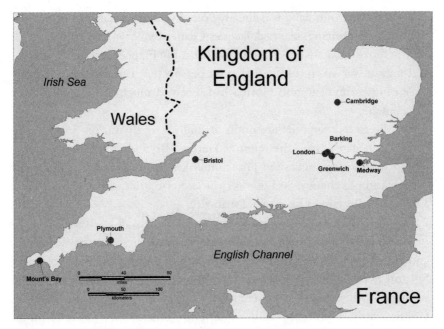

Figure 2.1. English places mentioned in Chapters 2 and 4. Figure by author.

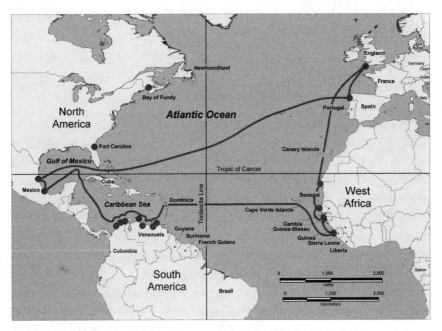

Figure 2.2. John Hawkins's third voyage and its major stops. Figure by author.

Coastal Newfoundland was already dotted with multinational fishing stations that no monarch claimed. Jacques Cartier explored and colonized the St. Lawrence River west of Newfoundland for France starting in 1534, so that region was taken from a European perspective. But the long coast between Newfoundland and Florida had received much less attention from the French.

For the time being, the attention of English royals was on political turmoil that began during the reign of Henry VIII, and the consequences of that turmoil for his successors. That tumultuous history retarded full English participation in the Age of Discovery. It also conditioned opportunities for a sailor like Ingram as he reached maturity.

English exploration was mostly left to fishermen and privateers for the time being. For their part, English seamen and their investors were often content to prey on the ships of other nations, particularly those of Spain. Spanish fleets returning from the Americas were often loaded with gold, silver, and other treasure extracted from the peoples of Peru and Mexico. Consequently, early proposals for English colonization were typically framed in terms of establishing outposts from which royally authorized piracy could be more easily deployed against Spanish assets. To these efforts were added England's entry into the slave trade, in which huge profits were possible even without seizing Spanish treasure.

Race-Based Slavery

The world's dominant religions share much of the blame for general acceptance of slavery as a legitimate institution. Christianity was familiar with slavery from its earliest roots in the Greco-Roman world that fostered its development, and there is plenty in the Bible condoning it. Islam neither explicitly approved nor condemned the practice, but Muhammad was himself a slave owner and trader. The Quran does have much to say about the proper use of slaves. Martin Luther did little to improve matters in the Reformation, saying, "Sheep, cattle, men-servants, and maid-servants were all possessions to be sold as it pleased their masters."[1]

Prince Henry the Navigator of Portugal (1394–1460) is often celebrated today for his promotion of marine exploration. However, as historian Will Durant pointed out decades ago, "The first major result of Henry's labors was the inauguration of the African slave trade."[2] The Muslims of North Africa were already old hands in the acquisition of slaves from sub-Saharan Africa, but they were equal-opportunity slavers, reticent only when it came to enslaving fellow Muslims. The Portuguese were not as fastidious, allowing that Christians could be slaves so long as they were also black. By midcentury there were thousands of slaves in Portugal. It was all made clear and official by the Catholic church. The papal bull, *Romanus Pontifex*, which was issued in 1455 by Pope Nicholas V, sanctioned the purchase of black slaves from infidels so long as they were converted to the Catholic faith.

We remember 1492 as the year Columbus first sailed to America, but it was also the year that Moors and Jews were rounded up and executed, enslaved, converted, or expelled from Spain, depending on local circumstances. Slavery remained potentially open to all, but while other slaves had some hope of redemption, blacks were condemned to hereditary servitude. It was a convenient distinction because while masters and slaves in Europe tended to look alike prior to the Age of Discovery, it was now easier to distinguish at a glance between white masters and black slaves. Heredity made the distinction permanent and conventional. Blacks thus came to be regarded by most whites as irredeemably less than fully human.

Bartolomé de las Casas, who sailed with Columbus in 1502, was a Dominican friar who was appointed protector of the indigenous Americans around 1516. Las Casas took this appointment seriously, and he did what he could to argue for the abolition of the *encomienda* system, which had legitimized the enslavement of indigenous Americans. As a consequence, the Spanish emperor, King Carlos V, issued "New Laws of the Indies for the Good Treatment and Preservation of the Indians" in 1542. These *Leyes Nuevas* forbade the enslavement of American Indians. However, the new laws were resisted in the colonies by *ecomenderos* who were profiting from the exploitation of indigenous Americans, so the effects of the new laws proceeded slowly. Las Casas published *A Short Account of the Destruction of the Indies* in 1552, and the gradual abolition of the *encomienda* system quickened. Las Casas successfully argued that indigenous Americans were fully human. No such reprieve was in store for Africans, at least not yet.[3]

Enslavement and the introduction of Old World diseases ravaged indigenous American populations in the decades following the voyages of Columbus. It appeared that even if indigenous American slavery were curtailed, the populations of these groups would continue to decline due to epidemics. Las Casas suggested that the negative economic effects of the end of Indian slavery could be offset by encouraging Spanish peasants to migrate to the Spanish colonies in America. But there were insufficient numbers of them in Spain to make this a realistic solution. Ferdinand and Isabella had granted permission to the colonists of the Caribbean to import African slaves in 1501, and subsequent Spanish monarchs continued this policy. As the *encomienda* system faded and immigration from Spain failed to make up the difference, the Spanish colonists came to rely on the increased importation of African slaves. It was a loathsome practice but a successful business plan, and in Plymouth, England, John Hawkins took the lead in exploiting it for his own profit. Hawkins became a major influence on the life of David Ingram.[4]

The Rise of John Hawkins

John Hawkins (1532–1595) is known today for introducing the delusional benefits of both racial slavery and tobacco smoking to English culture (Figure 2.3). This was with Elizabeth's tacit approval in the first decade of her reign. Hawkins used these and other less disgusting enterprises to enrich himself and his queen. Young David Ingram would become part of it all.

Like many leading figures of his time, Hawkins was a vain and violent man. He had killed a man by the time he was 20, and he was ready for bigger things. Hawkins was, like his father William, largely unburdened by strong moral convictions. Both were mariners who prospered by sailing with whatever religious wind was blowing as their Tudor monarchs lurched from Catholicism to Protestantism to Catholicism and back again. John was unusually adept at navigation, deceit, treachery, ruthless violence, and piracy, which made him a success in the business of privateering and in the new business of race-based slaving. His favorite practice was to sail to West Africa and either kidnap people or buy captives from warring chieftains, then haul them like cattle to be sold to Spanish colonists in the West Indies. This trade was forbidden by Philip II of Spain, not because the king frowned on the practice but because he wanted to maintain a monopoly in the slaving business in Spanish colonies.

Hawkins's technique was to sail into a port on the Spanish Main with a load of slaves, request a license to trade, then attack and kill a few people when it was refused. He then forcibly sold slaves and other goods under

Figure 2.3. John Hawkins. Public Domain via
Wikimedia Commons. National Maritime Museum,
Greenwich, London, and Creative Commons.

the guise of some contrived combination of ransom payments and damage
reimbursements.

Hawkins and Queen Elizabeth were nearly the same age, both in their
30s in the later 1560s. The tumultuous five-year reign of Queen Mary I,
Elizabeth's half-sister and predecessor, had included Mary's brief marriage
to Spanish king Philip II. This provided Hawkins with the convenient claim
that he had been a faithful subject of the king of Spain for the four years
Philip also had also been (sort of) the king of England. This became one
of his favorite arguments when trying to penetrate Philip's prohibition of
English trade with Spain's colonists in the West Indies.

1562: Hawkins's First Voyage

Hawkins's first two voyages set the scene for his climactic third voyage.
Hawkins set off from Plymouth on his first slaving expedition in 1562. He

had three ships, at least two and maybe all three of which were owned by Hawkins and his brother. Hawkins's young kinsman, Francis Drake, was probably aboard one of them.

A 20-year-old David Ingram was of an age to have been hired on to this voyage as an ordinary sailor. However, while it is possible, it is very unlikely that he sailed on this trip, as he would have had to make his way to Plymouth, 248 miles (400 km) from his home near London, in order to sign on. Hawkins sailed from Plymouth to Africa, then on to the Caribbean, before returning to England the following year with a large profit.

1564: Hawkins's Second Voyage

Hawkins took out a second slaving expedition in 1564. As late as the previous year, Queen Elizabeth had still been uncertain about the morality of the trade. "If an African were carried away without their free consent it would be detestable and call down the vengeance of Heaven upon the undertakers," she observed.[5] However, the promise of new wealth created by Hawkins on his first voyage helped the queen overcome her moral scruples. Elizabeth also enjoyed the pleasure of indirectly using Hawkins to annoy King Philip II of Spain, her former brother-in-law.

The queen was so optimistic about the second voyage that she loaned Hawkins the *Jesus of Lübeck*, a large warship she had inherited from her father, Henry VIII. For this, she expected a share in the profits. The *Jesus* was old and in poor condition, but it had the advantage of carrying 21 guns; it also had plenty of space for supplies, trade goods, and slaves going west and for loot coming home. Best of all from his point of view, Hawkins could legitimately fly the royal standard from a mast (Figure 2.4). Another of the queen's ships, the *Minion*, later joined the little fleet on part of the journey.[6]

David Ingram almost certainly sailed with Hawkins on this second expedition, because the *Jesus* was the queen's ship and was therefore stationed at London or at Medway on the lower Thames, not Plymouth. Ingram's home in Barking was near enough for him to be easily recruited. Later evidence will also show that on Hawkins's third voyage, Ingram probably knew things that he had picked up on this, the second sailing. Young Francis Drake was probably also again aboard one of the ships that sailed under Hawkins.

Figure 2.4. The *Jesus of Lübeck*. Public Domain via Wikimedia Commons. Photo by Gerry Bye. Original by Anthony Anthony.

Hawkins and his men repeated their previous practice of bullying Spanish colonists into buying slaves at stops in the Caribbean. On his way back to England in 1565, Hawkins stopped for fresh water at the French outpost of Fort Caroline on the River of May, what is now called the St. Johns River, near modern Jacksonville, Florida (Figure 2.5). It was probably here that Hawkins picked up American tobacco and the practice of smoking it. Smoking had already spread to continental Europe, but it was new to England. The French colonists, largely Protestant Huguenots, were short of food and not in good condition. Hawkins offered them passage back to France, but they declined. The St. Bartholomew's Day Massacre in Paris had not yet occurred, but to them an uncertain future on the River of May already seemed preferable to life in Catholic France.

Another reason to conclude that Ingram was a crewman on the *Jesus* on this voyage is that five years later on Hawkins's disastrous third voyage, Ingram would remember enough about the French fort on the River of May to think he might find refuge there as well as a way home. However,

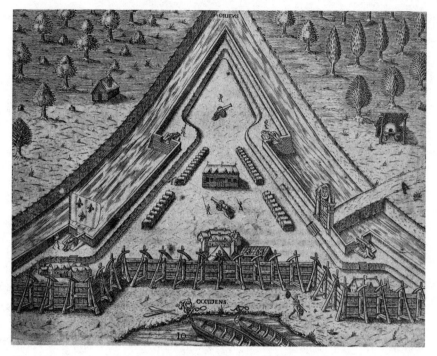

Figure 2.5. Fort Caroline, Florida. Alamy M2JG3R. Fort Caroline..

not long after Hawkins departed Fort Caroline for England, a Spanish expedition fell upon the French in their lonely outpost and slaughtered all but a few who could convince the attackers that they were Catholics.

The Spanish resettled the colony, renaming it Fort San Mateo. But the Spanish in turn were slaughtered in 1568 by an avenging French force led by Dominique de Gourgue. He was back in France by June 1568, having left no French garrison behind to hold the fort. The Spanish then returned and rebuilt Fort San Mateo. However, they abandoned the post again in 1569. By the time Ingram found out about this complicated series of events on the River of May, he would have to give up the idea of going there.[7]

1566: The Lovell Voyage

Hawkins followed up his second slaving voyage by sending out a relative, John Lovell, with four small ships in 1566. Hawkins did not go himself. However, Francis Drake was sent along on this expedition. Drake was young (26), but by this time he might have been a junior officer. It is unlikely that Ingram was on this voyage, because none of the ships sailed from the Thames River. Lovell commanded a small fleet that was once again sailing out of Plymouth, this time without any ships supplied by Queen Elizabeth.[8]

Lovell was a man of overweening religious convictions, and these prevented him from following the example of the duplicitous Hawkins and feigning polite friendship for Spanish Catholics he encountered. Like Hawkins, Lovell stopped in the Canary Islands for supplies, but he also used the occasion to deliberately offend the Spanish islanders, whose cooperation he could have enjoyed otherwise. Lovell then sailed on to Guinea, where he spent three or four months acquiring African slaves by hook or by crook. When he eventually reached the Caribbean, he was initially rebuffed by local officials, of course. He quickly resorted to the same forceful techniques previously used by Hawkins. These worked at first, but Lovell was rebuffed more decisively at Río de la Hacha on the north coast of modern Colombia. He then dumped about 90 older, sick, and starving slaves on the shore and sailed off.

Lovell went on to Hispaniola, but he was not successful there either. He ended up returning to England with some unsold slaves and little else to show for his efforts. He arrived back in Plymouth in September 1567. By this time, plans for a much larger expedition were well advanced. This new voyage was to be once again under the direct command of John Hawkins.

1567: Beginning Hawkins's Third Voyage

This time Queen Elizabeth invested again by leasing the *Jesus of Lübeck* to Hawkins, the largest of the four ships he had used previously on the 1564 second expedition (Figure 2.4).[9] The pretext John Hawkins concocted for this, his third voyage, was based on the claims of two Portuguese adventurers.[10] These men had been promoting themselves and stories of easy West African gold in Paris, Madrid, and now London, hoping to get hired as guides. John Hawkins was interested in their claims, if only because they provided him with a cover story for traveling again to West Africa, where the real money was still to be made acquiring slaves to be illegally sold to Spanish colonists in the Caribbean. The cover story was necessary to deceive and mollify the Spanish ambassador and his agents in London.

Various wealthy English backers were also interested in the venture, probably understanding the gold prospecting ruse as well as Hawkins did.

These included William Cecil, then still Queen Elizabeth's secretary of state. A syndicate was formed and backing was secured. In addition to the *Jesus of Lübeck*, Queen Elizabeth committed another of her own warships to the venture, the *Minion*, with which Hawkins had briefly consorted on his second slaving voyage. Both ships were overhauled and supplied on the River Medway, then moved up the Thames to the Tower of London. There Hawkins refined the armaments of the two ships. The *Jesus* was armed with 21 guns. David Ingram again signed on as a seaman, probably either at Medway or at London. Later evidence consistently shows that it is almost certain that he served again aboard the *Jesus*, rather than on the *Minion*.

The *Jesus of Lübeck* was old, leaky, and top-heavy, but it was still suitable to serve as Hawkins's flagship. Hawkins chose Robert Barrett to serve as the ship's master, a man having both plenty of experience at sea and a knowledge of both Portuguese and Spanish. The *Minion* was even older than the *Jesus* and plagued by bad luck, but although she had lost many men in the process, she had brought wealth back to England on previous expeditions.

Crewmen on slaving ships were paid better than ordinary merchant mariners, and they could also expect to make money in private trading along the way. This was probably an attraction for Ingram, then about 26 years old. A slaving expedition was dangerous, but it offered potential profits that sailors like Ingram concluded outweighed the risks. For his part, Hawkins traveled with a wardrobe of 50 changes of clothes and a beautifully furnished cabin. By this time his coat of arms featured a human crest, with a bound human slave depicted where a totemic animal typically appeared on most coats of arms (Figure 2.6).

There were a few men aboard who would survive the coming disaster and live long enough to report what would happen over the coming months. Hawkins himself would be one of them, David Ingram would be another. A third man who survived the voyage was Job Hortop. Hortop had been born in Bourne, Lincolnshire, and had been apprenticed as a powdermaker on the Surrey side of the Thames in London. From there he had been recruited into service as a gunner on the *Jesus of Lübeck*. Hortop's odyssey would prove to be a very long one, but he too would eventually return to England. Another man who would survive to return and tell his tale was Miles Phillips. He was a gentleman adventurer who would escape after a long captivity and eventually write his own contribution to the history of the voyage.[11]

Figure 2.6. John Hawkins's coat of arms, with its bound slave crest. Public Domain via Wikimedia Commons. William Harvey—College of Arms, United Kingdom.

The queen's two ships left London for Plymouth in August 1567, there to join four of Hawkins's own smaller vessels for the expedition to Africa and the Caribbean. Hawkins went from London to Plymouth by land, as did his two Portuguese guides. It was important that the fleet sail in autumn, before either the weather or their queen turned against the project. For uncertain reasons the two Portuguese guides disappeared, having probably figured out that they had been conned by the man they had tried to con. Hawkins then undertook to repurpose the voyage, sending an express letter to Elizabeth asking her permission to do so. This he entrusted to George Fitzwilliams, his right-hand man. Hawkins forged ahead with preparations while waiting for the queen's reply, stocking up on fine Rouen cloth that could not be sold in Africa but would return a good profit in the Caribbean. He also loaded a large store of dried beans, which could only have been intended as food to sustain slaves through the awful middle passage between Africa and Spanish America. Word of this reached the Spanish ambassador in London, and he immediately protested to the queen and William Cecil that Hawkins was planning another illegal slaving trip to the Caribbean. Both denied this intent, as did Hawkins himself, and the ambassador seemed to be placated—or at least was lulled into silence.

Hawkins and his brother, William, assembled their own ships in Plymouth. These included the *William and John*, the *Swallow*, the *Judith*, and the *Angel*. The *Swallow*, which was not the same ship as the *Swallow* that Lovell took out in 1566, towed a pinnace for close work inshore. Together the six ships in the fleet would carry 408 men. Among the officers again was Hawkins's young kinsman, Francis Drake, by now probably the captain of the *Judith*. Other men who had sailed with Lovell might have joined one or another of the crews, but turnaround time was short, and the ships might have been already fully crewed. As usual, crew lists have not survived.[12]

Fitzwilliams returned to Plymouth with the queen's approval of the voyage in his pocket. The Protestant Elizabeth was not about to yield to a Catholic Spanish monarch who thought himself empowered by the pontiff to share the Americas only with Portugal. With her permission in hand, Hawkins took his fleet to sea.

Sailing and navigation were largely unregulated emerging technologies of the sixteenth century. The distinction between entrepreneurial privateering and piracy was blurry, with venture capitalists taking huge risks and sometimes enjoying huge returns. Hawkins was backed by many investors in addition to the queen. At least 30 of them came along on the voyage, in part to protect their investments. Chief among these were Thomas Goddard, who had the advantage of being fluent in both French and Spanish. Others of them included Hawkins's brother, William; George Fitzwilliams; and Miles Phillips. Also aboard the *Jesus* was Captain Edward Dudley, with a detachment of marines. There were also various servants, including Hawkins's young nephew Paul, who served as cabin boy. There were 166 men and boys on the *Jesus*, another 99 on the *Minion*, and perhaps 143 more on the smaller vessels. Most of them would never see England again. There were also 40 to 60 African slaves left over from Lovell's voyage, but they were probably not counted among the total of 408.[13]

The fleet sailed on Monday, October 2, 1567. Four days out toward the Canaries they encountered gale-force winds, which lasted for another four days. It was nearly a disaster; the ships were scattered and in danger of sinking. The towed pinnace and the *Minion*'s longboat were both lost, along with their small crews. When the winds finally calmed, the *Angel* and the *Jesus* found each other and made for Tenerife in the Canary Islands. The *Judith* caught up to them, and the three ships anchored safely in the Santa Cruz harbor of Tenerife Island.[14] Meanwhile, the *Minion, William and John*, and the *Swallow* came together and sailed to the nearby island of La Gomara (Figure 2.7).

It was an uneasy stay of less than a week, despite the fact that Hawkins had some friends on Tenerife. Lovell's obnoxious behavior the year before was partly to blame. The English ships and their Spanish hosts were mutually distrustful, especially after the Spanish realized that this was the notorious Englishman they called Juan Aquines, who had already twice violated Spanish sovereignty in the Caribbean, three times if they counted Lovell's

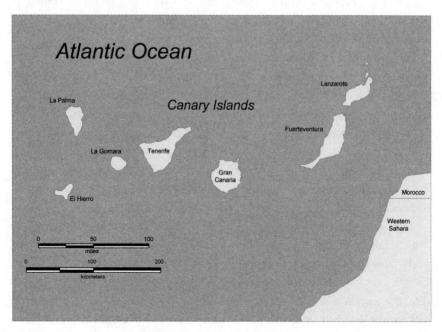

Figure 2.7. The Canary Islands. Figure by author.

voyage. On top of that, George Fitzwilliams quarreled with Edward Dudley, the captain of the detachment of marines Hawkins had brought along. This led Dudley to strike Hawkins, a grave offense for which Hawkins came close to executing Dudley.

There was ostentatious piety aboard the *Jesus* and the other ships, despite the piracy and slavery that were the purposes of the voyage. Hawkins ordered mandatory morning Protestant services. For his part, Fitzwilliams secretly went to Catholic Mass, as did at least one other man. The clandestine Catholics would find much later that they had a way to avoid execution by mollifying their Spanish captors in Mexico.

Suspicious moves by the Spanish caused Hawkins to leave the Tenerife harbor under cover of darkness and anchor farther along the coast, out of range of their guns. There he spent over two weeks refitting and resupplying. Then he moved westward to the island of La Gomara, hoping to find the rest of his ships. He did find them there, and by November 4 the six-ship fleet was assembled once again and ready to head for the African coast.

David Ingram later said nothing about the voyage up to this point. At least nothing about it is preserved from his interrogation. That changed when they reached Africa. As explained in Chapter 1, the first 18 entries in the State Papers Colonial manuscript and now in the New Transcript described what he saw and experienced in Africa, mostly in what is now Sierra Leone.

Hawkins headed his fleet eastward to reach the coast of Africa. When he saw land, the ships turned south toward Africa's Cabo Blanco, crossing the Tropic of Cancer (Figure 2.2). The cape lies where the border between the ? modern Western Sahara and Mauritania reaches the sea. Along the coast they met six French merchant ships. After a brief engagement Hawkins captured all six. One of them had a cargo of mullets according to Job Hortop. Five of them had certificates to prove their good intentions, but the sixth did not. Hawkins decided that this one was actually a French pirate ship that had recently raided Spanish settlements in the Canaries.[15]

The next day, the Frenchmen on the suspect ship, a caravel, offered to join the English slaving expedition. Hawkins agreed, but he did not entirely trust the French crew. He solved the problem by moving most of the French crew to the *Jesus*, and sending English crewmen to man the French ship, the *Don de Dieu*. Its captain, Paul Blondel, became "Captain Bland" in subsequent English and Spanish documents. He would survive and serve English interests in the next decade. His ship was renamed the *Grace of God* and incorporated into the fleet, a replacement for the pinnace that had been lost in the storm.

The addition of the French ship was important, because it entailed the addition of French sailors to the crew of the *Jesus*. These were men with their own considerable experience in the Caribbean and with Spanish colonists there. Their influence would be important to Ingram and others in the marooning that would follow the disastrous climax of the expedition in Mexico.

They sailed south another 380 nautical miles (704 km) to Cape Verde, the westernmost tip of Africa, at what is now Dakar, Senegal. Hawkins was more enthusiastic than cautious at this point in the expedition. He led a force of 150 men ashore, striking inland in search of people to enslave. The local people had plenty of experience with this kind of predation, and they put up stiff resistance. They used short iron-tipped spears, as well as bows and iron-tipped arrows to ambush and push back Hawkins's party of soldiers and sailors. Hawkins's men laughed off the minor wounds produced by the little arrows, but they later discovered that the arrow tips had been poisoned, and that the wounds were often lethal. Job Hortop later remembered that 25 men, including Hawkins himself, were wounded by the arrows. Hawkins and a majority of the other wounded men survived. However, eight of them, including marine Captain Dudley, died in agony a few days later.[16] Their deaths were protracted, with symptoms like those of tetanus. Hawkins had captured and enslaved a few Africans, but he had lost about the same number of his men. This was not an equation for success in the slaving business.

Hawkins pressed on, taking his fleet southeastward around the bulge of West Africa. Like Hawkins, David Ingram later did not talk much about this early unsuccessful part of the expedition's activities on land. However, he would have plenty to say about Africa, its resources, and its peoples along the Guinea Coast they now approached.

3

Ingram in Africa

We turn now to a reconstructed, chronologically correct recounting of David Ingram's story. Evidence shows that he began his 1582 testimony by describing what he saw in Africa, the first major stop in Hawkins's disastrous third voyage in 1567. Francis Walsingham and other gentlemen present for the interrogation were not particularly interested in Ingram's experiences in Africa and the Caribbean, but it appears that when they told him to begin with a summary, that is where he started. Only later in the proceedings did random questions and backtracking by the recorders begin to jumble what Ingram was saying and secretaries were recording.

In the end, everything Ingram said was represented by Hakluyt as describing what he saw and experienced on his long walk in North America, nothing else. However, by word count in the State Papers Colonial manuscript, 48 percent of what Ingram reported to his interrogators in 1582 pertained to his initial experiences in Africa.

To his credit, Ingram's views and descriptions of Africans were mostly sympathetic. However, Ingram was in Africa as part of a slaving expedition. At least some of England's new overseas ventures involved officially approved trading in African slaves, and there is no way to dress that up as a heroic contribution to the Age of Discovery. Hawkins's business revolved around the capture, enslavement, and transport of West African people. Ingram tells how Africans were enslaved in the autumn of 1567.

The West African Coast

Having failed in his first attempt to acquire slaves where his fleet first touched Africa, Hawkins decided to move past Cape Verde and try again.

They ran into Portuguese ships near and in the Cacheu River in what is now northwestern Guinea-Bissau (Figure 3.1). They alternately plied, cajoled, and bullied the Portuguese men they encountered. Robert Barrett, the Portuguese-speaking master of the *Jesus*, led an attack up the Cacheu, capturing several more caravels, small maneuverable ships with triangular sails. Hawkins followed with more ships and men, bringing the English force on land up to 250 men. Ingram was probably among them.

Barrett ran into trouble, but the river was too shallow for Hawkins to rescue Barrett and his men with boats he had available. After some preliminaries, a battle broke out and Barrett's detachment had to fight its way back downstream to the safety of the fleet. Hawkins lost four men killed and many others injured in this action.[1]

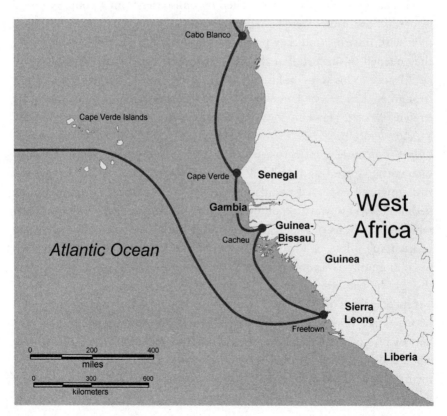

Figure 3.1. John Hawkins's third voyage and its major stops. Figure by author.

Portuguese slavers operating in the same area had allied themselves with some local tribes in order to use them as slaving intermediaries. They exploited local warfare by allying themselves with the stronger local leaders and buying captives from them. For the moment the Portuguese had the advantage over Hawkins, because their African allies helped them push back the English attackers. Hawkins's men were still able to bring out some captured caravels. Hawkins added one of them, the *Espiritu Santo*, to his growing fleet, renaming her the *Gratia Dei* (By the grace of God). He then decided to move on southeastward along the coast again, hoping to find less contested opportunities.[2]

Hawkins explored other rivers along the coast of what are now Guinea and Sierra Leone. Ingram and his shipmates encountered the delight of eating bananas and the terror of nighttime attacks by hippos. For weeks, efforts to capture slaves remained less productive than they had hoped for. Then Hawkins's fleet was approached by emissaries from a couple of local leaders whose armies were besieging an interior town. They needed English men with firearms, and they proposed that Hawkins provide the firepower they needed to succeed. For this they promised as many slaves as Hawkins could stow in his ships' holds. It was the same kind of deal they and other strongmen had reached previously with the Portuguese along this same stretch of coast. Hawkins formalized an agreement with them on January 15, 1567–1568.[3]

It was an agreement between strong charismatic leaders, who were simultaneously served and enabled by their subordinates. In exchange, the strongmen all expected mandatory loyalty and obedience from ordinary people. Hawkins was not different from the African leaders, having the same expectations of David Ingram and his shipmates as the Africans had of their subordinates. That tradition continues in autocratic regimes even today. Ingram was complicit in the awful business of slaving, but he probably thought he had little choice.

Once again Robert Barrett led a force, this time moving up the Sierra Leone River. Francis Drake, Hawkins's young cousin, was part of it as captain of one of the smaller vessels. Barrett was greeted by one of his new allies, and he was probably treated to a gourd of palm wine as part of the formalities. They settled on a joint strategy, one that made effective use of English tactical organization and firearms.[4]

West African Cultures

The contending African forces are today difficult to identify with certainty. The fighting took place on the island of Conga and elsewhere along the Sierra Leone River, inland from what is now Freetown, Sierra Leone (Figure 3.2). However, in 1567 there was much fighting between several local tribes and African invaders. Two of them were the Mendes, called "Manes" by the Portuguese, and the Temnes. The Temne people lived along the river that Hawkins and his men penetrated. It is clear from other sources that the Temnes were conquered around that time by the Mendes, who lived to the east of the Temnes. It is likely that the conflict that Hawkins took advantage of was part of that broader war.[5]

Today the dominant culture in this part of Sierra Leone is still Temne. It is probable that the people Hawkins captured were mostly Temnes, but his captives might conceivably have included Mendes or speakers of some other language of the Niger-Congo family. Historical matters are also confused by the numbers of political subdivisions. In the eighteenth century there were still 44 Temne chiefdoms. These were further divided into subgroups.

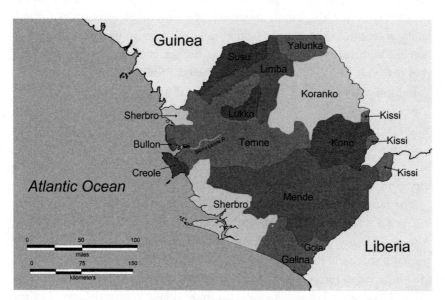

Figure 3.2. The cultures of Sierra Leone. Figure by author.

Ancient animosities between them persist today, but they are now often framed in contending religious terms.[6]

Ingram's Testimony about Africa

The People

What Ingram had to say about Africans reveals his curiosity about, and his empathy for, African people.[7] Ingram might have had a lot to say about the battle, but the seven topics in the charge of his interrogators did not call for that kind of information. The native uses of iron tools, cattle including milk cows, and guinea hens were responses to specific questions arising from the seven broad questions of Francis Walsingham's agenda.

Ingram said, "The people are of disposition courteously given if you use them courteously and do not abuse them either in their persons or goods. The killing and taking of their beasts, birds, fishes, or fruits, cannot offend them, except it be their domestic cattle, for they do milk some of them. They keep beasts about their houses, cows, guinea hens, and such like. Also that there are wild horses [zebras] of goodly shape, but the people of the country have not the use of them. If any of them do hold up both their hands at length together and kiss the backs of them on both sides, then you may undoubtedly trust them, for that is the greatest token of their friendship that may be. Which if they break, they die for the same."

Ingram was telling his story chronologically, often touching on specific topics separately when they related to other regions he had visited. For example, through the course of the interrogation, Ingram described birds he had seen at separate times in Africa, the Caribbean, and North America. By backtracking and lumping all references to birds, the recorder muddled observations made by Ingram at different times and in different places.[8]

The same sort of confusion prevailed in Ingram's discussion of the use of horsetails, which most later readers incorrectly assumed pertained to North America. "If any of them [Africans] happens come to you with a horsetail [zebra] in his hand then you may assure yourself that he is a messenger from the king, and to him you may safely commit yourself to go anywhere, or go to the king or anywhere else, or send by him any thing or message to the king, for those men are always either ensign bearers in the wars, or the king's messengers as aforesaid, who will never betray you."

Ingram saw zebra tail whisks, which came up again at the end of his trek through North America. "There was given to the Captain Champaigne of Le Havre in France for one of those tails, a hundred pieces of silver. And a piece is eight ounces as he said he had heard." Zebra or horsehair fly whisks are still made in Africa and used as ensigns of office. Jomo Kenyatta, Kenya's first president following independence, was often photographed with a ceremonial fly whisk. French Captain Champaigne could have told Ingram about fly whisks only after he had rescued Ingram and his two companions, sometime in late 1569. Champaigne must have had some experience in West Africa, for he told Ingram about the sale of a horsetail ensign, apparently during a conversation about their similar experiences there. That the sale was made for an astonishing 100 silver pieces of eight clearly impressed both of them.

African Silent Trade

Ingram said, "If you will have any of the people come aboard your ship, hang out some white cloth or thing on a staff, for that is a sign of amity. And if you will barter for wares with them, then leave the things that you will sell, on the ground, and go from it a pretty way off. Then they will come and take it, and set down such wares as they will for it in the place. If you think it is not sufficient, then leave their wares with signs that you do not like it, and then they will bring more until either they or you are satisfied or will give no more. Otherwise you may hang your wares on a long pike or pole's end and so put more or less on it until you have agreed on the bargain, and they will hang out their wares on a pole's end in like manner."[9]

Ingram was describing silent trade, a well-known practice later found to be common across West Africa. Ingram was impressed by the efficacy of silent trade, and he would later use this part of his African experience to make his way from community to community along the trails of eastern North America. He described silent trade as something to be recommended to future English voyagers. Ingram would also discover other techniques to facilitate trade in North America.

In connection with trade, Ingram said in one place that "Ballivo" was a greeting, like good evening or something like that. At another point in his testimony he said that word was *gwando*. It might seem encouraging to discover that many words begin with a "g" in both the Mende and Temne languages, but searching for words corresponding to *ballivo* or *gwando* in either language is a fruitless exercise, as is usually the case for most people remembering words heard a few times in the distant past.[10]

The two alternative words in what are otherwise identical sentences is probably also further evidence of the inabilities of separate recorders to hear and spell unfamiliar words. It is also further good evidence that the 12-year-old memories of exotic words by an illiterate English-speaking sailor are unlikely to provide useful evidence for linguists. That said, Ingram's recollection of some other words encountered in eastern North America proved to be more useful (see Chapter 7).

African Customs and Clothing

Ingram, like other English people of his time, was particularly attentive to practices that were the most exotic from his own cultural perspective.[11] Like others of his generation he was particularly fascinated by cannibalism and practices related to it. He was present when an African died, apparently from natural causes. He described the person's next of kin cutting the deceased's throat and distributing the blood for his kinsmen to drink as part of the ritual. It was his impression that none of the blood should be lost to the family. However, he was quick to add that these were courteous people who were not indulging in cannibalism, a subject he would return to.

The Englishmen referred to local African leaders as "kings," as they also often did in the English conquest of Ireland. Ingram noticed that these men were always elegantly clothed in colored garments so that they would stand out. He also noticed that leading men arrived for meetings carried on sumptuous chairs that were decorated with silver, crystal, and other kinds of precious stones. Important subordinate men typically wore large russet feathers in their hair to identify their high ranks.

African Tools and Implements

Ingram's questioners were interested in not just the kinds of people he had encountered and how they were dressed, but also in the sorts of implements they had and how they used them.[12] He described iron-bladed crooked knives that the West Africans used for expertly carving wood and bone. He even saw a kind of bugle that he thought had been carved from an elephant's tusk. Horn vuvuzelas were made in southern Africa, so it is possible that these are what Ingram saw.[13] Plastic versions of these are heard most often today at soccer matches. Making an African vuvuzela from solid ivory was possible with iron tools, but it would have been very difficult, and it is therefore unlikely. It is also possible Ingram saw a forest buffalo horn vuvuzela and incorrectly remembered that it had been made from ivory.

The vuvuzela was connected with other equipment used in warfare. The Africans used drums made from wood and hide. They carried dried wood-frame hide shields that had been thickened in salt and were strong enough to deflect arrows. They fought with short spears headed by socketed iron blades two fingers broad and a half foot long. They also used broad iron swords nearly a yard long. These were single-edge swords with broad backs. Ingram thought they were similar to English fencing foils but heavier.

They also used short bows strung with cordage and used to shoot yard-long arrows. These were headed with metal or bone. Ingram noted that the arrows were short range and low velocity. They could be deflected by a shield or a staff. However, he had also seen heavy volleys of lethal poisoned arrows that produced small but fatal wounds.

Ingram returned to the importance of horsetail ensigns, which he noticed were especially important to display in warfare. They were dyed in various colors, such as red, yellow, or green, and some of them had bits of glass or crystal affixed to them.

Crooked knives, swords, and arrow points of iron; artifacts made from elephant tusk; hide shields; and this additional reference to horsetail (zebra) ensigns all point to Africa. None of these existed in North America prior to extensive European trade. One could make a tortured argument that the items in this list, other than elephant tusk, could have been introduced and left over from the 1539–1540 portion of Hernando de Soto's expedition along the part of the Atlantic Coastal Plain of North America that Ingram later passed through. However, Ingram's evidence indicates that the artifacts were much too common and abundant for that argument to be credible. Ingram was speaking generally, and things like six-inch socketed iron spear points could not have been present at all, let alone in common use, in America at this time.[14]

Crime and Punishment

In Africa, men were allowed to have multiple wives, five to ten for successful men, as many as a hundred for a king. Adultery was severely punished. The guilty woman was compelled by magistrates to cut the throat of her guilty lover. This was followed by the guilty man's kin being obliged to cut the woman's throat. In another case, the guilty individuals were executed while lying on their backs with their hands and legs bound. An executioner knelt on their chests and executed both of them with a crooked knife.[15]

Ingram insisted that he had witnessed such executions, which seem tame compared to the gruesome executions that were common back home in England at the time. Grotesque public executions were a feature of Elizabethan England, albeit not for adultery. Heads were lopped off in the less elaborate punishments. Truly serious offenders could expect to be hanged, gutted, and dismembered in gruesome public displays. Ingram probably judged that what he said he saw in Africa was even worse. Like cannibalism, he probably viewed the drastic punishments he described as more evidence that these dark-skinned people were less than fully human. It was another convenient way to rationalize race-based enslavement.[16]

It appears that this part of Ingram's testimony created much agitation among the assembled gentlemen in 1582. Other sources indicate that there can be no doubt these dramatic events, or the fear of them, occurred in Africa. Ingram was profoundly impressed, as were others who witnessed it, by the surrender of an African man to Hawkins and inevitable slavery. The man elected to surrender himself into slavery to avoid the death penalty for adultery that Ingram described so vividly.[17]

Their Kings

Ingram observed and reported on the protocol required when interacting with a West African king.[18] "If you will speak with the king at your first approaching near to him you must kneel down on both your knees and then arise again and come somewhat nearer him within your length. Then kneel down again as you did before. Then take of the earth or grass between both your hands, kissing the backside of each of them, and put the earth or grass on the crown of your head, and so come and kiss the king's feet. Those circumstances being performed you may then arise and stand up and talk with him."

In addition to wearing very colorful clothes to stand out in a crowd of commoners, the kings wore what Ingram described as large red stone tablets, four inches long and two wide (10x5 cm), on strings around their necks. These were apparently bipolar tablets, each with curved sides and having a perforation at one end. The inexperienced Ingram said that he thought they might be rubies.

A king had one of the red tablets because of his office. But it was also the case that the red tablet caused its holder to be king. "If by any means whatsoever the stone is taken from him, by force or by slight, he who steals it shall be king in his place." Kingship was not the usually permanent rank enjoyed by English kings. Ingram estimated that most kings lasted only four or five years. In the best of circumstances, a deposed king could expect to be quickly replaced by his competitor; in the worst, he would be killed.[19]

The Specter of Cannibalism

Ingram returned repeatedly to the subject of cannibalism. Elizabethans were fascinated by the notion of cannibalism and Ingram did not disappoint. "You shall know the men eaters by their teeth, for their teeth are long and sharp at the ends like dog teeth." Filed teeth served as a way to distinguish between people who were truly irredeemable savages from those who were merely primitive.[20]

The practice of tooth filing is well known for West Africa, but it was very rare or absent in North America. Rare ritual cannibalism was later reported for a part of North America that Ingram visited. There are a few examples of a different form of native tooth filing from Mesoamerica, but few if any of them from the Eastern Woodlands. However, excavations in Mexico City in the 1980s turned up the skeletons of African people with teeth filed to sharp points, just as Ingram described. They were found when subway construction encountered a colonial-era hospital for indigenous people. Archaeologists have inferred that these people were slaves who arrived in the sixteenth century.[21] It is possible that these were African people who had been captured along with many of David Ingram's shipmates after the battle at San Juan de Ulua (Chapter 4).

African Industries

Ingram observed Africans heating and cooking with white peat they dug out of bogs.[22] His recorders heard different depths at which it was found, one writing "two or three feet," and the other writing that it came from a fathom (six feet) underground. Perhaps they both heard "fathom" but one did not know enough to convert it accurately. Ingram remarked on how wholesome, sweet, and aromatic the peat was. He made a small ball of the white peat and tied it to his hair so that it would hang in front of his nose. He understood why the Africans burned the white peat even though there was much wood available. The Africans also enjoyed healthy salt marshes near the ocean, which to Ingram helped account for the abundant marine fishery off shore.

Ingram saw many iron tools, and he concluded that the Africans were extracting it themselves from ore by heating it on perforated iron plates and allowing the molten metal to drop through and be collected. He saw this only at a safe distance from the heat, so it is not clear what he was observing. The Africans had been smelting iron and hammering it into tools for millennia. Local smiths used laterite ore, small furnaces, and hand-operated bellows to produce iron by means of a bloomery process. Charcoal fuel heated the ore to its melting point, producing a bloom of iron mixed with slag. Subsequent heating and smithing served to remove the slag and make iron implements.[23] Ingram told his interrogators much that was generally accurate about African industries that were missing from the Americas. African metallurgy, including iron, and the people's uses of other metals are good examples.

Ingram's Botany

Ingram talked about many productive tree species, particularly fruit trees. All three of the manuscript recorders of his testimony lumped all of the botanical entries in ways that Ingram could not have intended. Again, the confusion probably was prompted by the interests and questions of Ingram's interrogators.

Ingram made five statements about palm trees, four of which pertained to Africa.[24] He saw people tapping palm trees and using the sap, which "will yeald a wine in color like whey but in taste strong and somewhat like bastard."[25] He thought it was an excellent drink, but like strong wines it would make a man drunk if he drank too much of it. The Africans used gourd bottles to ferment the sap, leaving them hanging from convenient branches for anyone passing by. A traveler would drink the stalest, and thus strongest, of them, refill the gourd with fresh sap and hang it at the least fermented end of the queue.

The gift to Robert Barrett, the polyglot master of the *Jesus*, of a gourd containing palm wine in an African town was mentioned earlier. It is revealing if it is true, but it comes from an uncertain source.[26] Palm wine and its storage in gourds is widely attested in Africa. Making palm wine was then and still is common in West Africa. There are examples of gourd containers in the Caribbean, but it is likely that the practice of making palm wine was introduced there only later by the Spanish (Chapter 4).[27]

Drinking fermented beverages was rare and generally absent in sixteenth-century North America. Pulque was fermented from maize in central Mexico, as it still is today, but fermentation of palm wine was not indigenous anywhere along the route of Ingram's long walk in America. Ingram could have encountered the uncommon use of fermented agave in south Texas, or of fermented persimmon in Carolina, but not palm wine. Heart of the sabal palm was commonly eaten in America, but not in Africa.[28]

Ingram and the other seamen with Hawkins had much greater exposure to the use of poisoned arrows in Africa, although they would later discover that some were used in the Caribbean as well.[29] The difference was that the toxin used in Africa led to symptoms like those of tetanus, whereas the toxin used in the Caribbean was probably taken from the manchineel tree or some animal source. There was much interest in finding a remedy for infection by African poisoned arrows. Ingram noticed that a red oil sap from the root of one species of palm, probably the oil palm, was an effective antidote for African poisoned arrows and other weapons. Elsewhere we learn that Hawkins was advised by one of his party to treat his arrow injury with a clove of garlic. Thus, as it typically is with folk remedies, this one occasionally appeared to work, but more often these treatments were ineffective.

Recent research has shown that palm oil has active ingredients that have some therapeutic potential. Africans have traditionally used it not only to treat poisoned arrow and other wounds but also as a cure for gonorrhea, bronchitis, headaches, and rheumatism. Whether it is effective against any of these remains to be tested, but Ingram was at least correct in reporting its use.[30]

A final mention of the use of palm trees in Africa was Ingram's observation that African war parties tried to camp as near as they could to groves of palms so they would have them handy not just for treating arrow wounds but for palm wine as well.

Ingram became a big fan of bananas, which were quite new to him. He thought the fruit of the plantain tree tasted like pudding and was delighted that it could be eaten raw when it ripened and turned yellow.[31]

Ingram described plants that impressed him as exotic everywhere he landed. In Africa, more than a few of them were domesticates introduced by the Portuguese, who brought them from Indonesia and other places along their extensive trade routes. Bananas originated in Southeast Asia and New Guinea, but they were spread by Arab traders to the Indian subcontinent and Africa prior to the sixteenth century. Later, Portuguese and Spanish ships carried the plant to West Africa and the Americas. The banana plant survived transportation readily and eventually found its way to gardens surrounding colonies in Brazil and the Caribbean. Thus, it is remotely possible that bananas had already been introduced to the Caribbean by the Spanish by 1567. While that remains possible, it is much more likely that West Africa was where Ingram first encountered them.

There is considerable confusion about trees in the manuscripts. Ingram had a good eye for plants, large and small. He mentioned several of them when his questioners asked him to describe the fruitfulness of the country, and what sorts of plants could be found there. He mentioned a half dozen that he could only have seen in Africa, but these were lumped with Caribbean and American plants by the recorders and later editing.[32]

Ingram reported seeing many date palms, orange trees, lemon trees, and almond trees. All of these were native to West Africa or had been recently introduced by the Portuguese. None of them were native to the Caribbean or North America. He also reported an abundance of Brazil trees, probably including the Brazil pepper that is still invasive in the subtropics today. The many pepper trees he referred to could be any of several plants that are native to West Africa.

He made a point of describing what he called an "abundance of bombasine or cotton trees and bushes." These were the kapok trees (*Ceiba pentandra*) that are native to Africa. Ingram saw the commercial potential of yellow kapok fiber, which is light, buoyant, water resistant, and resilient. Until the invention of synthetic fibers it was important for stuffing mattresses, pillows, life preservers, and the like. Ingram thought there was enough of the product to fill an infinite number of ships.[33]

Ingram's Zoology

Unlike North America, Africa had many herd animals that Ingram took to be species of deer.[34] They came in white, red, and speckled colors, the

likes of which he had never seen previously. He was able to be more knowledgeable in the case of Walsingham's oddly specific agenda question seven
regarding whether Ingram had seen a beast much larger than an ox. Ingram
said he had seen many large buffalos, similar to oxen in shape, but with
drooping ears, curved horns, and shaggy hair on their ears, their breasts, and
elsewhere (Figure 3.3). Their eyes were very black and their hair very long
and rough like a goat. The hides of these were very desirable and expensive. Ingram had noticed that the buffalos kept company only by couples,
male and female. They always fought male to male and female to female
when they met. Ingram's descriptions, here and elsewhere, reveal a sharp
eye and a keen memory for the wonders of the natural world. Regrettably,

Figure 3.3. African forest buffalo (*Syncerus caffer nanus*). Photograph by Jamie
Lantzy. GNU Free Documentation License, Version 1.2 or any later version
published by the Free Software Foundation.

Walsingham's interest in oxen was prompted by John Walker's report of ox hides in what is now the state of Maine.

Ingram's description later led some historians to conclude that Ingram was describing American bison, even though bison do not sport long drooping ears. Ingram's description is clearly that of an African forest buffalo (*Syncerus caffer nanus*), the range of which includes Sierra Leone. The identification is made certain by his description of the forked iron tool used to hamstring (hough) the buffalo to put it down. Iron tools did not yet exist in North America. Ingram could only have seen such a tool and the hamstringing technique in Africa.[35]

Ingram also saw many other animals for which Africa is famous.[36] He saw herds of elephants, repeating that their tusks were used to make trumpets that the people used in warfare. He also encountered leopards, which were very dangerous. Somehow he learned that a leopard could kill people and would even follow an unarmed person up a tree to do so. That kind of observation indicates that Ingram was somehow communicating with and learning from the Africans he encountered. It was the beginning of his education in the ways in which a traveler can overcome language barriers with pointing, gestures, and nonverbal expressions.

Job Hortop later reported his experiences with hippos, which Ingram probably shared. Hortop was astonished by the overall size and the lethal tusks of what he called the "sea horse." The hippos, he said, sometimes came into the villages at night, seized a sleeping person, and dragged them to their deaths in the river. The Africans countered this by laying logs across forest trails, where they could corner and kill the cumbersome hippos. The hippos are still very dangerous to people in Africa.

Hortop also described how the Africans killed elephants with deadfalls. After noting a tree where an elephant liked to spend the night, they cut the trunk almost through at the height of the elephant, waited for it to topple and pin the elephant, then moved in quickly to kill the animal with spears. Hortop's words show that Ingram was not the only crewman with an interest in the natural world and a gift for cross-cultural communication.[37]

Ingram's concluding statements regarding Africa mentioned his surprise at seeing russet parrots rather than green ones.[38] All of the parrot species (*Psittacidae*) Ingram could have encountered in the Caribbean and in eastern North America would have been green with various markings, as any good bird guide will confirm.[39] When he mentions russet parrots he is clearly talking about what he saw in Africa. Guinea and Sierra Leone are home to one of two species of the genus *Psittacus*. The russet parrot is the timneh parrot (*Psittacus erithacus timneh*), which is closely related to the African gray parrots that are more widespread to the east (Figure 3.4). Both are often kept as pets today because of their highly developed abilities to mimic human language. The timneh is smaller and the darker of the two species, with a dark maroon tail and a patch on its upper mandible. Ingram correctly describes its color as "russet," which in Elizabethan English referred to homespun clothing that was coarse, rustic, and typically a dull reddish brown.

Ingram also talked about the guinea hens of West Africa. The latter are sometimes kept as novelties in modern America, but they were largely confined to Africa in the sixteenth century. Ingram's observations in Africa give ethnographers and other natural historians an early look at things later confirmed by European travelers. In some cases they added information that might not otherwise be known today, at least not for this early date. The information on cultural practices is a good example of this part of Ingram's contribution to modern ethnology.

This ends the African portion of Ingram's account. His descriptions of the people and their natural setting seem strangely sympathetic given the

Figure 3.4. The West African grey timneh parrot (*Psittacus erithacus timneh*). Public Domain via Wikimedia Commons. Photograph by Peter Fuchs. Licensed under the Creative Commons Attribution-Share Alike 2.0 Generic license.

purpose of Hawkins's third voyage and the way it played out in what is now Sierra Leone. Hawkins attacked his Portuguese competitors, and like them he exploited the ongoing warfare between African nations, allying with the African leader of one antagonist in order to acquire slaves from the other. English firepower and tactical organization ensured that the conflict would end as it did, and Hawkins would fill the holds of his ships with captives.

The battle for the besieged Temne town was brutal. The defenders launched clouds of poisoned arrows. The English fired their arquebuses, large heavy firearms. The Africans fought each other hand to hand in a confused battle. In the end the town fell to the attackers. The African victors initially seemed more interested in exterminating their defeated enemies than in turning them over to Hawkins. The Englishmen were appalled to witness not just massacre, but also some cases of ritual cannibalism, following the slaughter. Hawkins rued the loss of so many potential slaves, but he still ended up with hundreds of men, women, and children to fill his ships, while losing only a few of his own men.[40]

Along the way, Hawkins had recruited a French ship and seized some Portuguese ships, so that by the time he finished his raiding and buying in West Africa he had a larger fleet, with the cargo holds filled with 400 to 500 African people. With that, the slaving fleet set off once again, this time bound for the Caribbean.

4

Ingram in the Caribbean and the Gulf of Mexico

After stocking up on wood and water, the fleet set off for America on February 3, 1567–1568.[1] They had been hunting for slaves in Africa for over two months. At this point they had between 400 and 500 men, women, and children stowed away as human cargo. The passage was bad enough for the officers and men of the ship, but it was horrendous for the newly enslaved people kept in manacles in the hold. This awful journey was what came to be regularly referred to as the "middle passage" of what was a triangle trade route between Africa, America, and Europe.

The preferred sailing practice of the day led Hawkins to first head to the Cape Verde Islands, at a latitude of about 15.5° north. The fleet then let the trade winds carry them along that line of latitude to the islands of the Lesser Antilles. Once there they would pass through the island chain, the Leeward Islands stretching northward on their right, and the Windward Islands on their left. It was 53 days and nights before a lookout sighted land, March 27, 1568. This was the island of Dominica (Figure 4.1).

Ports of Call

Once through the passage into the Caribbean Sea, Hawkins steered his fleet southwest to the island of Margarita, off the coast of Venezuela. Hawkins was well received by the local governor, and there was trading in goods other than slaves amid much ceremonious dining and polite entertainment. There was probably trade in slaves and other contraband too, but none of that appears in the official records. Both sides knew that this would be in

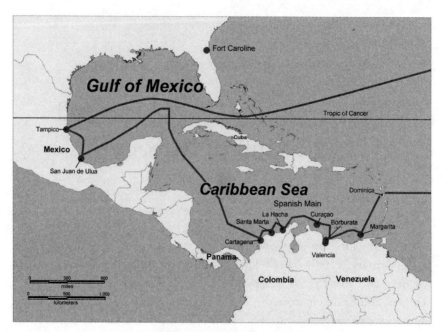

Figure 4.1. The clockwise route of the Hawkins expedition around the Caribbean and the Gulf of Mexico. Figure by author.

violation of orders from the king of Spain. It was better to leave it unrecorded. For the time being, practicalities protected Hawkins and his ships. The fleet stayed nine days at Margarita.[2]

Margarita

Margarita's coastline had an abundance of pearl oysters, and the Spanish were taking advantage of them. Ingram was impressed by their techniques.[3] "The people do dive and fish for pearl in three or four fathoms of water, which they have in oysters. They do cover, when they dive, their heads and upper parts of their bodies with leather to their waists, tied fast about their middles, whereby they take air under the water."[4]

Oysters of the *Pteriidae* family produce nacre, and they are consequently the source of both lustrous pearls and mother of pearl. Most species of this family are tropical, but the distributions of some of them extend to shallow coastal zones of higher subtropical latitudes. *Pinctada imbricata*, commonly called the Atlantic pearl oyster or the Gulf pearl oyster, is of a genus known mostly from the western Pacific, but it also occurs in southern Florida and Texas southward around the Gulf of Mexico and the Caribbean.

Columbus encountered pearls in Venezuela on his third voyage in 1498. He described women wearing pearls where he went ashore, and he managed to acquire 1.5 kilograms of them, the best of which became part of Queen Isabella's famous Venezuelan necklace. Cortés later also acquired pearls, along with gold, silver, and other Aztec treasures in Mexico. The royal houses of Europe became destinations for many of the pearls obtained by explorers during the sixteenth century. There they served as symbols of power, along with jewels and precious metals. Elizabeth I was a particularly avid collector; several portraits of her show pearls as important components of her dress and regalia.[5]

In 1568, pearls were being produced in large numbers both here and off the Pacific coast of Panama. There is no evidence to indicate that Ingram could have observed pearling either in West Africa or off Panama's Pacific coast. However, the fleet stayed over a week at Margarita, and here Ingram was able to observe the pearl divers. Ingram's description of leather equipment to extend dives seems a bit far-fetched, but it is consistent with and supplements a longer description provided by Herrera in his 1726–1730 *Historia General*. The pearls that they dived for on Margarita were the largest discovered up to the time. Herrera wrote:

> The Cacique Pedrarias made the natives dive for pearls in the presence of the Castilians, at their request. Many of those that the Cacique gave them were like hazelnuts, and some even larger. They were very skilled at going underwater, and they entered the sea calmly. They went in their canoes, using a stone tied with wicker as an anchor for each canoe. They plunged into the water, carrying bags tied to their necks, and from time to time the bags came up full of oysters. Sometimes they dove into ten *estados* [ca. 20 m] of water, because the bigger oysters are at the bottom. If they occasionally come up, it is for food, and they remain at work while they have it. The oysters stick to the rocks and to each other, so it is necessary to use considerable force to detach them. Many times it happens that the divers drown because they run out of air during forced dives, and because the sharks attack them. The bags for the oysters have ropes tied to them so they can pull them up out of the water. They found shells with ten, twenty, and thirty or more pearls, but small ones. The Indians did not know how to drill holes through them, so that decreased the value of those they brought back.[6]

A contemporary watercolor (Figure 4.2) is also consistent with Herrera's description. However, the French text with the image claims that the divers

CANAV·POVR·PE CHER·LE SPERLES

Figure 4.2. Pearl divers off Margarita. Drake Manuscript, folio 57, 261. The Morgan Library & Museum, MA 3900. Bequest of Clara S. Peck, 1983.

could hold their breaths up to 15 minutes. This is longer than the current world record for free divers. Perhaps Ingram's awkward description is of leather air bags used to extend their dives.

Borburata

From Margarita, the Hawkins fleet set off westward for Borburata, 130 kilometers west of modern Caracas. This was the eastern end of the stretch of Caribbean coast that is still known as the Spanish Main.[7] There Hawkins conducted more illicit business, bought supplies, and careened his ships for cleaning and patching. Ships in this era were not yet being clad with copper to protect their timbers from barnacles and teredo worms. This was not a serious problem for ships that stayed in colder northern waters, but the effects of these residents of tropical seas could turn the hulls of wooden ships into sieves with alarming speed. As a result, in these waters, ships had to be cleaned and recaulked frequently. But even then, the damage was swift and extensive in the Caribbean Sea. Hawkins's fleet was deteriorating simply because it was in tropical waters.

The governor of Borburata was a strict enforcer of the king's prohibitions on trade with the English, so Hawkins's letter to the governor had to be even more obsequious and deceitful than usual. He offered subtle bribes and exercised slaves ashore as means to attract interest. He also sent a letter to the bishop at Valencia, 22 miles (35 km) inland, for which he received back a polite reply. Hawkins took this to mean that the bishop would not discourage the sale of slaves.

Hawkins heard nothing from the governor, so he sent Robert Barrett with a detachment to Valencia to see what could be developed there. They found the town to be deserted. The missing residents even included the presumably friendly bishop. Meanwhile, covert trading and ship maintenance continued for two months at Borburata. These were probably the months of April and May in the Julian (Old Style) calendar. Such a long stay would have afforded them two new moons and at least one full moon, during which they could use the very low tides to careen their ships on the beach and clean their hulls. They started with the smaller ships, the *William and John*, the *Swallow*, the *Judith*, the *Angel*, and other craft that had been picked up off Africa.

Curaçao

The smaller vessels having had their hulls cleaned, Hawkins had his men turn to careening the *Jesus* and the *Minion*. He sent the smaller ships off northwestward to acquire beef and hides on Curaçao, where the Spanish had long since released cattle to run wild and propagate.[8] Ingram appears to have been aboard one of the ships sent to Curaçao. He was probably talking about Curaçao when he mentioned seeing many European domesticates that had been left to go wild and propagate there. He said, "There is great plenty of wild goats, also great plenty of kine [cows] and cattle like ours, but they are all wild. There is great plenty of wild horses, also great plenty of sheep like ours."[9]

There is a curious final paragraph that appears at the ends of the Tanner manuscript and of Hakluyt's 1589 published version of Ingram's testimony that is derived from it. It does not read like the paraphrased notes that comprise all the other entries in the three source manuscripts. Richard Hakluyt probably added this codicil after the interrogation was concluded.[10]

It is an important passage, not just for the information about the Spanish colonization of the island it contains but also for its probable later use by Shakespeare as a source for *The Tempest*.[11] This important passage is worth repeating, because it comes up again in later chapters of Ingram's story.

> Also, the said examinate saith that there is an island called Curaçao, and there are in it five or six thousand Indians at the least and all these are governed by one only negro who is but a slave to a Spaniard. And moreover the Spaniards will send but one of their slaves with 100 or 200 of the Indians when they go to gather gold in the rivers descending from the mountains, and when they shall be absent by the space of twenty or thirty days at the least every one of the Indians will nevertheless obey all the slave's commandments with as great reverence as if he were the natural king, although there be never a Christian near them by the space of one or two hundred miles, which argues the great obedience of these people and how easily they may be governed when they be once conquered.

The Curaçao story is consistent with events that occurred later during Francis Drake's return voyages to the Caribbean during the decade of the 1570s. By that time there were remote communities of escaped slaves that had successfully established themselves far enough away from Spanish communities to flourish independently. These were the Cimarrons (Sp. Cimarrones), hardy people of African descent who were numerous enough to hold the Spanish at arm's length and to resist their efforts to enslave the blacks anew. Drake was not surprised to encounter them, and he anticipated forming alliances with the Cimarrons based on mutual respect and common cause against Spanish interests. Drake would quickly establish working relationships with the Cimarrons in Panama when he landed there in 1571. This means that Ingram's assertion that Africans were succeeding on the Spanish Main, both as slaves and as outlaws, was not new information among seamen in 1582. Drake probably understood the opportunities afforded by the Cimarrons from his own experiences as a young captain on Hawkins's third voyage. However, Hakluyt's later inclusion of the codicil might indicate that it was still news to the more sheltered gentlemen of London.[12]

La Hacha

With his bigger ships cleaned, Hawkins decided to leave Borburata on the full moon at the beginning of June. They rendezvoused with the ships that had gone on to Curaçao, and the reassembled fleet headed for Nuestra

Señora de los Remedios del Río de la Hacha. This was the formidable name of a squalid little town that had suffered repeated depredations by pirates. Among them had been John Lovell, Hawkins's agent who had come by the previous year. The commander of the small Spanish force at La Hacha, Miguel de Castellanos, had been severely fined for having traded with Hawkins on one of his earlier voyages, so he had turned Lovell away just months ago. Curiously, Hawkins decided to send Francis Drake in advance to La Hacha on the *Judith* and with the *Angel* as well. This was despite the fact that Drake had been with Lovell, for the Spanish commander was almost certain to once again give him a hostile reception.

The Spanish predictably opened fire on Drake's ships as soon as they were in range. Drake returned fire, but then withdrew out of range to blockade the harbor. This the English ships did for five days, until Hawkins joined them with the rest of the fleet. Hawkins sent a letter ashore, forgiving the commander for his previous treatment of Lovell and his unfriendly reception of Drake, and proposing that all would be well if Hawkins could sell 60 slaves as a means to defray his current expenses. This was rejected, so Hawkins landed a force away from the town and attacked on land, under covering fire from his ships' guns. The Spanish defenders were dispersed into the surrounding forest.

La Hacha was at the time another center of the Caribbean pearl trade on the Spanish Main. At La Hacha, Hawkins cajoled, charmed, and threatened the obstinate Spanish under flags of truce. Eventually two escaped slaves came to Hawkins and told him that they knew where the Spanish treasury was hidden. They led Hawkins and his men to it, with the result that the English then held not just the town but all its portable wealth. Castellanos remained adamant, but Hawkins was driving a wedge between him and the leading citizens of the town. The citizens were tired of hiding in the woods and losing all their possessions to a man they thought only wanted to trade with them. Castellanos was forced to relent, and he sat down to negotiate with Hawkins. Castellanos created a plausible cover story to give to his superiors, and all was forgiven between the Englishmen and the Spanish colonists. Brisk covert trading continued under the terms of this ruse.

They cut a deal and made a show of amity. The English returned everything they had taken from the community and assumed liability for what had been destroyed. In exchange they were allowed to trade in goods and slaves. It was a large net gain for Hawkins. There were additional sales disguised as gift exchanges, including some involving pearls of high value. As part of the bargain, Hawkins treacherously handed over the two African men who had turned on the Spanish and had provided Hawkins with crucial help. Both of the men were brutally executed.

While they were at La Hacha, Job Hortop engaged in some jungle adventures, along with others of Hawkins's sailors. Hortop was very impressed by the jaguars and alligators. Using a pig as bait, they caught a huge alligator, which the ship's carpenter measured to be 24 feet long. The men killed and skinned the beast, then stuffed it for storage on board one of the ships. It was another trophy for display back in England.[13]

Once business was concluded, Hawkins sailed off, headed for the natural harbor at Santa Marta, below the snow-capped Sierra Nevadas on what is now the north coast of Colombia. He arrived there around the end of June 1568.[14]

Santa Marta

At Santa Marta Hawkins again conducted his usual charade, except that this time he and the savvy governor agreed on a contrived military confrontation at which the Spanish would pretend to resist then quickly capitulate, this to be followed by a brisk sale of slaves. In the end, Hawkins had only 50 slaves left, but the Spanish settlers could afford to buy no more.

Job Hortop was by this time an amateur natural historian, much like David Ingram. Hortop encountered a seven-foot rattlesnake at Santa Marta. The vivid memory of it stayed with him through his later decade of Spanish imprisonment. He reported that the snake was as big around in the middle as a man's thigh. The English sailors had never seen anything like it, as rattlesnakes are native only to the Americas. The huge snake had 13 large segmented rattles on its tail, indicating that it was that many years old, as Spanish informants told Hortop.[15]

Cartagena

Hawkins sailed on to Cartagena, but there he was rebuffed again. This time he faced formidable fortifications. Hawkins did not have enough men and arms to challenge the Spanish there. Moreover, it was late July, and the hurricane season was upon them. Knowing that, it made sense to begin the long journey home. Contrary winds kept them stuck at anchor for another week, during which time a small French boat that had been part of Hawkins's fleet decided to remain in the Caribbean. They set off on their own.

The larger *Grace of God* remained with him, but Hawkins had transferred the French crewmen of this vessel to the *Jesus*. By this time he had come to trust the Frenchmen enough to restore them to their former ship, from the *Jesus* back to the *Grace of God* and their familiar French captain. In exchange, the English crewmen who had made certain the *Grace of God* would remain with the fleet were transferred back to their home ship, the *Jesus*. Hawkins also decided to scuttle the Portuguese caravel he had taken off Cape Blanco; it had been riddled by teredo worms and was in no shape to recross the Atlantic. These changes would influence critical decisions that would have to be made later in the summer.[16]

The People

Ingram made several observations about the Caribbean in addition to those already mentioned. However, it is not certain where he was in each case. His audience was fascinated by his mention of the nakedness of Caribbean people. This was of particular notice to English seamen.

"In the southern parts of those countries they all go naked, saving that the noblemen's privates are covered with the bark of a gourd, and the women's privates with the hair or leaf of a Adalmita palm tree. Further that the men go naked saving only the middle part of them covered with skins of beasts, and with leaves."[17]

The use of gourd penis sheaths was common in New Guinea, but it was also known for parts of Africa and South America (Figure 4.3). It is not known to have been used in North America. To this entry, Hakluyt later added the observation that of necessity northern Indians dressed more warmly. Leaving that comparative addition aside, the context of the entry points to the Caribbean, and in this there is support from a source called the Drake Manuscript. Paintings in the Drake Manuscript are mostly labeled as depicting indigenous people, and most appear to reference the Caribbean. All of them are rather primitive compared to the paintings later made by John White at the ill-fated Roanoke Colony in 1587, but like White's illustrations they are very informative.[18]

Figure 4.3. Indian of Santa Marta, on La Guajira Peninsula, Colombia. Drake Manuscript, folio 87, 264. The Morgan Library & Museum, MA 3900. Bequest of Clara S. Peck, 1983.

Ingram's Botany

Less startling is Ingram's description of cassava (*Manihot esculenta*), also known as manioc, yuca, mandioca, and Brazilian arrowroot.[19] This tuberous domestic plant was widespread in South America and on the islands of the Caribbean, but it never became established in southern Florida. "Their bread is only made of the root of a cassado tree, which they do dry and beat it as small as they can, and then temper it with water, and so bake it in cakes on a stone." Ingram failed to notice an important step in the preparation of cassava. The cassava tuber had to be grated, soaked, *leached* to remove toxins, and then dried before it could be baked in cakes and eaten.

Ingram made note of a plant he identified as a pineapple.[20] Pineapple plants are bromeliads that are native to southern Brazil and Paraguay. Native South Americans spread the plant from there northward. It eventually spread to Mesoamerica and into the Antilles, where Columbus encountered it. It was cultivated there as well as on the Spanish Main and coastal parts of Mexico. The Spanish called pineapple *piña de las Indes*, for its similarity to a large pine cone and its cultivation in the West Indies. English sources called it "pinappel" for the same reason. The early presence of pineapples in the Caribbean is also confirmed by the Drake Manuscript.[21]

Ingram was taken by the delicate taste of the pineapple fruit, and he was impressed that he could smell the aroma given off by the plant at a distance. The Portuguese took the pineapple from Brazil to India by at least 1550, and they probably introduced it to West Africa around the same time. The Hawkins expedition fought with the Portuguese around their ports of slave trade, so it is possible that Ingram saw pineapples both there and in the Caribbean.[22]

Some of what Ingram told his interrogators was supplemented by know-ledge he picked up between his rescue in 1569 and his 1582 appearance before Walsingham. Ingram was aboard the *Elizabeth* in 1578 (Chapter 10). The ship was one of those in a fleet commanded by Francis Drake. The *Elizabeth*, captained by John Wynter, got separated from Drake's *Golden Hind* in the terrible seas of the Strait of Magellan. Wynter struggled to keep his men alive and healthy by harvesting penguins for food, and a local tree bark that the local indigenous people assured him would treat scurvy. He eventually despaired that the *Golden Hind* had been lost, and turned back to England.

As Ingram noted to his questioners, Wynter brought the peppery bark home along with some young specimens of the plant.[23] The bark still bears his name. Wynter's bark (*Drimys winteri*), *canelo* to the Spanish, is a slender, medium-sized tree that grows up to 20 meters (66 ft) tall. It is native to the coastal rainforest of southern Chile and Argentina, where it is a dom-inant species. The bark did turn out to be an effective remedy for scurvy, which explains Wynter's effort to bring whole plants home for cultivation in England. Ingram was impressed by it, as he was with so many other exotic plants he encountered. There is more to be said about David Ingram's time aboard the *Elizabeth* in Chapter 10.

Ingram's testimony regarding plants included a description of a deadly poisonous fruit that looked like an apple and grew on a tree.[24] This was the fruit of the manchineel tree (*Hippomane mancinella*), every part of which is very poisonous to humans. This plant, also called beach apple, death apple, or poison guava, is one of the most dangerous in the world. One can experience severe dermatitis merely from drops of rainwater dripping from its leaves or from the smoke of a fire burning its wood. Ingesting it can be lethal. It is poisonous to most other animals as well. A notable exception is the iguana, which can eat and digest the fruit. Little wonder that the fruit attracted Ingram's notice.[25]

The Spanish called it *manzanilla de la muerte*, death apple. Columbus encountered it on his second voyage to the Indies.[26] The manchineel is today regarded as the most toxic plant in North America, so it is allowed to persist only in remote parts of the Florida everglades and in the Virgin Islands National Park. Ingram was never that far south in Florida, so he probably saw the plant somewhere on the Spanish Main. The only inconsistency is that manchineel apples produce an extremely toxic milky white sap, not an inky black juice as claimed by Ingram. Perhaps he encountered a rotting specimen.

Manchineel trees are found around the Caribbean, including the territory of the Calusas of extreme southern Florida. They are also found in West Africa, so it is possible that it was there that Ingram first encountered them. Most of Ingram's experience with poisoned arrows occurred in West Africa, but there the toxin archers selected was different. African arrow wounds produced symptoms like those of tetanus while Caribbean ones did not. It is likely that these circumstances tip the balance toward the Caribbean as the region where Ingram encountered the manchineel. There the Caribs might have used manchineel to poison their arrows. Although poisons were used on arrows in eastern North America, there is no evidence that Ingram could have encountered manchineel later on his long North American walk.[27]

Ingram talked about various sweet woods he encountered in the tropics, saying little about them because of his unfamiliarity with them. However, in one case Ingram specifically referenced *Lignum vitae*, a very hard Caribbean species that is still used for crafting durable wooden tools.[28]

Ingram's Zoology

"There is a bird called a flamingo which is very red feathered, and is bigger than a goose, and billed like a shoveler, and which is very good meat."[29] Ingram remembered two particularly remarkable Caribbean birds. This one is clearly named as the flamingo. Flamingos feed head down, the tops of their bills below their bottoms. The closest analog Ingram could think of was the English shoveler duck (*Anas clypeata*). Ingram compared the flamingo to a goose, perhaps because flamingos are large and honk like geese in flight. Ingram's mention of the shoveler might indicate that he was confusing flamingos with the smaller roseate spoonbills, which are colored like flamingos but feed like shovelers.

Ingram never mentioned hummingbirds, which are widespread in the Americas but unknown in the rest of the world. While they were exotic, they were also tiny, and apparently escaped his notice. However, Ingram repeatedly mentioned larger exotic birds. In the case of the harpy eagle, the bird was so large that some later readers have dismissed it as a preposterous figment of Ingram's imagination.[30]

The harpy eagle is a huge raptor that is still found in the rainforests of Central America and northeastern South America (Figure 4.4).[31] Ingram could have seen these birds anywhere along the Spanish Main. The female of this species is larger than the male, weighing up to 22 pounds (10 kg), with a wingspan that can exceed the arm span of a man.

The harpy eagle was not formally described and scientifically named (*Harpia harpyja*) until Linnaeus did so in 1758. Similarly, large Asian relatives of the harpy eagle, the Philippine eagle and the Papuan harpy eagle, were not known to science until the nineteenth century. Recent studies have confirmed that the harpy eagle can kill and carry off sloths and adult monkeys, usually ignoring smaller monkey species. All three eagle species still exist, but in 1582 Ingram's description of this enormous bird conformed with nothing then known, and it must have struck his interrogators as extremely unlikely.

It was probably later in the hostile Mexican port of Veracruz that Ingram found out about the Spanish silk industry in Mexico.[32] He was impressed by the abundance of silkworms. In 1568, the people of Mexico made use of both native silkworms (*Gloveria psidii*) and imported Asian silkworms. This comment by Ingram was good news to Walsingham and the other

Figure 4.4. The harpy eagle (*Harpia harpyja*). Alamy CWCPM2.

investors at Ingram's interrogation. It might surprise modern readers to read that native Mexicans had already developed an industry that harvested the silk taken from native caterpillar cocoons to make containers and paper. Asian silkworms were introduced to Mexico by the Spanish in the 1530s and easily added to the native industry. Production continued until the next century, when the king of Spain banned the export of Mexican silk in order to protect Spain's home silk industry.[33] The use of the native silkworms has continued to the present day in Mexico.

The Tempest

When Hawkins's fleet eventually set sail in a favorable wind, they had no good idea about what they might encounter as they sailed northwest across the Caribbean. They knew it was hurricane season, but there was nothing on the horizon to indicate they were in any danger. They intended to sail between the Yucatan Peninsula and Cuba, then turn east to pass out of the Gulf of Mexico and through the Strait of Florida into the Atlantic, but the fleet never made it. The eight ships almost succeeded, but a supreme wind fell on them in the Gulf of Mexico (Figure 4.1).[34]

Ingram and everyone else in the fleet experienced a monstrous tempest, in which lightning and thunder were constant for 24 hours. Even amid the worst of the hurricane Ingram wondered about the cause of such an extraordinary storm. He thought that heat of the tropical climate was the culprit, long before modern meteorology confirmed it. He had seen the approaching edge of the massive hurricane cloud, an ominous predictor that he would never forget.

Hurricanes are still common in these waters, today more than ever. Like earthquakes around the Pacific Rim, fires in chaparral forests, and tornadoes in the American midcontinent, they are part of life in a dynamic environment. The season for hurricanes in the western Atlantic is June 1 to November 30, with the maximum threat from late August through September. Hawkins could not have picked a worse time to try to sail home. He and his crew had thought that the storm that had scattered the ships on the way to Africa had been serious at the time, but it was nothing compared to what they experienced in the Gulf of Mexico. The strength of Caribbean storms generally and colossal hurricanes specifically were not events that were taken lightly by sailors. They survived this one but it compelled them to seek shelter in a hostile Spanish port.

The old top-heavy *Jesus* was heaved about, her timbers springing wide enough to allow seawater and even small fish through great cracks in the hull. Chain pumps were unable to keep up with the leaking. Hawkins had no choice but to give up trying to beat against the howling northeast wind, to turn the *Jesus* around, and to run desperately before it. This he did, signaling the other ships in the fleet to follow. The *William and John* did not see the signal, and lost contact. The others began a long, terrifying flight southwestward across the Gulf.

Ingram and everyone else in Hawkins's fleet nearly perished in the hurricane. The ships survived, but they were so badly damaged they had either to put into port quickly for repairs or sink. When the wind abated, Hawkins found himself deep into the unfamiliar waters of the southwestern Gulf of Mexico. It was already September 11, and they were low on food and water. They needed to find a safe harbor to resupply and repair the ships for what they expected would be a rough autumn crossing of the Atlantic.

Mexico

The next day they intercepted a small Spanish ship and learned that there was a serviceable harbor called San Juan de Ulua at Veracruz, on the Mexican coast. The good news was that they could reach it in a few days. The bad news was that the annual Spanish treasure fleet, the *flota*, was due to arrive soon at the very same port. Not only would the annual fleet be arriving any day, but its well-armed ships were delivering the eminent new viceroy of New Spain before loading up accumulated treasure to take back to Spain. Hawkins thought he might be able to just barely get in and out again before the *flota* arrived.

Hawkins's ships barged unannounced into the harbor at San Juan de Ulua on Thursday, September 16, 1568. The *Jesus* led, followed by the *Minion*, and then the smaller ships. Together they brought about 60 guns to bear on the Spanish ships and shore installations.[35] Spanish lookouts at first mistakenly reported that these were the lead elements of the *flota*. The Spanish garrison happily allowed the English ships to sail in, thinking they were the Spanish fleet from Seville that so worried Hawkins. Hawkins was in the harbor and in charge of it before the appalled defenders realized that the ships were English. The harbor was not much more than a section of coastline protected by a low offshore island. Hawkins brazenly pulled his ships in and anchored in the lee of the barrier island before the stunned Spanish could react.

Robert Barrett was sent to talk with Captain Antonio Delgadillo, whose bad luck it was to command the defense of the island. Barrett apologized for the intrusion and explained the dire condition of the English ships. He requested permission to remain only long enough to repair damages and take on water. Barrett spoke good Spanish and it was all very polite. Delgadillo had no choice but to comply. It took the rest of the day to get all the ships moored behind the long protective island, alongside the Spanish ships that were already there.[36] Hawkins took over the port and repairs on his ships were begun under the baleful eyes of the overmatched Spanish garrison.

Unfortunately for the Englishmen, the Spanish *flota* arrived the very next day, a Friday. Delgadillo sent a pinnace out to warn Admiral Francisco de Luxan of the situation. The notorious English pirate John Hawkins, who they called Juan Aquines, had taken over the port. Luxan informed his distinguished passenger, Don Martin Enriquez, the newly appointed viceroy of New Spain, that there was a hitch in their plans. Delgadillo met with Hawkins, then conveyed the Englishman's conditions to the admiral and viceroy. The Spanish noblemen were nearly overcome with indignation. Through Barrett, Hawkins insisted on a precautionary exchange of hostages, 10 from each side, and time to complete his repairs. The Spaniards agreed, but they expected that they would violate the arrangement as soon as it was convenient to do so.

It was actually Tuesday, September 21, before contrary winds switched and allowed the *flota* to enter the port. This allowed Hawkins a few extra days to carry out some frantic repairs. Then the Spanish ships entered and moored side by side, but separate from the similarly lined-up English ships, all of them with their bowsprits sticking eastward out over the low island. Between the two lines of ships was an unmovable dismasted hulk. The *Minion* was closest to the hulk, but with a prudent space left separating her from it. The *Jesus* was next to the *Minion*. Closest to the hulk on the Spanish side were the two heavily armed warships of the *flota*, their largely unarmed transport ships safely arrayed farther along.

If Ingram said anything at all about the battle at San Juan Ulua the interrogators left no record of it. However, it is clear that Ingram and his shipmates Richard Browne and Richard Twide were aboard the *Jesus*. Everyone was desperately busy trying to make her and the other English ships seaworthy as rapidly as possible.

The Spanish held a council of war and decided to attack on Thursday morning, September 23, 1568. During the night preceding the planned attack they moved 200 soldiers into the hulk that separated their warships from the English ships. Despite their best efforts, they were unable to do this in complete silence, and Hawkins surmised that an attack was imminent. He made one last try to talk his way out of danger, even having one of the senior Spanish officers join him for an early dinner aboard the *Jesus*. It all fell apart when a steward spotted a dagger in the Spaniard's sleeve.

Everyone scrambled in alarm. Hawkins bolted out to the main deck of the *Jesus* and ran across to the *Minion*. There he could see that the Spanish were attempting to pull the hulk close enough to the *Minion* to board her. The truce was over, and the fighting began.[37]

Guns on each end of the little island were still held by Hawkins's men ashore, but they were about to be overwhelmed. His sailors cut the ships' mooring lines at their bows. The *Minion* and *Jesus* started moving away from the hulk as frantic sailors hauled on stern anchor hawsers to pull the ships back away from the island. The ships were moved far enough out to prevent boarding, while allowing their guns to fire on the Spanish warships. All but the *Swallow* got free, but at that point the island guns were taken over by Spanish gunners. The English gunners were captured and the English ships started taking devastating fire from the cannons ashore.

In the confusion, an English ball found a barrel of powder on one of the Spanish warships and blew it up, but the English ships were still badly outgunned. Francis Drake on the *Judith* was farthest from the action, nearest the southeastern end of the island. The *Minion* and the *Jesus* were taking a beating, still unable to set sail and extricate themselves. The Spanish ignited a fire ship, then another, and set them both loose on the north wind toward the English ships. The fires fizzled out before reaching their targets, but it was only a short respite for the English.

The *Angel* was holed at the waterline and sank quickly. The foremast of the *Jesus* fell, and the mainmast was so weakened by shot that it could not carry canvas. The *Grace of God* was dismasted and her French crew rowed her pinnace over to the *Jesus*, hoping for salvation there. Hawkins signaled the *Minion* to come alongside the *Jesus* in order for her to gain shelter from the guns on the island. The old *Jesus* could do little more than provide cover by this time. Drake joined them with the *Judith*, taking cover behind the *Minion*. Hawkins's crews frantically began shifting food, water, and stores from the *Jesus* to the two smaller ships. The *Judith* soon had all she could carry, and Hawkins ordered Drake to take her out of range of the Spanish guns and wait. Drake made a run for it and escaped into the Gulf.

The Spanish launched another fire ship, and it bore down on the *Minion*. This time it was looking like the tactic would succeed. The *Minion*'s desperate crew uncoupled from the *Jesus* and unfurled her sails. Those who could scrambled across from the helpless *Jesus*, abandoning 45 slaves, many shipmates, and what was left of stores and treasure on the flagship. The sailors who made it to the *Minion* included David Ingram, Richard Browne, and Richard Twide.

Hawkins leaped on to the *Minion* with them, not knowing that his 11-year-old nephew Paul, the cabin boy, had been left behind on the *Jesus*. The *Minion* crawled toward the safety of the open sea on a north breeze as night fell, leaving most of what was left of Hawkins's fleet behind, ravaged and sinking. The Spanish fire ship drifted harmlessly past what was left of the *Jesus*.

There was no trace of Drake and the *Judith* at dawn the next day. The *Minion* managed to make good her own escape, taking temporary refuge in the lee of Isla de Sacrificios, now called the Isla Parajos, a scant two miles (4.4 km) southeast of San Juan de Ulua. The Spanish took possession of all the remaining English ships still afloat in the harbor, along with slaves, surviving crewmen, treasure, the Spaniards who had briefly served as hostages to the English, and the cabin boy, Paul Hawkins.

Hawkins tallied his losses aboard the *Minion*. He had left Plymouth a year earlier with six ships and just over 400 men. Along the way he had added the French *Grace of God* to his fleet along with some other disposable vessels. The *William and John* had disappeared in the hurricane. Francis Drake had escaped with the *Judith*, and that ship was also missing. Both of those ships might have survived, but from Hawkins's point of view it was just as likely that both had gone down with all hands. In either case neither ship was at Hawkins's disposal. The queen's *Jesus of Lübeck* was a hulk in the Spanish harbor. So too were the smaller *Swallow* and the still smaller *Angel*. Half of the men who had sailed with Hawkins the previous year were dead, prisoners, or missing. It was bad, but it would soon become worse.

Hawkins took the *Minion* northward. The overloaded ship sailed from Isla de Sacrificios to just north of Tampico, a distance of 380 miles (610 km). It took them two weeks. The *Minion* had a fraction of its original crew, just those men who had not been killed or captured over the months or in greater numbers the day of the battle. To these were added Ingram and other survivors from the *Jesus* who had scrambled aboard at the last minute, along with various men from the other ships that had been lost. David Ingram was one of the lucky men, but their good fortune was only temporary. Drake and the *Judith* had disappeared with around 50 men. Hawkins was left with around 200, all of them with him on the poorly supplied *Minion*.

Once they were out of immediate danger of annihilation, Hawkins took stock and realized that there were not nearly enough supplies to get 200 men safely back to England on the *Minion*. At best, there was only enough food and water for about half the 200 men on board to survive. Men were already eating hides, rats, cats, pet monkeys, and any other emergency food they could find. He decided to put the key question to his crew. They could go ashore and take their chances, or they could stay aboard the *Minion* and risk death from starvation on the long voyage home. Which would it be? On Friday, October 8, 1568, with the Mexican shore in sight, Hawkins put the hard choice to the ragged men on the *Minion*.

There was mortal risk involved in either choice, but each man had to decide whether to stay aboard or go ashore, taking his chances against poor odds in either case. Hawkins preempted the loss of the key men he needed to sail the *Minion* by declaring them ineligible to go ashore. David Ingram, a refugee from the *Jesus*, was not among the essential seamen. Neither were Richard Browne or Richard Twide.

There was a strong tendency for the *Minion's* surviving crewmen to be inclined to stay aboard and encourage the men from the *Jesus* and other ships to take their chances ashore. There were still 12 Africans chained in the hold. Hawkins did not put them ashore, not out of compassion, of course, but thinking that he might be able to exchange them for food somewhere along the way.[38]

It was in the nature of the hard choice that every man had an interest in being in the minority. Friendships were also at play as men changed their minds or dithered in indecision. It was the kind of choice that is still of interest to modern game theorists. If enough men could be persuaded to go ashore, those remaining on board would have better chances for survival. If too few took the offer, those going ashore had relatively better odds. Each man had to evaluate the decision in terms not just of the risks inherent in each choice but also in terms of how those risks shifted as decisions changed. Finally, and predictably, they separated into two nearly equal groups of about 100 each. Those who elected to remain aboard were tasked with rowing the others to shore, a job the *Minion* men were only too happy to carry out, so long as it could be accomplished quickly.

Hawkins embraced each of the soon-to-be marooned men in turn. To each of them he gave six yards of Rouen cloth to use in trading, as well as money to those who demanded it. The money would be worthless for trading or much of anything else, but the cloth later proved to be very important. Hawkins promised that if he made it home, he would return for the marooned men in a year. He advised them all to leave books and other unnecessary possessions behind, and to take only a single gun and a couple of old swords for hunting and butchering game. To have taken more weapons could appear threatening to the indigenous people and to the Spanish colonists they were likely to encounter. Hawkins appointed Anthony Goddard, a gentleman investor who spoke Spanish, to lead them. Trips in the two remaining pinnaces were needed to ferry the glum men ashore. Two French sailors from the *Grace of God* drowned when the boat crew forced those in the last load to swim ashore from outside the breakers.[39]

The Landing

About the beginning of October 1568, David Ingram, with the rest of his company, being [about] 100 persons in all, were set on land by John Hawkins, about six leagues to the west of the river La Mina, or Rio de Minas, which stands about 140 leagues west by north from the Cape of Florida.[40]

So begins Richard Hakluyt's 1589 version of David Ingram's relation of his year-long walk. The estimate of 140 leagues turned out to be an underestimate by about half. Ingram's later estimate that his long walk covered at least 2,000 miles (3,200 km) was also much too conservative.

In fact, David Ingram and 111 others, not counting the two Frenchmen who drowned, were put ashore near modern Tampico.[41] The town lies on the north side of the Panuco River, where Hawkins assured the men that they would find a Spanish settlement if they decided to take their chances there. This was the coastal territory of the Huastecs, speakers of a Maya language long separated from the main region of Maya speech of modern southeastern Mexico, Belize, and Guatemala. This was also the uttermost northern limit of Mesoamerican cultures along the Gulf. Northward beyond what is today called the Rio Soto la Marina lay the thickets and scrub desert of coastal Tamaulipas.

This was a dry region still unsettled by the Spanish, the domain of a thin population of fierce Coahuiltecan hunter-gatherers. These were lumped in the consciousness of more civilized Mesoamericans with others of what the Aztecs, and later the Spanish, referred to as the Chichimec barbarians of the northern deserts. The Chichimec people lived in impoverished environments having few resources. They were typically hostile to outsiders, having nothing to trade, no reason to be friendly, and every reason to simply rob strangers rather than to help them.[42]

The more sedentary Huastec farmers might have been of some help, but they had abandoned the coastal zone earlier in the century. The Huastecs were no friends of the Spanish colonists. Hernan Cortés had established the first Spanish colony among them in 1522. Two years later, the Huastecs burned the settlement to the ground and sent the colonists packing. Spanish retribution followed. This included the execution by burning of 400 leading men of the Huastecs, the enslavement of many survivors, and their deportation to the Antilles during the years 1526 to 1533. A Franciscan friar eventually ended the terror, but by this time the surviving Huastecs had taken to the hills, well away from the coast and unlikely to be of much help to stranded English sailors.[43]

Plenty of fresh water was found ashore, and the men gathered shellfish and berries for food. The people the sailors encountered ashore the next morning were Chichimecs, hostile nomads who had spread into the formerly Huastec territory. They attacked almost immediately, killing eight of the Englishmen. The nearly defenseless men remaining surrendered. Those with colored clothing were stripped. Curiously, those who happened to be wearing black were not. Ingram later implied that he had not been stripped of his clothes or of his Rouen cloth. With that, the Chichimecs pointed out the way to the nearest Spanish settlement, and left them. The marooned men were down to 103.

Anthony Goddard decided that they should start working their way south as suggested by the Chichimecs. Half the men, including Miles Phillips, followed him. The rest, including David Ingram, Richard Browne, and Richard Twide, chose John Hooper as their leader and started heading north. With that choice, every man was once again taking a life-risking gamble.[44]

Some of the Frenchmen from the *Grace of God* had argued that they could make for the Huguenot settlement at Fort Caroline on the River of May in Florida (Figure 4.1). Hawkins had stopped there on his 1564–1565 voyage, and sailors who had been with him back then also supported the idea. These included David Ingram. None of them knew that the French Huguenots at that colony had been massacred by the Spanish soon after they had visited it, and if there was anyone left there at all they were almost certainly not friendly. Not knowing this, setting off for the River of May seemed like a good idea to at least Ingram and a few others. Ingram would not get the bad news about Fort Caroline until he reached what is now northern Florida.

Within two days, the northern group was attacked again, and this time, John Hooper and two other men were slain. About half of this party then decided that they had made the wrong choice just two days prior. Twenty-five men split from the others of the northern group, turned around, and went southward in search of Goddard and his party. The two groups found each other, and the reunited men pushed south toward Tampico. Job Hortop was with this group.

Ingram and 26 others continued northward. This smaller group later fragmented again, men striking off on their own singly or in small groups. Ingram, Browne, and Twide began their long trek together. As for the others, they were probably killed or taken in by one or another of the Chichimec bands that eked out an existence in this vast desert. Ingram and his two partners never saw any of them again. They were the lucky three who eventually made it through this hostile country and returned home.[45]

South of them, Phillips and the rest of Goddard's party, largely naked and plagued by mosquitos and no-see-ums eventually made their way to the Spanish outpost. By this time Goddard had 76 men with him. Most would not survive what was going to happen to them over the next decade. They were taken to Mexico City, where they joined the men who had been captured at San Juan de Ulua.

Job Hortop was one of those who made it to Mexico City. Two years later he was shipped to Spain, where he was imprisoned along with Robert Barrett, the master of the *Jesus*, and John Gilbert. Hortop was sentenced to be a galley slave for 12 years. He was later released into servitude in Spain. He eventually escaped and made his way back to England. There, like Ingram, he would tell his story. A few others, like Hawkins's nephew Paul Hawkins, were young enough or convincing enough to be forgiven and thus gain their freedom in Mexico, where they learned the Spanish language and transitioned into colonial Spanish society.[46]

Hawkins Sails Home

Back in the Gulf of Mexico, Hawkins and the *Minion* had hung around for a week, sending teams ashore for fresh water and whatever food they could find. They lost track of those who had gone ashore as the marooned men split up and moved out. At last, on Saturday, October 16, the *Minion* set sail on favorable winds and headed for the Florida Channel. The grim return voyage lasted through 76 days of near starvation and scurvy, punctuated by deaths. On the last day of December 1569, the *Minion* limped ironically into the harbor of Pontrevedra, Spain, unable to push on to a friendlier port (Figure 2.2). Only about half of the men who had left for home in the *Minion* were well enough to appear on deck, but Hawkins made sure the emaciated crewmen were properly dressed, it being more important to look good than to feel well. They obtained supplies, but some sickened and died from the shock of eating rich food.

Hawkins remained at Pontrevedra as long as he dared, but he feared that if the Spanish detected how weak he really was, it would prompt them to seize the *Minion*. This led Hawkins to move on, with a serviceable crew reduced to only about a dozen men. He sailed to nearby Vigo, Spain, where he could hide the *Minion* among English merchant ships and hire additional crewmen from them to help him sail home. On January 20, the *Minion* cleared the Bay of Vigo and headed for England.

Two days later, Francis Drake sailed the *Judith* into Plymouth Sound. He had given up ever seeing Hawkins again the night following the battle at San Juan de Ulua, and he believed that he and his crew were all that was left of the English fleet. Hawkins sailed into Mount's Bay near the Land's End tip of Cornwall on January 25. There most of his crew took their very first opportunity to get off the cursed *Minion* and walk on English soil (Figure 2.1). It was still 1568 because Elizabethan England did not mark the start of the new year until March.

When Hawkins sat down to write William Cecil, then still the queen's secretary, he had a lot to account for. Of the six vessels he had left with, only three made it home. The *William and John*, separated from the fleet by the hurricane, had returned earlier via the Azores and Ireland, but like the *Minion* she was so damaged that she disappeared from history. Why it took so long for Drake to get the *Judith* home has never been explained, but she at least was sufficiently intact to remain in the Hawkins fleet.[47] Hawkins had suffered many losses, including the queen's bigger ship, the *Jesus of Lübeck*. Beyond that, he had lost a majority of his company, including his own nephew. At least he had a substantial amount of gold to cart to London and present to the queen, and for that she was pleased. Behind them in America, David Ingram, Richard Browne, and Richard Twide had only one recourse. They continued walking north and east to confront the unknown perils of what Columbus had called an "other world." The three survivors were astonishingly lucky.

Fourteen years later, Miles Phillips would escape Spanish captivity and seek out David Ingram in London. The two of them would repeatedly sort through the details of their experiences in an effort to account for all the men who had gone ashore. By then, neither of them would remember all their names, but Ingram was sure that the 23 unaccounted for in the groups that had headed north had been alive when he last saw them.[48] However, they had all been on short rations for two weeks before the landing, and since then their nutrition ashore had not been much better. It is possible that Ingram, Browne, and Twide were the three most able to travel, and the others simply could not keep up. Ingram's uncertainty about the rest of the men suggested nothing positive about their subsequent survival. Like the randomly fortunate survivors of so many forgotten disasters, Ingram, Browne, and Twide would later credit their good fortune to the capricious grace of a benevolent god.

5

The Long Walk: Autumn 1568

In 1589, seven years after David Ingram's testimony before Francis Walsingham and his panel of gentlemen, Richard Hakluyt published his version of "The Relation of David Ingram of Barking." Hakluyt provided only the most general description of the long walk.[1] He was certain that the trek had begun on the Gulf Coast of northern Mexico. He knew that Ingram and his two companions had walked northeastward through a major portion of North America before arriving where Ingram had estimated was about 50 leagues short of Cape Breton, Nova Scotia. The walk had taken the men about 11 months, roughly seven of which were near the Atlantic Coast, on trails running north from the River of May. This river, now called the St. Johns, is in northeastern Florida. Ingram had estimated that he traveled a distance on land of at least 2,000 miles (3,219 km). The three men never stayed more than three or four days in any of their stops, except in the "city of Balma," where they stayed about a week.

This was the beginning of the long walk that so many historians have found difficult or impossible to believe. Ingram testified that he, Browne, and Twide walked for 11 months. However, evidence in Ingram's testimony allows the identification of 38 trail and canoe legs, each having geographic and seasonal markers that clarify both the tracing and the timing of their probable route. Mapping legs against a backdrop of the aboriginal trail network of the Eastern Woodlands reveals their route in that larger context (Figure 5.1).

The legs of their long walk are grouped into four seasonal segments in this and the following three chapters. Known trails, topography, and clues in Ingram's testimony allow a detailed understanding of both the route and the required elapsed time needed to complete the long walk and the final legs completed by canoe. There are 12 named locations for which the evidence

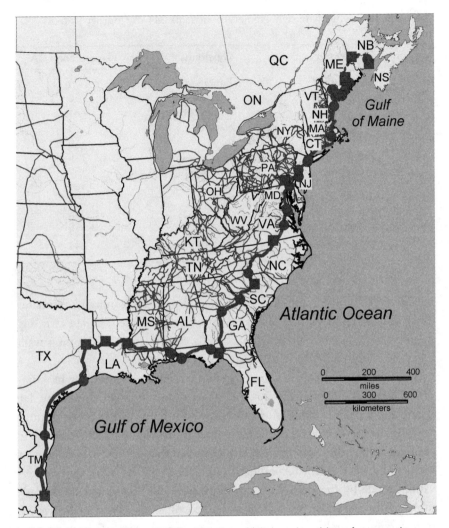

Figure 5.1. A general map of the junctions (•), waypoints (▪), and connecting probable legs of Ingram's long walk, shown against a backdrop of known trails. Figure by author.

is so compelling that it is reasonable to define them here as high–probability waypoints. Between the waypoints are less certain junctions at known trail intersections. It has been possible to reconstruct the entire route by first connecting the highly likely waypoints and then adjusting less certain but still likely junctions in between them, mostly using known sixteenth-century trails. The three men most probably took a route that turned out to

Table 5.1 Twelve highly likely waypoints on Ingram's 244-day journey by foot and canoe.

Segment	Season	Waypoints	Elapsed Days
1	Autumn	Tampico	0
2	Autumn	Nacadoches	56
3	Autumn	Natchitoches	64
4	Autumn	Natchez	72
5	Winter	Iniahica	120
6	Winter	Cofitachequi	139
7	Winter	Occaneechi Town	159
8	Spring	Balma	181
9	Summer	Upsegon	225
10	Summer	Caiocama	226
11	Summer	Guinda	235
12	Autumn	Bay of Fundy	244

be about 3,651 miles (5,876 km) long, much longer than Ingram's estimate.[2] They did this mostly on foot but occasionally by canoe. The last two segments were apparently completed not as a continuation of the long walk, but almost entirely by birchbark canoe (Table 5.1).

Many armchair historians have scoffed at Ingram's story that he completed a 3,651-mile journey in only 11 months.[3] Often implied but left unsaid has been the assumption that the three men had to walk through the territories of many hostile American Indian nations. But this too is contradicted by the evidence. Ingram observed that while the nations were often in conflict with each other, his evidence and evidence from observations made by the de Soto expedition show that exotic strangers could move easily and unthreatened from one town to the next, particularly if they carried desirable trade goods. While the early legs of the long walk entailed a dangerous passage through desert thinly populated by hostile hunter-gatherers, later legs turned out to be on long-established and well-worn trails between welcoming farming towns in the Eastern Woodlands.

While a trek of over 3,600 miles in a single year may seem impossible to sedentary historians, many people have completed similar or longer hikes at that speed. Holly Harrison, whose trail name is "Cargo," set off to hike from Tierra del Fuego to Prudhoe Bay, Alaska, on December 17, 2016. Harrison, a 57-year-old thru-hiker from North Carolina, set off from Ushuaia, Argentina, intending to complete the 15,000-mile trip in record time. He initially averaged 15 miles a day, but he later stepped up his pace, reaching Nevada in a year. There a heart attack stopped his progress. After surgical repairs and recuperation, he set off again and reached his goal in June 2018. His daily average before the heart attack was 20 to 30 miles (32– 48 km) a day, which most thru-hikers can manage.[4]

Another thru-hiker, Richard Nathan, reproduced Ingram's long walk in reverse. On August 18, 1999, Nathan set out walking from Guysborough in Nova Scotia. On May 14, 2000, nine months and 3,300 miles later, he arrived in Barra del Tordo, a tiny fishing village in Tamaulipas, on the Gulf of Mexico.[5]

Google Maps uses 5 hours and 15 miles (24.1 km) per day as the standards for computing time and distance typically covered by a hiker. Both modern data and historical accounts support these reasonable standards.[6] The California Trail was about 3,000 miles (4,800 km) long, and many people walked rather than rode it in the nineteenth century. A legacy of that average is that the farming towns of America's prairie states tend to be about 15 miles apart, for this was the average distance people could walk per day alongside ox carts in the nineteenth century. Inns and small hamlets sometimes grew up about halfway along these 15-mile trails, providing convenient midday stops for food and rest.

At 15 miles a day on land and estimates for days of canoe travel, Ingram's entire journey of 3,651 miles would have taken 246 travel days. Eleven months equals about 330 days. That means that Ingram and his companions had at least 87 days for periodic delays, recuperation, and resupply. Ingram said they never stayed more than three or four days in any stopping place, except the town of Balma, where they spent six or seven days. The conclusion has to be that they in fact completed their 3,651-mile-long walk in 11 months, and that the reconstructed route is highly likely.

To hike 3,651 miles was and is no stroll in the park, but as Holly Harrison, historic travelers, and dozens of thru-hikers on the Appalachian Trail every year demonstrate, neither was it improbable. The principal hazards for the three sailors turned out to be mainly uncertainties about how they would find clothing, food, and shelter along the way.

The records clearly show that Ingram, Browne, and Twide initially intended to head for the French Fort Caroline in northern Florida. Only after getting close to this initial goal did they discover that it had been destroyed by the Spanish, at which point they resolved to head north to Cape Breton. They had to know that it was a very distant goal, but it was the only other place on the Atlantic coast where they could be sure to find friendly ships. Although a few historians have argued for a more rugged interior route, neither the evidence nor informed opinion refutes this generally accepted route.

The First Segment of the Long Walk

The three men completed the first major segment of the long walk during the course of autumn 1568. This segment covered 1,326 miles (2,134 km), which would have taken them 88 days to complete.[7] They could have taken a total of 31 days for periodic rest and resupply. This segment has been divided here into seven legs. The trails of this part of northeastern Mexico have not been mapped in any detail, but topography narrowed the choices then as it still does now. The rugged north-south Sierra Madre Oriental mountain chain lies just inland to the west of the Gulf of Mexico coast in the state of Tamaulipas. The coastal plain is only about 20 miles (32 km) wide, too rugged in the west and too swampy in the east for easy travel. Ingram and the men with him probably hiked northward along or close to the current routes of Mexican national highways 180 and then 101. Here, as in much of the rest of North America, later roads followed ancient paths.

The Gulf shore near Tampico is stipulated as the beginning point of the long walk, the first, and probably the most certain, of 12 waypoints on the long walk. In 1568, there were most probably established (if perhaps fading) Huastec trails that Ingram could follow northward to the previous limit of Huastec territory, marked by the Rio Soto la Marina. It was as much as 123 miles (198 km) north of the spot where they had been put ashore. This, the first leg of their long walk, would have taken them eight days (Figure 5.2).

Fourteen years later, after Miles Phillips escaped Spanish captivity and sought out David Ingram in London, the two of them repeatedly sorted through the details of their experiences in an effort to account for all the men who went ashore. Neither of them could remember all their names, but Ingram was sure that 26 of them had headed north. Ingram, Browne, and Twide had survived. Ingram insisted the 23 unaccounted for had been alive when he last saw them.[8]

The Rio Soto la Marina was known as the Rio de las Palmas in the sixteenth century. Northward beyond this river lay the thickets and scrub desert of coastal Tamaulipas, a dry region then still unsettled by the Spanish. It was the domain of a thin population of fierce Coahuiltecan hunter-gatherers,

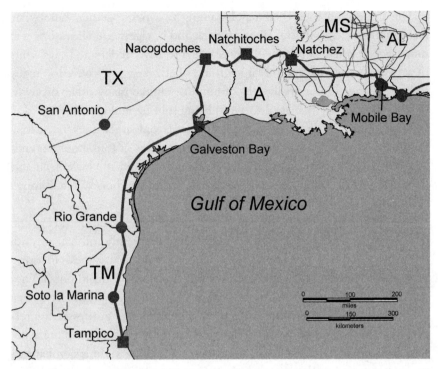

Figure 5.2. The junctions (•), waypoints (▪), and probable legs of the Autumn 1568 segment of Ingram's long walk, shown against a backdrop of known trails. Figure by author.

lumped in the consciousness of more civilized Mesoamericans with others of what the Aztecs and later the Spanish referred to as savage "Chichimecs." These people lived in impoverished environments having few resources. They were typically hostile to outsiders, with little to trade, no reason to be friendly, and every reason to rob strangers. Their reported contacts with the Chichimec hunter-gatherers they encountered indicate that what little the Englishmen had the Chichimecs would have attempted to acquire through seizure rather than trade.

Ingram, Browne, and Twide kept pushing northward across a desolate and often hostile landscape, along trails left by millennia of Huastec and Chichimec travelers. The trails were probably sketchy but discernible. The distance from Soto la Marina to the Rio Grande was 170 miles (274 km), a distance that would require 11 days to cover. The three were unarmed and too few to be much of a threat, but they were consequently also vulnerable. It might have been the worst leg of their long walk.

The three men used their naval training to work together. Sailors had feet toughened by barefoot labor on deck and in rigging in all seasons, and minds accustomed to routine. They also had to have understood that while they were too few to fend off large groups of attackers, they were too many to be challenged by a small party of hunters. Unlike many other survivors of the century, they managed to avoid being split up and captured by small Indian bands, and they were lucky enough to avoid larger ones. Their long shipboard experience had involved a constant series of four-hour watches. Without a clock, or even an hourglass, the men would still have been able to keep to their shipboard routine, taking turns standing watch through each long night.

Ingram, Browne, and Twide had started out with the trade cloth Hawkins had given them when they disembarked. They apparently still had 18 yards of Rouen cloth between them. Their subsequent survival suggests that they were able to hold on to at least some of the cloth as they hiked north. They had also seen silent trade in action in West Africa, and they would have been able to start using it as soon as they encountered small groups of hunter-gatherers. Ingram's description of how this transpired is contained in his description of African silent trade (Chapter 3), which he and his companions probably applied at this time in North America. However, because of the impoverished environment, there was probably not much useful trading in this early portion of their journey.

Making fire also was an important skill in the unforgiving environment of northern Mexico and Texas. Ingram describes a friction technique for igniting kindling. Except for where iron pyrite and chert were both available to strike sparks, the fire drill would have been necessary. Flint and iron strike-a-lights were unavailable in North America, so the technique he had previously described for Africa could not have pertained to this part of Ingram's journey. Instead, for what he saw here, the fire drill made sense for America.

The men would have been able to find canoe transportation across the Rio Grande, as they would other rivers they encountered. Dugouts were typically left unattended at points where rivers blocked well-established trails all across the Eastern Woodlands. Once across they continued their long walk, hiking northeastward parallel to the long curve of the South Texas coast. Their intent was still to hike to Fort Caroline, and as the days passed, they were undoubtedly heartened as the bending trail pointed more and more toward the morning sun.

It might seem like it would have been easier for the men to hike along the high-tide line on the long string of barrier islands found along this part of modern Texas. There was also plenty of food there in the autumn, especially in the lagoons between the islands and the mainland. Tubers, nuts, seeds, birds, mussels, scallops, oysters, turtles, dolphins, and fish abounded, and the men would have been able to take at least some of them. However, barrier islands were discontinuous, and existing inland trails would have been a faster and more secure way to travel. At least the trails were adequately defined. Trails were not a new phenomenon, and the men had the advantage of bypassing the broken and sometimes swampy geography of the coastline.

A plaque in Kingsville, Texas, also implies agreement that Ingram probably stayed on trails a few miles inland. Their route seemed clear enough to the citizens of Kingsville. The plaque commemorating "Englishmen in South Texas, 1568," which was erected by a state committee in 1973, stands about a third of the way from the Rio Grande to Galveston Bay. It is the only such plaque anywhere along the route of Ingram's long walk.[9]

The leg from the Rio Grande to Galveston Bay was 378 miles (608 km) long, and traveling this would have taken them 25 days. By then they had been walking for about a month and a half. Around Corpus Christi Bay, the men passed into the territory of a friendlier indigenous nation, people who had more resources and better technology than the Chichimecs.

They must have picked up shell and other coastal trade items where they could. These items would later prove to be nearly as much in demand inland as their stock of high-value cloth. The history of European trade in North America reveals that just a narrow strip of colored high-quality cloth would have yielded high returns in bartered food and clothing. Hawkins had prepared them with their stock of trade cloth, but unknown to them, an earlier Spaniard had prepared the market for what they could offer the people of the Texas coast. They must also have quickly discovered that the people they met preferred to couch trade as mutual gift-giving, a polite way to keep the process civil.

Ingram's Ornithology

Ingram's notice of North American birds continued on his long walk as it had in Africa and the Caribbean. Some North American species were to him as remarkable as some of those he had witnessed before. He mentioned the long-billed curlew (*Numenius americanus*), which he would have seen along the Mexican or Texas coast. He compared this bird to the European curlew (*Numenius arquata*) that was familiar to him back home. The long-billed curlew winters on this part of the Gulf Coast beginning in the fall, which is consistent with when Ingram and his companions passed through. The observation thus supports both the timing and the route of these early legs of the long walk.

Curlews also appear on the list of "commodities found in North America" that Walsingham had compiled from other sources prior to Ingram's interrogation.[10] Precisely how he and the other interrogators used the list of over two dozen bird families is unknown, but it is not difficult to imagine a process like the one followed by modern birders. They typically share the results of their field observations at meetings after organized species counts. In the 1582 interrogation, someone probably read down the list of family names and Ingram responded when curlews were mentioned.

Ingram's Botany

Ingram briefly described a small tree or bush that produced red seeds, which the people pounded and made into a drink, and which they stored in wooden vessels. Two recorders both heard and wrote down the same basic description. This was a thorny bush that produced red berries in pods two to four inches long, which Ingram compared to the European sloe tree.

This is a good description of the honey mesquite (*Prosopis glandulosa*), an important native food source that still grows in Tamaulipas and southern Texas. It is a small to medium-sized legume, a thorny shrub or small tree. Ingram's description of the seeds, their pods, and the thorns is accurate, although he puts the lengths of the pods at the lower end of its size range. While it is known from a later source that Texas Indians used honey mesquite to make ritual drinks, there is no indisputable evidence that they fermented it to make wine, which is the word Ingram used to describe the drink. Many people of the Eastern Woodlands used sugar maple sap, strawberries, and other fruits to prepare pleasant drinks, but without fermentation. However, the Catawba Indians of the Carolinas, whose territory Ingram almost certainly passed through later on, are known to have fermented persimmons into a kind of beer in the sixteenth century. Other fruits could have been used similarly.[11] If they truly made a fermented drink of mesquite seeds, Ingram is our only source for the practice.

Ingram said he remembered that the honey mesquite berry was called *guyathos*. The word is unlikely to mean anything to linguists familiar with languages of the region. Ingram's long-term memories of words he encountered more than a decade earlier only rarely proved useful later on. In this particular case the term would later be contorted by George Peckham, one of Ingram's interrogators, for his own purposes. It is very likely that Hakluyt was prompted to insert a reference to *guyathos* by Peckham, who was grasping for terms that he could claim were of Welsh origin. Peckham seized upon the term, altering it to *Gwynethes* to make it appear more Welsh. The latter is a Welsh word now seen mainly as a female given name. As modified by Peckham, it appears to have an English plural. Without the English plural it means "white" or "fair" in Welsh, which otherwise has little to do with why someone might use it to name an exotic berry.[12] This is discussed further in Chapter 11.

Hakluyt and Peckham might actually have heard something like *Guyathos* from Miles Phillips, further evidence that all three were present at Ingram's interrogation. In his own report, Phillips said, "Here our men were very sick of their agues, and with eating of another fruit called in the Indian tongue, Guiaccos."[13] Hakluyt's spelling is two steps removed from the Spanish term *guayabo* (guava tree), which may be the source of the term Phillips remembered as *guiaccos*.

Setting the word games aside, it is clear that Ingram accurately described the red seeds of the honey mesquite. These were used for food and medicine by East Texas people living both in and beyond the range of the tree. This is important, because Ingram would later use honey mesquite products in trade. Like discoidal marine shell beads, mesquite seeds were small, portable, and in demand away from the coast. So too were mesquite thorns, which Ingram would discover were used as tattooing needles by some of the indigenous Americans.[14]

Following Cabeza de Vaca

Ingram could not have known it, but his trio had the assistance of a Spaniard who had been marooned on the same Texas coast in 1528. It was six years before the man made his way back to New Spain (Mexico City) on over-land trails.[15] He spent almost two of those years as an itinerant trader, first among indigenous coastal people and later with people in the interior, the same nations Ingram later encountered.

Álvar Núñez Cabeza de Vaca's surname was Núñez, the "Cabeza de Vaca" that followed being a title he had inherited from his mother. Most modern authors refer to him by his amusing title rather than by his name. In 1527 he served as royal treasurer for King Carlos V of Spain, and he sailed with the disastrous expedition led by Pánfilo de Narváez that year.

Despite Narváez's previous failed attempt to rein in Hernán Cortés a few years earlier, Carlos V of Spain saw fit to appoint him Adelantado, "gov-ernor," of a force of several hundred men, large enough to explore the northern arc of the Gulf of Mexico all the way from the Rio de las Palmas (now Rio Soto la Marina) to the Florida peninsula. The Rio de las Palmas was the river David Ingram later crossed at the end of the first leg of his long walk.

After an inauspicious beginning that involved a hurricane, Narváez set off for Rio de las Palmas in five ships, with 600 men and a few women. Contrary winds and currents blew the fleet in a direction opposite the one intended, and it ended up landing in Tampa Bay. After a series of disasters ashore, the expedition found itself marooned in Apalachee territory in nor-thern Florida. The Apalachees were the same people who would later be reluctant hosts for the de Soto expedition, and still later would be visited by David Ingram and his companions.

About 250 men of the Narváez expedition first ate all their horses, then in desperation built five large rafts on which they hoped to make it by sea to the western end of the arc of the gulf they had intended to explore in the first place. All five rafts washed up on the Texas coast, most of the men dead or dying.

Cabeza de Vaca survived this and years of other misfortunes, after being cast away naked and defenseless with other men near Galveston Bay Island on November 8, 1528. Some of those who survived were taken in by one or another of the bands of people all later known as the Karankawas. These were friendlier people than the Chichimecs living in less productive cir-cumstances south of them. They were robust people who had dugout ca-noes and pottery and other modest advantages. However, the terms of their adoption of the marooned Spaniards were harsh once the natives discovered the men had nothing to offer but their labor.

Cabeza de Vaca and others were made servants, and they were required to haul wood and water in exchange for sharing whatever food was collected along the coast. The Spaniards named the island "Malhado" (ill fate), an appropriate choice. The hunter-gatherer bands near the coast and the larger tribes in the interior were often at war with one another. However, after a year of drudgery Cabeza de Vaca realized that a foreigner with things to trade could move easily and unmolested between mutually hostile indigenous communities.[16]

Cabeza de Vaca left Galveston Bay Island to go live with another band on the mainland, probably on the lower Trinity River. There he used his language skills and ingenuity to promote himself as a trader. He managed to stay in touch with three other Spanish survivors, and between them they picked up the basics of six native American languages. But as Cabeza de Vaca's business as an itinerant trader emerged, he found there were more regional languages, too many for him to master.[17] This problem also had a solution.

Cabeza de Vaca, like Ingram years later, must have picked up the sign language used by other itinerant traders as he went along. It was a means of communication that would have served him well, as it later would serve Ingram, Browne, and Twide in the course of their long walk. There is plenty of historical evidence that a conventional sign language existed along the Gulf Coast and inland in the sixteenth century. Although North American Indian sign language is best known from many nineteenth-century sources about the Great Plains, there are many earlier references to a more widespread standardized sign language in the Southeast as well, particularly this part of the region. The words of Núñez Cabeza de Vaca's 1542 relation provide the first clear evidence of a phenomenon found all across eastern North America.[18]

We passed through a large number of diverse languages; with all of them God our Lord favored us, because always they understood us and we understood them; and thus, we asked (went along asking) and they responded by signs, as if they spoke our language and we theirs; because, although we knew six languages, we were not able to take advantage of them everywhere, because we found more than a thousand differences.[19]

My principal wares were cones and other pieces of sea-snail [whelk], conchs used for cutting, sea-beads [shell disk beads], and a fruit like a bean [honey mesquite] which the Indians value very highly, using it for medicine and for a ritual beverage in their dances and festivities. This is the sort of thing I carried inland. By barter I got and brought back to the coast skins, red ochre, which they rub on their faces, hard canes for arrows, flint for arrowheads, with sinews and cement to attach them, and tassels of deer hair which they dye red.[20]

This was how Cabeza de Vaca worked himself out of servitude, learning native sign language and facilitating trade between tribes. As a strange-looking but harmless Spaniard he could travel wherever he wanted, and he was fed and lodged as a guest in the villages he visited. Every contact led to a new introduction and a new invitation as his reputation preceded him. A man with highly valued things to barter for a reasonable return was always welcome, and no one wanted to put future trade in jeopardy by seizing his goods or otherwise treating the trader poorly. Cabeza de Vaca understood the basics of the law of supply and demand. He knew that as he carried his goods along well-established trails, the things he carried became more valuable as the distance back to their sources increased. At the same time, the things he was offered in exchange were cheaper for him to acquire the closer he came to their sources. The trick was to carry small things of high value. Bulky commodities were not appropriate for long-distance trade and exchange for traders traveling on foot.

Cabeza de Vaca might have been unknowingly following trails used by earlier Aztec *pochteca* merchants or other foreigners with highly valued things to trade. The *pochteca* had long used the same business logic to supply the Aztec nobility with luxury goods from the north. Mexican obsidian blades, tropical bird feathers, and chocolate went north, while things like turquoise and marine shell came back to central Mexico from the lands beyond the northern deserts. Theirs was also a barter economy, although cacao beans were sometimes used as a kind of standard currency.[21]

A critical question is what goods had value? The answer is that it depends, because the issue is more culturally bound and less easily grasped than is immediately obvious. This is especially true for barter systems that lack currencies. To the Spanish, gold and silver were highly valued, for they were both rare and easily transformed into coinage that was widely accepted as a medium of exchange in Europe. But in North America there were no true currencies.

Rarity was a factor in native North America, but so was the perceived magical power of certain objects and materials. While the Spanish probably placed value on gold because of its rarity and convertibility to currency, American Indians put more value on marine shells and beads because of their perceived supernatural power and their rarity inland. This was true across most of the continent in the sixteenth century.[22]

Cabeza de Vaca happened to have been marooned in the mesquite *bosque* of southern Texas. This put him in the source area for the shells and mesquite seeds that interior tribes desired. He probably ranged at least 60 miles (100 km) to the source of red ochre near Nacogdoches, maybe twice that far into north Texas given that he reported seeing bison.[23] In addition to the ochre, he returned to the coast with high-value skins, chert (flint), and other compact items that were in high demand there.

He made this work for him for nearly two years, and he might have become a permanent immigrant to one or another of the communities he knew had he been a solitary castaway. However, his longing to return to Spain grew too strong to resist, and he still had contact with a few other Spanish survivors. He joined three other former shipmates and they set off overland, through the domain of the Chichimecs and toward colonial Spanish settlements. They eventually made it to Mexico City in 1536, after many more adventures.

Cabeza de Vaca returned to Spain just as Hernando de Soto was finalizing his plans to explore North America, two decades before Ingram and the other men of the *Minion* were marooned on the western Gulf shore. Cabeza de Vaca would die in Seville in 1560, but his legacy of the strange-looking but benevolent trader must have remained in the memories of older native people still living along the Texas Coast in 1568.

From Galveston Bay, the three English sailors apparently followed the example of Cabeza de Vaca, probably without knowing it. The Karankawas would have headed them in the right direction, as they had Cabeza de Vaca decades earlier. Ingram might also have encountered an interior trader to imitate and to use as a guide, but that much good luck was not necessary. More likely they simply took advantage of encouragements they received from other travelers they encountered along the well-used trails. The men would have headed north along the Trinity River, probably leaving the river at what is now Livingston and striking northeast toward Nacogdoches, just as Cabeza de Vaca probably did 40 years earlier. And like him, they found that as strange-looking aliens having gifts but no involvement in regional conflicts, they could travel freely and be welcomed warmly.

Ingram's decision to head north toward what is still known as Nacogdoches had to have been determined not just by trading opportunities but also by the hazards of sticking to a more coastal route. The Atacapas lived eastward of the Karankawas along the coast, an area dominated by vast swamps along the lower Sabine River. The Atacapas were destitute hunter-gatherers like the Chichimecs, with little to trade. There were also fewer good trails in that direction because of extensive swamps. The choice was easy. Ingram and his companions almost certainly traveled north to Nacogdoches. The constraints they faced forced a choice that made Nacogdoches the second highly probable waypoint of the long walk.

It would have taken them about 12 days to walk the 178 miles (286 km) to this trading center at an intersection of the trail from the coast with the bigger San Antonio–Nacogdoches Trail. This bigger trail would later become the Camino Real of Spanish colonial Tejas. In Nacogdoches they would have found a ready market for what they carried, and they would have exchanged it for things like food, lodging, and new clothing.[24]

Their arrival in Nacogdoches brought them to a new culture. This was the domain of Caddoans, a set of related nations found in adjoining portions of Texas, Oklahoma, Arkansas, and Louisiana. Here too it is likely that some older people remembered Cabeza de Vaca.[25] The Caddoans were prosperous farmers living in large permanent towns having earthen platform mounds on which temples and the houses of leading people were built. Their crops included maize, beans, squash, and sunflowers, domesticated foods of the Eastern Woodlands that would become familiar to Ingram in the coming months. So too would the important roles of women in this and other farming societies Ingram would pass through, all the way from east Texas to northern Florida and beyond.[26] Ingram was impressed by the maize. "They have a kind of grain the ear of which is as big as a man's wrist of his arm, the grain is like a flat piece. It makes very good white bread." Ingram must have encountered tortillas and other Mexican foods at San Juan de Ulua, but this was probably his first exposure to the staple crops of North American agriculture that made such foods possible.

The Caddoans had matrilineal social organizations, in which descent was reckoned along female lines. Families organized around senior women were grouped into exogamous clans; young people were required to marry outside their birth clans. However, clans probably served not so much to regulate marriage as to facilitate trade with neighboring nations. Trade transactions were couched as mutual gift exchanges, and clan names allowed fictive kinship to facilitate trade, even between people who did not share a common language. Curiously, Caddo political offices tended to follow male lines, even though that inheritance necessarily crossed clan lines.[27]

De Soto's expedition had reached interior Caddoan towns farther to the northeast in 1541, but there had been no Europeans in Caddoan territory since then. Ingram and his partners were well received, and it should be no surprise to modern readers that the Caddo language was the lingua franca of the region at the time.[28]

Ingram, Browne, and Twide did their best with the unexpected welcome they received from their first Caddoan hosts. As usual, Ingram referred to the leading man of the town of Nacogdoches as a "king." His memory of it was that the name of the man's domain was "Giricka." The king had the three men stripped of their clothing so their hairy white skin could be examined by those present. There was general curiosity and discussion about these three strange men, but no evidence of malice. The king allowed them to get dressed, conduct their trading business, and move on without harm or ill-will. The three men were as novel to the Caddoans as the Caddoans were to the Englishmen. Nudity was not necessarily inappropriate or shameful here, so examination of their pale skins where the sun did not usually tan them was a harmless curiosity, not a calculated indignity.

Ingram reported that there were many large communities in the region. Major centers were scattered 100 to 200 miles (160–320 km) from each other, and their leaders seemed to be in constant conflict with one another. As peaceful traders, the three men could pass between these major towns and the smaller ones between them without difficulty.

Trails of the Eastern Woodlands

From Nacogdoches eastward, Ingram would have been on the well-known network of ancient trails of the American Southeast. Many of the Indian trails of the Eastern Woodlands have been mapped and published. Figure 5.2 shows the beginnings of known trails of the Southeast region.[29] However, the use of this evidence has been controversial, and that has led some historians to doubt this version of Ingram's story. Disease and warfare in the later sixteenth and seventeenth centuries so reduced and disrupted populations that many large towns were abandoned and whole regions were depopulated. Vast tracts of the Eastern Woodlands that had been dotted by communities surrounded by farming fields and linked by well-worn trails reverted to wilderness. The Euroamerican settlers who later reoccupied these regions often cleared regenerated forests, not virgin ones. The evidence for earlier American Indian occupations was by that time nearly all archaeological, and thus largely invisible.

The causes of the temporary restoration of wilderness are well understood. The infectious diseases that later leaked across the Atlantic were kept alive by shorter voyages and the presence of children in colonizing families. The Caribbean islands and the Southeast were the first regions to experience the resulting native depopulation. There were over a million people living in the Eastern Woodlands at the beginning of the fifteenth century. The overall population of the Southeast probably declined about 23 percent by the end of the century, while other regions of the continent did not start to decline until the following century or later. Claims that there were simultaneous catastrophic pandemic declines all across North America in the sixteenth century have been discredited. Nevertheless, the significant declines experienced by the Indians of the Southeast in that century are sufficient to raise legitimate questions about the trail evidence, which was gathered much later.[30]

It is understandable that some scholars argue that the trails followed by sixteenth-century travelers could have been erased through the course of the seventeenth century and that the trails mapped after that were new ones not necessarily related to the earlier network. However, the evidence consistently shows that the regional trail map published by William Myer nearly a century ago was as accurate before the epidemics as it was much later.[31] Myer's work was remarkable, the whole network looking as dense as a modern highway map. Figure 5.1 shows the portion of the larger network that is relevant to this chapter.

The evidence that Eastern Woodlands trails were well established and much traveled in the sixteenth century and beyond is compelling. Charles Hudson and Jerald Milanich used abundant archaeological evidence to reconstruct the probable route of the 1539–1543 de Soto expedition across 10 modern states of the Southeast. Their reconstructed trails are largely links between the over 20 towns named in accounts of the *entrada*, which in turn can often be securely identified by archaeological means. They then reconstructed the locations of the trails with adjustments for major rivers and topography. De Soto's long route compares well against a map of trails that still existed later in the seventeenth and eighteenth centuries, after wilderness had come and gone again. This is because like later settlers, American Indians preferred settlement locations in agriculturally productive areas that were also convenient to major river confluences. Topography also constrained trail placements. Pedestrian travelers avoided swamps and steep hills then as they usually do today. Thus, the thorough and detailed tracing of de Soto's 1539 trek northward through Florida and beyond has shown that the expedition usually traveled along Indian trails that were still in use in the 1830s, despite the catastrophic intervening native depopulation of the peninsula. Recent archaeological research also provides ample evidence that the trails mapped after the arrival of Europeans had been extensively used for trade for thousands of years. All of this leads to the conclusion that the historic trail evidence can be assumed to have existed in its historic form well back into prehistory.[32]

At Nacogdoches, the second waypoint of their long walk, the three English sailors turned itinerant merchants continued on the vast trail network of the Southeast. Their goal of hiking to northern Florida, and the geography of Tamaulipas and Texas, leave no reasonable alternative.

The unavoidable next stratagem would have been to follow what would later be a continuation of the Spanish Camino Real eastward to Natchitoches, a town still known by that name in what is now Louisiana.[33] This took the men eastward through friendly Caddoan territory. From Nacogdoches the trail went to San Augustine, Texas, across the Sabine River to what is now Robeline, Louisiana, and on toward Natchitoches. They left behind the trails previously trod by Cabeza de Vaca, but they were armed with new knowledge that would serve them well.

Natchitoches, another Caddoan town, was 107 miles (172 km) away from Nacogdoches, and the journey would have required a week to complete. Natchitoches, the third high-probability waypoint of the long walk, turned out to be a center for the production of cakes of salt, another compact high-demand trade good that Ingram and his partners could add to their stock. Acquiring it might have taken a stay of two or three days.[34]

Ingram would later say that the big towns tended to be 30 to 40 leagues (90–120 mi., 145–195 km) apart, closer to each other than the Caddoan towns had been. At this point, they were following easy trails along the northern edge of the coastal plain. It would turn out that from East Texas to Virginia they would be on a broad landscape covered by an open and easily traversed forest of longleaf pines (*Pinus palustris*). Natural food was plentiful, even for men with few hunting skills or equipment. For example, gopher tortoises (*Gopherus polyphemus*), an abundant keystone species, could be caught easily, a single one providing an excellent meal for three men.

The Spanish later intended that this main east-west trail would eventually extend all the way from Mexico City to what would become St. Augustine, Florida, along these same existing native trails. Native traders were certainly familiar with all of them, and the three Englishmen would have had little difficulty getting directions eastward, toward the rising sun, the River of May, and (they hoped) rescue at the French outpost of Fort Caroline.

The main trail continued on to Vidalia on the west bank of the Mississippi, a distance that would have taken another nine days. They probably stayed on the Texas-Natchez trail, reaching the Mississippi opposite Natchez after hiking 132 miles (212 km). The great river is only about a half-mile wide at this point. There the men might have needed a little time to find transport by dugout canoe to ferry across the river to the site of modern Natchez, Mississippi, just as Ingram later described. Natchez was the fourth reliable waypoint for the reconstruction of Ingram's route.

In Natchez they encountered another new language and more trading opportunities. Natchez is a language isolate not certainly linked to any larger American Indian family. Fortunately, the men were gaining greater fluency in the sign language that facilitated communication and exchange between the nations of the Eastern Woodlands.[35]

From Natchez the three sailors were probably told to take the Natchez to Mobile Bay Trail that led eastward across southern Mississippi.[36] The trail covered 238 miles (383 km) and it would have taken them 16 days to reach the bay. They were once again close to the Gulf of Mexico. From here they could eventually pass through the sites of future Pensacola and Tallahassee, and on to the River of May.[37] Their goal would have led them to keep moving toward the rising sun, staying near the Gulf. This then would have been the most probable of a small set of possible routes between Natchez and Iniahica (Tallahassee), the fifth highly probable waypoint along the long walk.

By this time, they were in the country of the Choctaw Nation, whose members spoke a language of the Muskogean family. Muskogean nations included the Chickasaws, Apalachees, and Creeks as well as some others scattered across the Southeast. These and other nations of the region were probably feeling the first effects of European contacts. The populations of the region were already beginning to decline as a result, but the evidence for it in the Southeast is today visible only to archaeologists, in the form of abandoned villages and towns.

Ingram and his companions must have hiked past or through at least a few recently deserted towns. However, Ingram did not allude to them, and they were apparently not noticeable to him. As bad as it was, this first wave of influenza, scarlet fever, and other childhood diseases from Europe appears not to have included smallpox; that terrible disease would come later. The reason the Southeastern Indians were spared smallpox for the time being is that the disease could not gain a foothold until permanent Spanish colonies complete with children were established in the region. Until then, the adult male explorers from Spain were either men who could not be smallpox carriers because they had survived the disease as children and were subsequently immune, or they had been effectively quarantined on their long Atlantic voyages.[38]

While he apparently missed noticing the silent evidence of the earliest epidemics, somewhere along this segment of Ingram's route he became aware of tornadoes, which he called "great winds like whirlwinds." Then as now they occurred with little warning during warm months in the Eastern Woodlands. That Ingram mentioned them at all suggests that he experienced them firsthand. His memory favored unusual sights and dramatic events, but he was careful to insist that his observations were not secondhand.

The three men were still moving eastward toward the River of May. They still imagined the prospect of salvation at Fort Caroline. But before long they would learn some very bad news.

6

The Long Walk: Winter
1568–1569

I ngram, Brown, and Twide had the good fortune to pass the winter on the warm Gulf Coast of North America. They were on well-worn trails, encountering other travelers from time to time. There were some cold nights, but nothing like those of more northern latitudes. The season began with December and lasted through January and February. It was the custom to start the new year on Lady Day, March 25, in Elizabethan England. For the three Englishmen, 1569 would not arrive until winter was past.

Heading for the River of May

This segment of the long walk has been divided into ten legs, all of them completed during the winter months (Figure 6.1). One of them was a water crossing that probably required an entire day. This segment of the long walk covered a total of up to 1,056 miles (1,700 km), a distance that would have required about 71 days travel, with about 25 days available for rest and re-supply.[1] Behind them, Natchez was the fourth highly probable waypoint of this segment of the long walk. Ahead of them they would not reach the next likely waypoint until they reached the town de Soto called Iniahica, at the site of modern Tallahassee. What follows here are the most probable legs they would have taken to Iniahica, the meandering path along known trails approximating a straight line between the two waypoints.

At this point, they had their first large bay to cross. Ingram later remarked on the lengths of this and other crossings. The canoes in this century were wooden dugouts, common all the way north to the Gulf of Maine, cumbersome but serviceable. Ingram said that "they passed over many great rivers

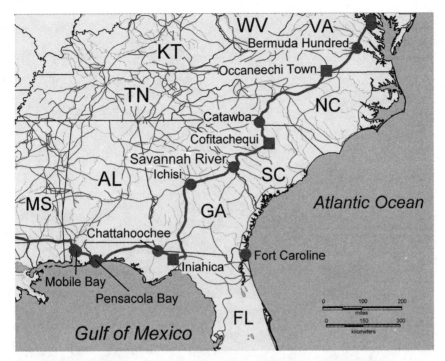

Figure 6.1. The junctions (•), waypoints (▪), and probable legs of the Winter 1568–1569 segment of Ingram's long walk, shown against a backdrop of known trails. Figure by author.

in those countries in canoes or boats, some 4, some 8 some 10 miles over, whereof one was so large that they could scarce cross the same in 24 hours."

Dugout canoes were an ancient form of watercraft in North America (Figure 6.2). Stone tool evidence shows that they were made and heavily used in New England and the Maritimes 5,000 years ago, presumably elsewhere in the Eastern Woodlands as well.[2] Many later examples are known for both the east and west coasts as well as for the rivers of the interior of North America. Dugouts would have been numerous at river crossings all along Ingram's route, from Mexico to southern New England. Some of them were very large, made from towering straight-trunked trees. Not having iron saws or axes, the Indians made dugouts by first felling a tree by burning and chopping it at the base of the trunk with stone axes. The trunk was then trimmed and hollowed by further burning, a long but effective process during which charred wood was constantly adzed or scraped away with shell scrapers or ground-stone gouges.

Figure 6.2. The manner of their fishing. Watercolor drawing by John White. British Museum. John White ca. 1585. 00672760001

In 1524, Giovanni da Verrazzano described some dugouts that were big enough to accommodate 15 men. The canoe illustrated by John White was smaller but sufficient for conveying small parties across major rivers. In the prosperous years before the catastrophic spread of diseases, native people were numerous, settlements were thriving, and travel was extensive.[3] Because of traffic on the trails, there would have been enough other travelers for the three sailors to find transportation across any river or bay they encountered.

It is eight miles (13 km) across the bay from Mobile to what would later be named Spanish Fort. The broad Mobile Valley to the north is a swampy estuary that could not be crossed easily either on foot or by dugout canoe. The best way across would have been a shorter trip by boat at the top of the bay. There must have been plenty of canoe traffic there to accommodate three white men bearing gifts, but it probably added a day to their journey. The hike from the east shore of the bay to Pensacola on the trail from Upper Creeks to Pensacola was 51 miles (82 km), which would have taken them an additional three days.[4]

Pensacola was the site of a short-lived Spanish colony founded by Tristán de Luna y Arellano. This settlement, which lasted from 1559 to 1561, has been identified by archaeologists at the University of West Florida.[5] The colony had been on Emanuel Point in Pensacola a scant seven years before Ingram passed through, and the local native Americans might have indicated it to Ingram. They would also have pointed out the way east.

Pensacola Bay is about 17 miles (28 km) across, but the three men would have more easily hitched a ride across the short paddle to the long barrier peninsula that separates the bay from the Gulf of Mexico. From there the Old Trading Path from Pensacola to Savannah stretched eastward across the sandy landscape of the Florida panhandle.[6] Their route took them through the domains of people known to archaeologists as Pensacola and Fort Walton cultures. The three men came upon another fork in the road at a point very near modern Chattahoochee, 155 miles (249 km) east from Pensacola. This leg of their journey would have taken them 10 days of walking to complete.

It may have been in this part of his long walk that Ingram saw manatees (*Trichechus manatus*), which against all odds still survive in the wild (Figure 6.3). During the cold months, manatees retreat into rivers that have their sources where underground rivers come to the surface. Such streams are relatively warm compared to other rivers or the sea during the winter. Ingram would have had opportunities to see manatees at Wakulla Springs,

Figure 6.3. Adult manatee. Photograph by author.

Florida, and in other smaller freshwater springs. The main spring at Wakulla is the world's largest and deepest freshwater spring.

Ingram's description of a manatee was remarkably detailed and accurate. He described it as a "strange beast bigger than a bear. It had neither head nor neck. His eyes and mouth were in his breast. This beast is very ugly to behold, and cowardly by nature. It bears a very fine skin like a rat, full of silver hairs."[7] However, this description was comically misinterpreted by sixteenth-century illustrators trying to make sense of Ingram's words (Figure 6.4).

Manatees are in fact bigger than bears. Adults weigh 880–1,210 pounds (400–550 kilos). They range from 9.2 to 9.8; feet (2.8–3.0 m) in length, but can grow up to 16 feet (4.6 m). They carry so much fat that they appear not to have necks. They are very gentle herbivores that avoid confrontations. Their skin is indeed sparsely covered with silver hairs, just as Ingram described. These are called "vibrissae" by biologists. They are dense around the mouth but more thinly distributed on the rest of the body. The vibrissae

Figure 6.4. An imaginative but clumsy sixteenth-century attempt to illustrate the description of a manatee. Public Domain via Wikimedia Commons. Sebastian Münster.

contain nerves; thus they are sensitive to currents and other tactile stimuli that the manatees use to navigate.

The men were still focused on reaching the French Huguenot colony of Fort Caroline on the lower St. Johns River near modern Jacksonville, and the obvious decision at the trail junction was to bear southeast rather than continue to follow the Old Trading Path toward Savannah. The new trail, a segment of what was later called the Trail from St. Augustine to the mouth of the Flint River, took them into the territory of the Apalachee nation and got them to a cluster of towns in and around what is now Tallahassee. The available evidence makes it very likely that the town at this important trail intersection was the one called "Iniahica" by de Soto.[8] Ingram was on the east-west trail across North Florida that would much later become the eastern end of the Spanish Camino Real.[9] This leg was 42 miles (68 km) long, and it would have taken them three days.

It was here that Ingram's route crossed the north-south trail taken by Hernando de Soto on his *entrada* three decades earlier. Ingram's encounter with the Apalachees is important because it establishes another (fifth) high-probability waypoint on the long walk. It was probably here that Ingram and his companions got some very bad news. The Spanish had destroyed the French colony at Fort Caroline, and the three sailors could no longer hope to find rescue there.

Most likely, it was the Apalachees who persuaded the three Englishmen to revise their travel plans. The three men almost certainly turned north at Iniahica rather than venturing any closer to what might have been left of Fort Caroline, still an 11-day walk away on the Atlantic Coast.[10] Their new goal was the dauntingly distant Cape Breton in what later came to be known as Nova Scotia. It was the only other place on the eastern coast of North America that the three men knew could offer some chance of being rescued.

The Apalachees were speakers of a language of the Muskogean family. East of them lived their enemies the Timucuas, whose domain stretched all the way to the site of the now destroyed French settlement. Ingram probably encountered some Timucuas because otherwise he would not have known the details of their culture that were later published by French sources.

In 1568, Florida was generally considered to extend north all the way to Chesapeake Bay. This was a stretch of coastline that received considerable attention from both French and Spanish ships in the years leading up to 1568. Fort Caroline had been established on the River of May 1564, four years before the English sailors were marooned. However, much had happened there in those years. Things would have been very different for Ingram in northern Florida had the French colony at Fort Caroline not been destroyed by the Spanish in 1565.

The brief but complex history of Fort Caroline had much to do with the events of the decade, more than just those of Ingram's long walk. The French explorer Jean Ribault had organized an expedition that stopped briefly at the River of May in 1562. He met with Saturiwa, chief of an eastern branch of the Timucuas. Ribault might have been tempted to establish a colony there at that time, but instead he continued on northward. Ribault sailed to the coast of what is now South Carolina, and established a small settlement on Parris Island that he named Charlesfort. He left 28 men at Charlesfort and returned to France. The French Wars of Religion delayed Ribault's planned return with supplies, and things did not go well for the 28 settlers he had left behind. They consequently abandoned the colonizing effort, successfully sailing back to France in a small open boat.

Meanwhile, René Goulaine de Laudonnière, previously Ribault's second in command, organized his own colonizing venture. The idea was to establish a colony in Florida for French Huguenots looking for a refuge from Catholic persecution in France. The Charlesfort venture had failed, but Laudonnière's impression of the River of May in 1562 encouraged him to go there.

In 1564, de Laudonnière sailed to the River of May with 200 settlers and founded Fort Caroline. It was the very sort of American settlement that Englishmen like George Peckham were hoping to establish, in his case for Catholics seeking refuge from Protestant persecution in England. These were the beginnings of what would become a long tradition of American colonies created by and for religious refugees of various kinds.

The importance of this for Ingram's story is that when Laudonnière established Fort Caroline, he was determined to learn what he could about the region and its native people. He subsequently did his own ethnographic research. He also had with him the artist Jacques le Moyne, who had been engaged to sketch and paint watercolors of the Indians of North Florida to illustrate Laudonnière's written descriptions.[11]

Laudonnière found the Timucuas in possession of gold and silver, which they beat into armlets and plates for adornment. These metals, they said, had come from wrecks of Spanish treasure ships that had been found on Florida's southern coast. The ornamentation corresponds closely to Ingram's description.[12]

When pressed, the Timucuas also speculated that there might be gold and silver mines in the Appalachians, five or six days' travel away, a claim that Laudonnière convinced himself had some merit. If anything, the Timucuas were talking about native copper, which occurs in the mountains of northern Georgia and adjacent states.[13] Spanish sources reported eight shipwrecks along the Atlantic Coast between 1528 and 1564. There were probably more unreported. Thus, Laudonnière's information that local gold and silver came in quantity from shipwrecks is entirely believable. That he hoped he would also find the precious metals mixed with copper in the Appalachians is understandable.[14]

The Timucuas knew how to work nuggets of copper, pounding and annealing the metal to make bracelets and other adornments. The same heating, annealing, and beating techniques would have enabled them to hammer ingots and coins of gold and silver into the sorts of ornaments recorded by le Moyne. They actually valued copper more highly than either gold or silver.[15] The reason was that Europeans used scarce gold and silver as a portable medium of exchange, while the Americans did not. Copper knives held a sharp edge better than did those of gold or silver. Abundance and utility, rather than rarity and beauty, was what mattered for the Timucuas.

Laudonnière also reported that the Timucuas had "exceeding fair pearls, and two stones of fine crystal, and certain silver ore," which they traded for French goods he regarded as trifles. The Indians indicated that quartz crystal and what Laudonnière took to be silver ore (actually mica) came from sources in the mountains, 10 days' travel away.[16] Laudonnière said in another place in his account that he obtained some pearls of small value, explaining that they had been burned. These were probably disk beads made from mother-of-pearl that had been darkened by the fire over which the oysters had been cooked.[17] Like other enthusiastic Europeans, Laudonnière was ready to look at the copper, mica, and marine shell that the Indians valued and to convince himself that they promised gold, silver, and pearl.

After such a promising start, the venture had not gone well. Both the local Timucuas and Spanish colonists farther to the south turned hostile, and this led to hunger and mutiny at Fort Caroline. John Hawkins had come by in July 1565, at the close of his second slaving expedition to Africa and the Caribbean. Ingram and some of the others who were later marooned in Mexico on his third voyage were with him at the time. Hawkins left his smallest ship with Laudonnière in exchange for powder, shot, and fresh water. Hawkins also acquired tobacco, which the French settlers had picked up from the Indians. Hawkins subsequently was probably the first to introduce the supposed therapeutic benefits of tobacco smoking in England.

Hawkins sailed home, and at the same time, Ribault was sending more settlers and supplies to Fort Caroline. By coincidence, this was also the moment when the Spanish colonial authorities decided to destroy the French colony. There was fighting at Fort Caroline just two months after Hawkins's visit. The action was initially indecisive and ended with the Spanish commander, Don Pedro Menéndez de Avilés, retreating southward to the place where he founded St. Augustine. Ribault arrived in time to pursue the Spanish attackers, but he was unexpectedly caught up in a hurricane, which forced him to abandon the counterattack. Meanwhile, in late September 1565, the Spanish marched overland, caught the French settlers at Fort Caroline by surprise, massacred all the men, and subjected the surviving women and children to slavery. Ironically, Ribault had saved himself from the hurricane by making it to the coast, but his luck was about to run out.

Ribault and other survivors of the hurricane were marooned ashore, and they started walking northward. They too were later caught by the Spanish and massacred. The Spanish then returned to the River of May, rebuilt the fort, and renamed it San Mateo.

Laudonnière and le Moyne had left before this complicated catastrophe unfolded, and they made it back to France with possibly at least some of their ethnographic notes and pictures. It appears that none of these events were known to the marooned English sailors in 1568. Had they been aware of what had happened on the River of May, Ingram and his partners would not have regarded it as a promising destination. Their ignorance regarding the events around Fort Caroline is explained by the timing of previous voyages. Hawkins had spent 1566 organizing his third slaving expedition. He had left England for Africa in 1567. He had been busy in Africa, then in the Caribbean, and had suffered his own disaster at San Juan de Ulua. All of this activity and the lack of prompt additional reports after Laudonnière and le Moyne successfully returned home kept the English from knowing what had happened to the French who were left in Florida. Every French settler left behind at Fort Caroline was dead or captured, and timely news from either French or Spanish sources was not forthcoming before Hawkins's third voyage began.

The French certainly became more aware of the disaster at Fort Caroline after Hawkins had already sailed for Africa in 1567. Dominique de Gourgues led a 1568 French expedition to take revenge on the Spanish, burning their fort San Mateo and slaughtering Spanish prisoners in reprisal for the 1565 massacre of the Huguenots on the same spot. That done, the French abandoned the ruined fort and sailed away. Following that, the Spanish returned and rebuilt the fort yet again, but they too would abandon the expensive effort to maintain it in 1569. Most of this was observed by the Timucuas in the winter of 1568–1569. It was still fresh in the minds of native Floridians when Ingram showed up. At that point they knew that the Spanish were still holding the fort. Ingram was lucky to learn about it while he was still at a safe distance from the River of May.

Much later, Jacques le Moyne would become friends with the English artist John White in the decade following Ingram's interrogation. The two artists exchanged and copied each other's work during the later 1580s. In some cases, the only surviving versions are copies made by one of the artists from originals produced by the other. In several other cases the originals do not survive at all, but we know them from black-and-white copies made for publication by the lithographer Theodor de Bry.[18] One of the reasons for these losses of valuable original art was that both White and le Moyne regarded their watercolor originals as merely drafts that the lithographer would later use to produce the final commercial products, reproduceable black-and-white lithographs. Le Moyne's paintings, White's watercolor copies based on le Moyne's work, and de Bry's lithographs provide us with our only views of what Ingram must have seen in North Florida.

Figures 6.5 and 6.6 were painted by John White, presumably based on le Moyne's originals. The Timucua man wore plates of copper or gold on his chest, arms, and legs. He was extensively and intricately tattooed, and he wore his hair in a topknot, his high status causing the addition of a raccoon tail (Figure 6.5). The woman wore her hair long and was dressed in a cape of Spanish moss. Like Timucua men, she was extensively tattooed.[19] Ingram saw what Laudonnière and le Moyne had seen in Timucua country. Ingram later said that "about the midst of their bodies they [Timucua women] wear leaves, which have growing there one very long, much like hair." His description is difficult to visualize until one sees the woman dressed in Spanish moss in Figure 6.6.

It is possible that Ingram or Hakluyt somehow got information from le Moyne, but probably not Laudonnière. Laudonniére wrote his narrative in the 1560s, well before his death in 1574, but it was not discovered and published until four years after Ingram's interrogation.[20] Le Moyne moved to London in 1581 and lived there until he died in 1588. During those years he collaborated with John White and perhaps Richard Hakluyt (Chapter 11). Le Moyne's own narrative was not published until 1591, but Hakluyt could have had it before publishing his version of Ingram's testimony. There is no evidence that Ingram ever met either le Moyne or White before his interrogation, but he might have.

Setting aside failures to communicate in 1582, Ingram's description of what he saw in the winter of 1568–1569 is remarkably consistent with what Laudonnière had observed just a few years previously. The native Floridians wore copper plates as well as *manilions*, hoops, and bracelets of gold and silver.[21] Ingram said that "the women of the country go appareled with great plates of gold covering their whole bodies much like unto an armor. . . . And likewise about their arms and the small of their legs they wear hoops and chains of gold and silver." Laudonnière said much the same thing. "They told me that when the women of that area went to dance they wore around their waists large plates of gold as big as saucers and in such numbers that the

Of 'Florida.

Figure 6.5. Timucua Man of Florida.
Watercolor drawing by John White, after
Jacques le Moyne. British Museum. John
White ca. 1585. 00025914001.

weight hindered them in their dancing, and that the men had gold in similar
quantities."[22] Perhaps these statements were not independent. However, the
recorders of the two contemporary 1582 source manuscripts independently
recorded what Ingram said at that time. It is not something Hakluyt could
have gratuitously added to the Tanner manuscript after the interrogation.[23]

"Bracelet" is a general term for any chain, string of beads, or solid metal
worn on the wrist, arm, or ankle. Many bracelets could have been, and
probably were, made of strung beads of marine shell and native copper.

Figure 6.6. Timucua Woman of Florida. Watercolor drawing by White, after Jacques le Moyne. British Museum. John White ca. 1585. 00026161001.

To these, the natives had recently added gold and silver as described. The Timucua man in Figure 6.5 wears a large plate, probably copper, on his chest and several smaller ones on his arms and legs. The women often appear to wear none at all; the large plates said to have been worn sometimes by women must have been mainly for important occasions.

Like Laudonnière, Ingram's questioners were keenly interested in the prospects for gold and silver mining. Spanish, French, and English explorers all earnestly hoped that they would find mines like those of Mexico and Peru. Hernando de Soto had also sought precious metals in the Southeast decades earlier, and without success. Either de Soto had missed the evidence or the precious metals sought so avidly by Europeans did not exist there. Ingram wanted to help his interrogators, so his apparent inability to distinguish gold and silver from pyrite and mica in what the people communicated to him influenced his testimony. He told his interrogators that there were many rivers flowing out of the mountains of the interior of North America, and that there was an abundance of gold and silver in their headwaters. Lumps of gold as big as a man's fist, or an egg, or a man's thumb could be picked up there where they had been washed out of their sources. This sounds more like iron pyrite than copper, but it hardly matters. The Timucuas had earlier been clear that native copper and mica came from the mountains, but that gold and silver had been acquired from Spanish shipwrecks. In his interrogation, these specifics were muddled by Ingram's eagerness to please and the gentlemen's eagerness to believe. The resulting miscommunication was seasoned by fragments of knowledge and ignorance on all sides.

Ingram saw palms along the Gulf Coast of North America, all the way from Mexico to North Carolina. Today the dominant native sabal palm (*Sabal palmetto*) is found nearly everywhere in Florida. Ingram described these accurately as having long fibers in their fronds, which often hung all the way to the ground. The Timucuas and others used these fibers to make ropes and cordage for their beds and for many other purposes. Uses of the sabal palm are well documented across its range in North America.[24]

The sabal is also called "cabbage palm," and for good reason. Ingram discovered that the heart of the palm just below the branches was excellent food. He needed only to have the ability to pare away the bark. Hearts of palm are still canned and sold as a delicacy. They are grown commercially for that purpose alone, because removal of the heart kills the palm.

"Their buildings are weak and of small form. They build their houses round like dovecotes and have in like manner a louver on the tops of the houses."[25] This brief entry, which has been pulled out of most but not all of its bogus context, is all that Ingram said about Timucua houses. Hakluyt and others combined this description with separate descriptions of large and impressive Northern Iroquoian longhouses. All three recorders of his testimony combined what he said about very different houses in this way. Fortunately, what is now known about native North American architecture allows the contradictory descriptions to be divided into separate coherent statements.

Figure 6.7. Timucua village. Alamy CTR3B0.

Timucua houses were indeed usually like dovecotes, most often round in floor plan with pitched conical roofs; they were lightly built compared to English houses (Figure 6.7). What was missing was the little cupola or louver for ventilation typically found on English dovecotes. The Timucuas tended to cook outdoors and had little need to build smoky fires indoors for heat. It is most likely that Ingram was referring only to Northern Iroquoian long-houses when he mentioned louvers (Chapter 7).

Figure 6.7 illustrates a round Timucua house with a thatched conical roof. The house is reasonably accurate. Other illustrations of Timucua houses confirm that they had no smoke holes or cupolas at their peaks, and thus no interior fires for heating and cooking. In the foreground is a Timucua dugout canoe like those that conveyed Ingram and his companions across major rivers and bays all the way from Texas to New England.

Following Hernando de Soto

Just as Ingram had unknowingly followed Cabeza de Vaca for a portion of his hike through Texas, the disappointment of having to abandon his intention to go to Fort Caroline put him on the trail previously taken by Hernando de Soto. Researchers agree that the documentary evidence indicates that de Soto constantly used Indian guides and that he almost always followed Indian trails. Moreover, documentary evidence confirms that his army marched at a speed of about five leagues (*legua común*) per day, which converts to approximately 17 miles (21 km).[26] The league actually varied in length because it was more a measure of time of march than of distance. A march of five hours at the rate of one league per hour was assumed.[27]

Like Hernán Cortés, Francisco Pizarro, and many other *conquistadores*, de Soto was from the tough Extremadura region of western Spain. De Soto was familiar with the earlier exploits of Cortés in Mexico and was himself a fearlessly brutal captain under Pizarro in the even more lucrative 1532 conquest of Peru. De Soto returned to Spain a wealthy man in 1536. There he set about organizing his own expedition for exploration and conquest in the Americas, where he hoped to become a landed *marqués* like Cortés and Pizarro. To that end, King Carlos V made him governor of Cuba, already a growing Spanish colony, from which de Soto was expected to annex a major portion of southeastern North America.

De Soto studied earlier expeditions to La Florida, mainly Ponce de León's 1513 and 1521 trips and the failed Narváez expedition of 1527. He was impressed by the account of Cabeza de Vaca, who was discussed in Chapter 5. In 1539, de Soto set off for Florida with around 700 Spanish, Portuguese, and African adventurers, 237 horses, 200 pigs, large war dogs, and other livestock, all stuffed into nine ships. They also carried tons of weapons, armor, and other equipment for what de Soto expected would be a four-year expedition. Some of the details of that expedition allow a better understanding of Ingram's more brief descriptions.

De Soto landed at the mouth of Tampa Bay in May in 1539, close to where Narváez had landed a dozen years earlier. After leaving some men and ships to establish a colony there and sending the rest of the ships back to Havana for supplies, he began his overland *entrada*. De Soto and his men moved north, at first roughly following a route parallel to that taken a dozen years earlier by the lost Narváez expedition. While some men were mounted, most were on foot and weighed down with equipment and stores. On days when they marched, they typically advanced the standard five leagues per day, slightly more than is assumed here for Ingram and his companions.

Soon after landing, they came across Juan Ortiz, a Spaniard who had been searching for Narváez over a decade earlier but then had become marooned himself. By this time Ortiz had gone native and spoke two local languages, including one of a family of languages spoken by the natives of northern Florida. Ortiz's experience was very much like that of Gerónimo de Aguilar, a Spaniard who had been marooned in Yucatan, became a member of a local Mayan community, and then later was fortuitously found and picked up by Hernán Cortés. Like Ortiz, Aguilar had become enculturated and was able to serve as a translator and guide.[28] These and other known cases demonstrate what often became of marooned Europeans and Africans in sixteenth-century America. Many melded into receptive indigenous communities, and it is possible that this was the fate of some or all of the 23 unaccounted-for men who had started north with Ingram, Browne, and Twide 30 years later. The difference was that while solitary castaways were often taken in and enculturated, groups of them were more likely to retain their cultural identities and seek to get home. Cabeza de Vaca had nearly converted, but he joined other marooned Spaniards and reached Mexico City. Similarly, Ingram, Browne, and Twide never lost each other's company, made key decisions together, and never abandoned their efforts to find rescue.

Ortiz recruited additional bilingual guides as the expedition tramped northward. They got particularly lucky when they came across a talented teenager named Perico (Pedro), who spoke several languages, including Timucua. While it was de Soto's practice to enslave Indians to serve as porters, Perico got much better treatment because of his language skills.

De Soto's techniques also involved taking hostages from leading families of the towns he entered and holding them until he was safely guided to the next village, where he repeated the exercise. He seized food wherever he could to feed his hungry army. There were some pitched battles in which the superiority of Spanish weaponry and cavalry produced death or enslavement for hundreds of the Americans. By October they had reached the large town where Tallahassee now stands. There de Soto decided to evict the residents, confiscate their food, and settle in for the winter.[29]

The town that de Soto called "Iniahica" has been located by archaeologists in downtown Tallahassee. De Soto wintered there in 1539–1540, and it is possible that the Narváez expedition had stopped there too, a dozen years earlier.[30] Thus it was a crossroads community, where the main east-west trail, by which Ingram later arrived, intersected the north-south trail followed by de Soto.

De Soto sent a detachment back to Tampa Bay to bring the men and ships left there up to rejoin the main expedition. At the same time, Ortiz was working hard to acquire intelligence about the lands to the north and west. The Spanish were, as always, especially interested in gold. In a pattern that would become familiar to European explorers, the Indians consistently pointed out trails leading to ever more distant wonders. Their intent, of course, was to keep the Spanish predators moving. Meanwhile, what seemed like minor illnesses carried by de Soto's men were beginning to have lethal effects on the indigenous people in close contact with them, and Spanish soldiers were finding that once again they had to carry their own equipment, due to a shortage of porters. Some of the pigs escaped, multiplied, and have feral descendants still living in the Eastern Woodlands. There is no evidence that any of the much more valuable horses escaped and survived in the wild.[31]

When spring arrived, Ortiz was told that a distant town called Cofitachequi was a desirable place to visit. His informant was a young man from that town who was in the employ of a team of traders who had come south to Timucua country. There were also more rumors of gold, but all of what little real gold de Soto secured, the Floridians had salvaged from shipwrecks.[32]

Cofitachequi turned out to be near Camden, South Carolina, 410 miles (660 km) distant. It would take the invasion force about a month to reach it along the network of existing trails. De Soto later would claim that he had found huge quantities of pearl in Cofitachequi and other places along his 1540 route of exploration in eastern North America.[33] It was there, after an arduous journey, that de Soto would encounter the local chieftain, who turned out to be a woman borne on a white litter. Like royalty everywhere, she was on display to be admired and envied. De Soto had described the proper way to approach "kings" in this region. Ingram also talked about the protocols for approaching kings, but most of what he described involved the more elaborate protocols he observed in Africa (Chapter 3). For the American Southeast, de Soto describes only the kissing of such a person's hands. Whatever Ingram saw in the same region appears not to have warranted mention by him.[34]

As usual, de Soto made the chieftain a hostage. Despite large quantities of supposed pearls they found there, they found none of the gold they had hoped for in Cofitachequi. After a few weeks of rest, de Soto and his men took their captive host and headed northwestward through the mountains.

She eventually would escape, and de Soto's expedition would continue its meandering journey to the Mississippi River and beyond.

Marine Shell

The team of Cofitachequi traders told de Soto what was being traded, and how. They said that pearls, mother-of-pearl beads, red ocher, and feathers were all portable and in high demand. Shorter trading trips involved bulkier salt, hides, and clothing.[35] De Soto's description of large quantities of pearls in Cofitachequi might seem to provide support for Ingram's later reporting of much the same thing. A major problem with both reports of pearls is that there is very little, if any, evidence of marine pearls in archaeological contexts anywhere in the region. Even pearls from freshwater mussels do not occur in such quantities, and none of them reach the huge sizes described by Ingram.

Ingram later said "they have among them in some of those countries a great abundance of pearl. . . . In every cottage you shall find pearl, and in some houses a quarter, in some a pottle [2 quarts], in some a peck, more and in some less." Many had been as large as acorns. He said that he had 27 pearls, every one as big as his thumb, and that Richard Brown had found a huge one in a canoe, which he gave to the French captain who eventually saved them. He also said that Timucua women wore chains of pearls along with their gold and silver.

The famous pearl named the "Peregrina" was found off the Pacific coast of Panama in 1513. It was the largest known at the time, and nothing larger was found until centuries later. The pear-shaped Peregrina is 2.6 cm in its longest dimension. It is an impressive jewel, seen in many photographs of Elizabeth Taylor, who owned it in the twentieth century. However, even the Peregrina is not even close to the size of a man's thumb.

What both de Soto and Ingram saw were shell beads, which looked much like very large pearls and were traded in great numbers throughout the region. Many marine shell beads have been recovered from archaeological contexts. For example, some rare and presumably expensive ones have been found in New York State and other places distant from their sources in the Gulf of Mexico.[36] If Ingram truly had Caribbean pearls in his possession during his long walk and he spent them very sparingly, he could have used them along with other high-value things to acquire food, supplies, and clothing along the way. But it is much more likely that he and the others were carrying marine shell beads as trade goods. The "large pearls" referred to by Ingram were made from the inner columns of whelks (*Sinistrofulgur perversum*). Whelk shell beads could easily reach the size of a man's thumb. Archaeologists have found many shell beads in the region, but only rarely have they found small freshwater pearls.[37]

The most likely explanation for such large accumulations of marine shell is that the association of marine shell with supernatural power led to hoarding by leading individuals. The similar patterns of shell distribution observed by archaeologists in the American Southwest cannot be convincingly explained by standard models of trade and exchange. Both there and in the Eastern Woodlands, a more likely inference is that marine shell hoarding was driven by a desire for the accumulation of its presumed supernatural power.[38]

Ingram's New Destination

The segment of de Soto's march between northern Florida and Cofitachequi is important because David Ingram almost certainly followed it three decades later. Just as important, de Soto's records show that long-distance trading along the trails of the coastal plain was easy and commonplace. Just as Cabeza de Vaca had prepared the way for Ingram and his partners to travel eastward safely as traders, the records of de Soto's *entrada* show that traders were also common on the trail northward from modern Tallahassee. This had to be good news for Ingram.

Ingram and his companions had no choice but to abandon the goal of reaching the River of May. Their only option now was to trek northward, toward the distant revised destination of Cape Breton. Excellent fishing brought English, French, and Basque ships there and to the Grand Banks and Newfoundland every year. This was common knowledge among English sailors. No other part of the North American coast was visited by friendly ships with enough regularity to offer the hope of rescue. Ingram consistently underestimated distances, and it seems unlikely that he truly understood how long their hike would turn out to be.

The leg from Iniahica, or some nearby Timucua town, to the town de Soto called Ichisi was the fifth of the 10 legs of the winter segment of the long walk. It was 212 miles (341 km) to Ichisi, a distance that would have taken the men two weeks to walk. Here, Ingram was at last entering the Atlantic coastal plain, the area of greatest interest to his interrogators. He must have detected this much later in his interrogation, because he provided them with more detailed responses to the seven questions in their agenda.

As they made their first northward leg, Ingram noticed that the best land, where most of the indigenous American people sensibly lived, was in the Appalachian foothills, six or eight days' travel into the interior from the coast. These were near the uplands where the Timucuas and others told him copper and mica could be found. From his own observation, Ingram could see that the grass was better there as well.

The grass of northern and central Florida seemed stunted and scorched by comparison. As he traveled, Ingram also became aware that fewer people lived near the seacoast so far as he could tell. This, he thought, was be-cause low country was rank and infertile, its grass tending to grow quickly through the summer then wither into a thick brown mass that new shoots found difficult to penetrate. Ingram passed through one region that he de-scribed only as "the backside of the Cape of Florida." Here the land was comparatively barren and unproductive. He noted that the people there were correspondingly "churlish and cruel."

However, for the most part the countryside was beautiful, fertile, and pleasant as the three men made their way north. These observations taken together indicate that the three men kept to a trail that ran near the Appalachian fall line, where the foothills meet the coastal plain. Along that route they passed over large grassy plains separated by densely wooded for-ests. In some places there were great pastures surrounded by natural hedges of delicate trees, which he found difficult to believe were not planted by people. This was exactly the kind of encouraging information Ingram's questioners were hoping for in 1582.

There were many dugout canoes of varying sizes, often left unattended at points where the trail was interrupted by a major stream. Ingram noticed that they were sometimes equipped with bailing scoops made of pieces of flat mica sheets stitched together by leather thongs or cordage. In houses along the way Ingram saw beautiful thin wooden dishes carved from wood, and ceramic pots made from clay that looked as fine as a potter could find in Venice.

By keeping to the main trail along the fall line, Ingram and his two part-ners followed the inflection point where rivers flowing down out of the

Appalachians abruptly slow down because their gradients flatten. Rivers are easier to cross near these points because they are slower and shallower than in the piedmont, narrower and less swampy than farther out on the coastal plain. Generations of indigenous Americans had established the easiest routes through trial and error. River crossing places tended to be the highest points for river navigation, the places where many new colonial towns were later laid out.

The route north parallel to the Appalachian Mountain chain took them to Ichisi, at what is today Macon, Georgia (Figure 6.1). What they found when they got there is today one of a group of large native town sites surrounding modern Macon. One of these, Ocmulgee, is now a National Monument, but the town that de Soto called "Ichisi" was probably on the nearby Lamar archaeological site. Whichever of the town sites was occupied in 1568, it was so large that Ingram would have considered it a city.

Ingram's Ornithology

Ingram's interrogators were interested in the birds of America, but the list they brought with them contained what were to them familiar birds.[39] Their questions probably prompted Ingram's responses in these cases. However, Ingram also remarked about unfamiliar exotic birds he saw, such as the harpy eagle and the flamingo in the Caribbean, or the Guinea fowl in Africa.

Ingram reported another bird species in the Southeast. As with the curlews of southern Texas, the larks he saw farther east struck him as larger than those in England. Ingram identified the horned lark, the only North American lark species. Their coloring is similar but not identical to the Eurasian skylark, the only lark Ingram would have seen in England. Perhaps he was tipped off by their very similar behaviors. Larks feed on the ground, spending almost all their time there, and they walk rather than hop. His observation of horned larks on their winter range is important to the story of the long walk because they confirm that he was in the Atlantic coastal part of the Southeast during the cold months of late 1568 and early 1569.

These observations are remarkable because they reveal that Ingram had an eye for the subtleties of bird watching. Anyone would have been struck by large exotic birds such as flamingos and harpy eagles, but Ingram saw and remembered more than that. Under questioning he later said that there were many kinds of birds in North America, as in England, but that there were many strange ones that he did not recognize as well.

He probably saw the now extinct Carolina parakeet along this segment of his long walk. He might also have seen and heard the large ivory-billed woodpecker along the Gulf coast, now also extinct. The similarly large and loud pileated woodpecker is still common and widespread in the Eastern Woodlands, but Ingram did not mention them either. It is surprising that Ingram also did not comment specifically on tiny hummingbirds, which are both striking and unique to the Americas.

Itinerant Trading

By this time, Ingram was mastering American Indian sign language, which he must have encountered first in Texas. Adair mentions it in his 1775 discussion of the Southeastern nations as well. "Two far-distant Indian nations, who understand not a word of each other's language, will intelligibly converse together, and contract engagements, without an interpreter, in such a surprising manner, as is scarcely credible."[40]

Traders were clearly welcomed in the towns of the Southeast. A few strangers who strode confidently into a town were not regarded as a threat, even though they were invariably armed. Neither were they robbed, for that would have put future trading at risk. They were fed and made comfortable, and typically the natives sought to establish some prior connection. This repeatedly involved the strangers' clan identity and the seeking out of locals having the same or similar identity. Although clans appear superficially to have served mainly to manage marriages, games, and other activities internal to towns, those functions were probably not the initial stimulus for their development. They probably arose long ago as fictive kinship, to facilitate ties and exchange between strangers from distant communities. Once it was established that a stranger was, say, a bear clan man, a local bear clan member would be found and the two would assume the relationship of blood relatives. The pretense of kinship on one or both sides of the relationship smoothed the way for successful business.[41] Whether three strange-looking sailors were accorded this treatment is uncertain but probable.

At a larger scale, the pattern of trade and exchange observed by archaeologists indicates that although trade might have been more controlled among the Mississippian chiefdoms to the west in interior North America, it was more independent in the Appalachian piedmont and along the coastal plain.[42] Ingram was fortunate to be traveling on trails well away from those that converged on powerful interior Mississippian towns and cities. There the chances of walking into hostility were greater.

For Ingram and his partners, sign language and fictive kinship thus facilitated trade and exchange, which otherwise would have been silent. Every leg of their long walk presented new trading opportunities. In the Southeast, people who lived inland could furnish mica, copper, pipestone, chert, and angelica (*Angelica atropurpurea*) roots to people on the coast. They also provided roots of New Jersey tea (*Ceanothus americanus*), which provided a red dye. Coastal people in turn provided marine shell, dried fish, yaupon holly (*Ilex vomitoria*) for black drink, and salt. Deer hides, beeswax, honey, and bear oil also moved through these trade connections. Marine shell beads were still in high demand, as they had been in de Soto's day. The polished inner column of a whelk shell would still be worth four deer hides as late as 1775 according to Adair.[43] These profit margins kept the trio of English traders moving north smoothly, even if they realized the full values of only a fraction of the goods they carried.

The trail to the Savannah River was 116 miles (187 km) long, and traversing it would have taken them eight days. This was a segment of what would in later years be called the Lower Creek Trading Path.[44]

People they encountered along the way, as well as the clarity of the well-worn trail they were on, led them to the beginning of the Occaneechi trail on the northeastern bank of the Savannah River, opposite what is now Augusta, Georgia. This was a major intersection of trading trails. The heavily used Occaneechi trail took them to the major town of Cofitachequi, then on to Catawba, Occaneechi Town, and eventually to the vicinity of Bermuda Hundred at the head of the James River estuary in eastern Virginia. This first leg on the Occaneechi trail was 114 miles (183 km) long, and traveling it would have taken them eight days to reach Cofitachequi, just south of modern Camden, South Carolina.[45]

After Cofitachequi, decades earlier, de Soto had pushed west into the mountains, because that is where his knowledge of Mexico and Peru predicted gold and silver could be found.[46] However, this was not the last the people of this town saw of Spanish conquistadores. A new *entrada* occurred just a few years before Ingram's visit. In 1564–1565, Pedro Menéndez de Avilés founded Spanish colonies on the coast of South Carolina, first San

Agustín, then Santa Elena on Parris Island. This was intended to facilitate renewed exploration for the rumored silver mines in the mountains to the west. In 1566, fewer than three years before Ingram would pass through the same countryside, Juan Pardo landed a force of 125 men at Santa Elena and set off for the mountains. At Cofitachequi he intercepted and then followed de Soto's route westward, establishing a series of short-lived *presidios* along the way.[47]

Whether Ingram was aware of the earlier Spanish visits by de Soto and Pardo cannot be determined from his testimony. The people of Cofitachequi probably remembered both Spanish expeditions, and their memories of Pardo must have been especially fresh. Ingram apparently encountered nothing remarkable resulting from the two *entradas*, further evidence of the ease of travel and trade in the region. Archaeological interest in this important town on de Soto's route allows Cofitachequi to also be defined as the sixth very probable waypoint on Ingram's long walk.

Unlike de Soto, or Pardo more recently, Ingram stayed on the fall line trail beyond Cofitachequi. He almost certainly stayed on the well-worn Occaneechi trading path that followed the fall line northeastward to Catawba and then on toward the trading town of Occaneechi, located near modern Hillsborough, North Carolina. Catawba was 56 miles (90 km) distant from Cofitachequi, and this leg probably took them four days to complete.

From Catawba, the sailors continued along the Occaneechi trail, through the towns of Saponi and Eno, to reach Occaneechi Town. It was a distance totaling 207 miles (333 km). Completing it would have taken them about two weeks. The Occaneechi Island trading center was near modern Clarksville, Virginia. The site was strategically situated on the Roanoke River in southern Virginia, where three trade routes came together. Thus, it was a major trading center in the seventeenth century, and it most probably had the same distinction a century earlier. The Siouan language spoken there was the lingua franca for a wide area.[48] The site of Occaneechi is well known to archaeologists. Its location at the hub of well-traveled trade routes makes possible the conclusion that it was a logical seventh waypoint on Ingram's long walk.

"They have also in many places vines which bear grapes as big as a man's thumb." Ingram was referring here to the muscadine grape (*Vitis rotundifolia*), which is widespread across the Gulf of Mexico and Atlantic coastal plain as far north as Delaware. As its scientific name suggests, the muscadine grape is large and plump, up to an inch (2.5 cm) in diameter. Giovanni da

Verrazano was impressed by these grapes when he saw them on the Carolina coast in 1524.[49] Thomas Harriot, when later describing North Carolina to Walter Ralegh, also noted that there were very large sweet grapes there.[50]

The town of Occaneechi was such a substantial trading town that the men might have stayed for two or three days. After bartering for food and supplies they would have headed northeast along the final leg of the Occaneechi trail to Bermuda Hundred.[51] This northern terminus of the Occaneechi trail was at the head of the tide, well up the James River from where Jamestown would be founded in 1607. Bermuda Hundred was near modern Petersburg, Virginia, which would still be an important military and trading hub during the American Civil War in the nineteenth century.

It was probably almost March by this time. The three hikers were following the movement of spring northward. The walk from the trading center at Occaneechi to the tidewater of the James River was 95 miles (153 km), and the men would have taken nearly a week to complete it. The coastal plain was narrowing as they moved north, and the trail thus took them closer to the coast every day. In the distance off to their right were the Outer Banks, where Ingram's interrogators of 1582 would eventually try and fail to establish a permanent English colony on Roanoke Island in the later 1580s (Chapter 11).

The three men passed bustling communities of speakers of languages of the Siouan and Iroquoian families. Nearer the coast were villages of Eastern Algonquians, the southernmost in a string of linguistically related cultures that extended all the way to Ingram's new goal, Cape Breton. The Carolina communities would have been visited and described by the leaders of the doomed Roanoke Island venture of the 1580s. Thomas Harriot, a scientist, and John White, the artist, were by then both working for Walter Ralegh. They would go back to England with descriptions and paintings that confirmed what Ingram had said previously in his interrogation.

Algonquian Communities

Eastern Algonquian communities lived as far south as northeastern North Carolina. Behind the Algonquians, in the interior, straddling the fall line of the Appalachians, were a series of Siouan and Iroquoian nations (Figure 6.8). The Iroquoians living here were in at least some cases related to the Northern

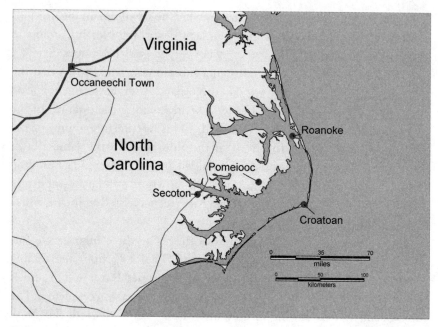

Figure 6.8. Carolina Algonquian villages of 1585–1586 mentioned in the text. Figure by author.

Iroquoians, whom Ingram would encounter farther north. These were the Tuscaroras, who had been visited by Spanish explorers before 1522.[52] However, Ingram had not yet reached any of the Northern Iroquoian communities having the very large longhouses that would impress him and cause him to linger for a week. The Iroquoians he might have encountered in North Carolina had smaller arched houses like those used by Virginia and Carolina Algonquians, as later illustrated by John White in the 1580s.[53]

The Eastern Algonquians of coastal North Carolina lived in bark or mat houses framed with light wood frameworks. The houses resembled in shape the larger longhouses built by Northern Iroquois nations but were much smaller in size, lacking both wide center aisles and interior fires. Figure 6.9 shows that the houses there were not nearly as large as Northern Iroquoian longhouses. While Pomeiooc (Figure 6.9) was palisaded for protection, the village of Secoton was not.[54]

The Carolina Algonquian houses had rectangular floor plans, unlike the circular floor plans of Timucua houses in Florida. The two house forms were alike in keeping fires and cooking outside. As Ingram continued northward into colder climates, he would find housing that had interior fires for

Figure 6.9. The palisaded Indian village of Pomeiooc. Watercolor drawing by John White. British Museum. John White ca. 1585. 00025869001.

heating as well as cooking. Both Northern Iroquoian longhouses and those of the Eastern Algonquians of New England featured large interior hearths, whereas those in the Southeast did not. Interior fires required smoke holes in house roofs, equipped with covers or roof lanterns so that rain would not enter. White's watercolors clearly show that the houses he saw did not have smoke holes. Archaeologists have long since confirmed these differences by examining excavated house floors.

Much is known about the Algonquians from records deriving from the later Roanoke (1585) and Jamestown (1607) colonies, both of which were established before smallpox decimated the native communities. Ingram was the first to describe these people.

John White's sketches and watercolors illustrate what Ingram saw in Carolina and Virginia. These people were similar to the Timucuas of Florida in some ways, but different in others. The topknot hairdos sported by Timucua men were absent, and the ornaments of gold and silver recovered from Spanish shipwrecks were also missing. Southern marine shell beads were in demand among the Eastern Algonquians, and Ingram's trading party no doubt enjoyed a brisk business.

Roanoke Island, North Carolina, later became the site of the famous Lost Colony. Leaders of the expedition who returned soon after its establishment provided confirmation of many of the things described by Ingram for the same part of the coast. The report of Ralph Lane is one such source.[55] Ingram's description was different from but consistent with Lane's. Ingram's repeated references to marine shell beads as pearls and the reference to vessels of massy silver (mica) were at least consistent. Mica sheets were used prehistorically for centuries in the Eastern Woodlands. The production of mica cutouts and inclusions with burials is well known for the earlier first-millennium Hopewell culture, which was centered in southern Ohio.[56] Stitching slabs of mica together to make scoops and containers is less widely known and for that reason Ingram's description provides information not otherwise known or understood.

Figure 6.10 is a later watercolor drawing by John White, a portrait of a man of the Outer Banks. This was a leading man, with body paint and feathers in his hair. The body painting might appear to be tattoos, but they are very different in style and coverage from the tattoos Ingram saw on the Timucuas in North Florida. In addition, Ingram refers to these decorations as varying colors of body paint, not tattoos. These Carolina men shaved the sides of their heads, leaving a crest or roach on the top. In this too they differ from the topknotted Timucua men.[57]

Figure 6.11 depicts the wife and daughter of a chief of Pomeiooc. The daughter appears to be eight to 10 years of age.[58] Like the man in Figure 6.10, the arm decorations look like tattoos, but they probably were temporary painted decorations. Ingram left no sketches, but he did provide descriptions of these people. Were it not for Ingram, we would not know that unlike the Timucuas, the Roanokes and their neighbors sported temporary body paint but not tattoos.[59]

Ingram admired the people he encountered in what would become known as Virginia. "The people commonly are of good favored features, and shape of body. The people are of growth tall and thick, above five feet

Figure 6.10. Man with body paint. Watercolor drawing by John White. British Museum. John White ca. 1585. 01613648696.

high, somewhat thick like Turks, with their faces and skins of color very red or like an olive, and towards the north somewhat tawny. But many of them are painted with diverse colors. They are very swift of foot. The hair of their heads is shaved or cut in sundry spots and the rest of the hair of the head is traced." All of this was later confirmed by White and Harriot.

Figure 6.12 depicts a Roanoke chief in 1585, possibly the man called Wingina. Like other chief men, he cut his hair short on the sides, leaving a roach. Lower-ranking men wore their hair long but gathered into a knot at the rear. This man has a square copper plate on his chest, along with a

Figure 6.11. Woman and child of Pomeiooc,
Watercolor drawing by John White. British
Museum. John White ca. 1585. 00672778001.

string of shell beads. Strings of shell and copper beads usually hung from
their ears. Senior men walked with their arms folded as a sign of wisdom.
Perhaps most significantly, this leading man is shown with no body art at all,
despite his apparent high status.

The square copper plate in Figure 6.12 is significant. In 1586, the Indians
told Ralph Lane about copper sources in northern Virginia, a country they
called Chaunis Temoatan. This report confirmed what Ingram had said four
years earlier. Still later, Arthur Barlowe confirmed that senior men mon-
opolized trade in copper and other goods, and that they could be easily

Figure 6.12. A Roanoke chief in 1585, possibly Wingina. British Museum. John White ca. 1585. 01613648694.

distinguished from commoners by their behaviors and the copper plates they wore.[60]

Examples of copper plates like that shown in Figure 6.12 are known from archaeological sites, such as the Trigg site in western Virginia. Historic sources later reported Algonquians wearing large copper plates on their chests as far north as Maine. It is clear that copper was plentiful in the Middle Atlantic region. Some of it was soft and pale native copper and some was redder copper cut from trade vessels that were by then being supplied by Europeans. Lane said that the Indians preferred the redder trade copper because it was harder and kept a sharper edge. The native copper of eastern North America is alloyed with a little zinc, giving it some of the properties of brass. European copper was more often alloyed with tin, turning it into harder bronze.[61]

Spring 1569 was at hand. The three men started out again, hiking through what for North America was a densely settled coastal environment. The communities they passed through were small, but there were many of them. To the north was Chesapeake Bay, its shores dotted by Eastern Algonquian farms and villages. They headed northward on trails that would take them up the west side of the great bay.

7

The Long Walk: Spring 1569

The spring 1569 segment of their long walk took Ingram, Browne, and Twide from Bermuda Hundred to Saco, near the southern tip of Maine.[1] It was a total of 797 miles (1,283 km), which would take them 53 days of travel, with about 19 additional days available for rest and recuperation. The first three of this segment's 10 legs probably took Ingram and his companions along the west side of Chesapeake Bay, on now unknown trails that took them past where Annapolis and Baltimore now stand. The western shore of the great bay is deeply indented by the estuaries of several rivers and many smaller streams. The trail going north probably stayed a dozen or more miles west of the bay in order to avoid broad river crossings (Figure 7.1).

Chesapeake Bay

There they were passing through another countryside that already had been visited by Europeans. During the 1550s, French activity along this part of the Atlantic Coast had made the Spanish increasingly alarmed. Spanish treasure fleets caught the Gulf Stream flowing north on their homeward voyages, and new French colonies there would have allowed French pirates to intercept and plunder them. As mentioned in Chapter 6, the principal consequence was the brief establishment of Fort Caroline in northeastern Florida, although this had been more a project designed to provide refuge for French Protestants than a pirating enterprise.

The Spanish had the advantage of having found a young marooned Englishman named John on a stop at Campeche, Mexico. Like the marooned Spanish men found by Cortés and de Soto, John was a survivor

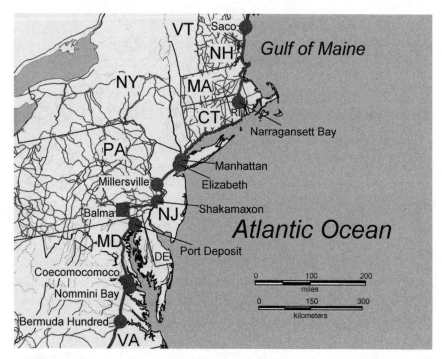

Figure 7.1. The junctions (•), waypoints (■), and probable legs of the third segment of Ingram's long walk, shown against a backdrop of known trails. Figure by author.

who had learned much about America in his time ashore. He had sailed from Bristol, England, as a cabin boy. His ship had found a very large bay at 37° north on the east coast of North America in 1546, and John seemed like someone who could guide Spanish exploration of the same section of the Atlantic coastline. The sources are fragmentary and confused, but Spanish ships appeared to have sailed into Chesapeake Bay in 1559 or 1560. They named what is now called Virginia "Ajacán,"[2] and they named the Chesapeake "St. Mary's Bay." There they kidnapped a young local Indian, whom they named Don Luis.[3]

There might have been earlier Spanish explorations of Chesapeake Bay, but just who found it and named it St. Mary's Bay is not important for the current discussion. What matters here is that Spanish Jesuit missionaries went there in 1570, a year after Ingram passed through. They landed near the site of the later English Jamestown colony and hiked across the peninsula from the James River to the York River, where they established a mission downstream from the main Powhatan Indian village. Don Luis had served as their interpreter and guide in this effort, but he soon turned on the mission-aries. The mission ended when the Powhatans killed all of them. There was a Spanish relief expedition sent to the bay in 1571. They were too late to save the missionaries but arrived soon enough to figure out what had happened. This was predictably followed by a punitive expedition the next year. These colonizing efforts having failed, the Spanish gave up on St. Mary's Bay for many years to come.[4]

Part of the importance of the failed Spanish mission in Powhatan ter-ritory on the west side of Chesapeake Bay is that it was part of a larger pattern of Spanish exploration of the Bay for several years both before and after 1570–1571. The missionaries failed because they had been chronically low on supplies, and the Indians were not interested in taking them on as demanding charity cases.

Also important is that all the Spanish maps of this period refer to Chesapeake Bay as St. Mary's Bay.[5] Ingram appears to have been familiar with this usage. He mentioned the St. Mary's Bay three times, and St. Mary's River once, but in ways that have long confused readers. Two of the comments clearly refer to St. Mary's Bay, Newfoundland, where Ingram later stopped on his way back to England. There he saw reddish English sheep that had been allowed to run wild like the feral domesticates the Spanish had introduced on the island of Curaçao. These two instances are discussed in Chapter 9. However, the other two instances where Ingram mentioned St. Mary's Bay just as clearly refer to Chesapeake Bay and the Susquehanna River.

There is no archaeological evidence for sheep around Chesapeake Bay in the 1560s. A survey of archaeologists who specialize in paleozoology and are knowledgeable about the Chesapeake region produced not one who knew of any sheep bones dating prior to the founding of the ill-fated Roanoke Island colony in the 1580s.[6]

Ingram also mentioned the St. Mary's River and claimed that there were rich silver (mica) mines on a mountain he called "Bauchoovan" 30 leagues from the coast.[7] As usual, the place name cannot be associated with any par-ticular American Indian language. However, a distance of 30 leagues converts to roughly 30 hours travel. This claim, in which Ingram again mistakes mica for silver, probably refers to the native metal deposits in the Appalachians of northern Virginia. There is nothing to link this reference to Newfoundland. In context, Ingram's mention of the St. Mary's River had to refer to a major stream flowing into Chesapeake Bay. He tied the comment to his discussion of maneaters rumored to live to the north, which is explained below as referring to the Mohawk nation of what is now eastern New York.[8] Consequently, this mention could have referred only to the Susquehanna River, which the three Englishmen approached as the season warmed.

Historians, particularly David Quinn, have tended to conclude that all four of Ingram's mentions of St. Mary's Bay or River refer to his observations in and around Chesapeake Bay. No other example shows better the confusion among Ingram's questioners, their recorders, and the historians who have tried to make sense of it all. David Quinn assumed that all references to St. Mary's involved Chesapeake Bay, and that this was further damning evidence against Ingram's testimony.[9] However, a closer look reveals that Ingram referred to two different bays named St. Mary's, and either he was unclear or his recorders failed to catch the distinction.

Ingram's Botany

By this time spring was in bloom, and Ingram noticed the flowers. Dame's rocket (*Hesperis matronalis*) is a Eurasian wildflower popularly known in England as the gillyflower. Dame's rocket is today an invasive plant in the Eastern Woodlands, having been introduced sometime well after Ingram's 1569 trek. It blossoms in the late spring, around the time Ingram completed this part of the long walk, but it would not have been part of the landscape in 1569. What he saw was phlox.

Native *Paniculata* or tall phlox of the phlox genus is a very similar native American wildflower found in the Eastern Woodlands. Like dame's rocket, it has a mix of white, pink, and purple blossoms. Phlox is easily confused with dame's rocket because their general sizes and shapes and the colors of their flowers are very similar. However, while dame's rocket blossoms have four petals, phlox has five. Thus, Ingram probably saw phlox plants and identified them as "gillyflowers like ours in England." A few species of phlox flower in May and June, but fall phlox does not flower until July through September. Ingram could have seen phlox frequently as he made his way north through the course of those months.

Ingram also remembered seeing wild roses in the spring of 1569. Wild roses occurred at the time in Eurasia and North America, but not West Africa or the Caribbean. Roses emerge a little later than phlox in the Eastern Woodlands. Most flower in June through August. Ingram probably would have seen them late in this segment of his long walk, and perhaps into the next one (Chapter 8).

Northward to Balma

Ingram said almost nothing about the long walk segment northward from Bermuda Hundred. The details of his itinerary were of little interest to his interrogators. The legs that took him northward to the top of Chesapeake Bay have to be inferred from topography from here to the next waypoint, a place that Ingram called "Balma."

The hike northward from Bermuda Hundred to Nomini Bay took them through or past a large number of Powhatan towns and across the broad estuaries of eastern Virginia. It was a distance of 83 miles (134 km). This leg took them at least six days, probably with many stops and river crossings.

They reached the Potomac estuary at Nomini Bay. They had the option of going northwest to a narrower crossing, but the estuary is so long that it would have required an additional two or three days of walking. They would have needed more than the usual amount of time to get ferried across to the north side of the estuary. This shorter route was a distance of at least 11 miles (18 km) by canoe, followed by a hike to the town of Coecomocomoco on the north side. This waterborne leg and the subsequent hike to the town had to have required a day of effort, as well as help from native boatmen.

From Coecomocomoco they probably hiked through the dense string of Patuxent towns east of modern Washington, past the site of modern Baltimore, to what is now Port Deposit at the mouth of the Susquehanna River. The distance was 118 miles (190 km), which required another eight days of travel.

When Ingram reached the mouth of the Susquehanna, he must have found out about the big town three days' walk upstream into what is now southern Pennsylvania. This would turn out to be a large Northern Iroquoian–speaking town. Most Northern Iroquoians lived far into the interior, in modern New York State, Ontario, and Quebec. The town that Ingram saw just three days away, and later described, could only have been a nation of Northern Iroquoians who had recently moved south to escape the conflict in their previous homeland. These people had to have been the Susquehannocks, people very unlike the Eastern Algonquians among whom the Englishmen had been traveling for weeks.

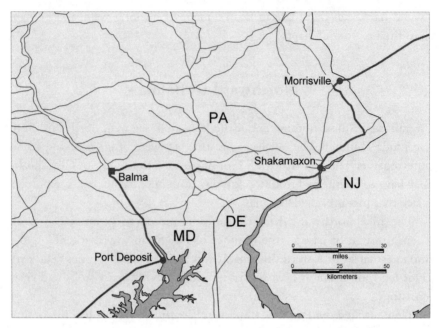

Figure 7.2. The trails, junctions, and the Balma waypoint in northernmost Chesapeake Bay and southeastern Pennsylvania. Figure by author.

The sailors took a detour upstream away from saltwater that put them on the trail network of southeastern Pennsylvania.[10] Here Ingram reached the place he called "Balma" when he talked about the distance he had covered on his long walk (Figure 7.2). He listed seven specific town names, but Balma clearly stood out among them as the big Susquehannock town.[11] The distance to Balma was 40 miles (64 km), and it probably took them almost three days to reach it from Chesapeake Bay. Balma was one of a list of seven town names mentioned by Ingram. The fact that three of them are identifiable as waypoints indicates that the whole list was mentioned in chronological order, with one exception that is explained in Chapter 9. Balma was the third town on Ingram's list of seven and the first that can be identified with a known archaeological site.[12]

The Susquehannocks

Ingram and his companions rarely stayed anywhere along their route for more than three or four days. However, they lingered for about a week at

Balma. It was an imposing town, and Ingram and his partners were so fascinated by its people that they stayed longer there than they had any other
place along their route. When questioned, Ingram said that far into the land
there are many people in towns and villages. At Balma he saw a town a half
mile, almost a mile, long. The town had streets broader than any street in
London.

At Balma, Ingram had come upon a town of large Northern Iroquoian
longhouses. Outside a village perimeter were agricultural fields that had
once been forested, but by 1569 they were cleared spaces except for the
standing dead skeletons of large girdled trees. Crops of maize, beans, and
squash sprouted from small hills of mounded soil where women did most
of the farming. Here and there among the fields were small houses where
people spent their summers hoeing and chasing off or harvesting deer and
other animals trying to feed on the crops. All of this was on rich land along
a river. The town, its scattered fields, and field houses could easily stretch a
mile and a half (2.4 km).

The lack of domesticated draft animals meant that manure fertilizer was
not available to Northern Iroquoian farmers. Wheeled transport did not
exist, so if alternative fertilizers were known, they could not be economic-
ally transported to the fields.[13] Consequently, unfertilized fields declined in
productivity every year. To make up for the declines, new fields were opened
every year, ever farther away from the core of the community. Firewood also
had to be gathered from increasingly distant sources. At the same time, bark-
covered longhouses wore out and the growing or shrinking families that
occupied them needed reorganization in new quarters.

Consequently, every couple decades these gradual changes prompted a
relocation of the community and the building of new and better housing.
The new village was not necessarily built very far away, but far enough to
allow for people to hike shorter distances to new fields, find firewood closer
to home, and construct fresh new longhouses more appropriately sized for
their growing extended families.

Balma's longhouses and their large sizes leave no doubt that it was a
Northern Iroquoian town. Figure 7.3 shows a reconstructed Northern
Iroquoian longhouse. The doorway, which is about 6 feet (2 m) high, provides scale.[14] By 1569, many such towns were medium to large-sized communities. A typical town might have had a dozen huge longhouses, built
with room to allow additions at their ends; these were often aligned with
public spaces like streets between them. The cores of the towns were often

Figure 7.3. A reconstructed longhouse, based on ethnological and archaeological evidence. Huron-Maison-Longue-Reconstituée-Extérieur_01. Public domain photograph by Pierre5018. Image via Wikimedia Commons.

palisaded for defense as this one was, the fields lying beyond the palisade and extending across cleared zones to the edge of the woods.

Balma was the only Northern Iroquoian town near enough to Ingram's route to have been the one he visited, and its identity as the place known to archaeologists as the Schultz site seems certain given his descriptions. It was a substantial palisaded town, which makes it the only high-probability waypoint for the spring 1569 segment of the long walk.[15] Balma and later Susquehannock town sites are well studied by archaeologists. However, until now there has been no clear evidence that Ingram had called it Balma or that a town the size of Balma was established on the site as early as 1569. The earliest of several well-informed estimates is that the first big Susquehannock town was not founded at the Schultz site until around 1575. However, Barry Kent, the originator of this estimate, said 1575 "at the latest," leaving room for adjustment. Ingram's evidence shows that Balma was well established six years earlier than that initial estimate.[16]

The thing that struck Ingram most forcefully were the large sizes of multi-family Susquehannock longhouses. These were typical Northern Iroquoian longhouses, much larger than any houses Ingram had seen up to this point. It is clear that Ingram went on at length about them in his interrogation. Fortunately, excavations in Pennsylvania, New York, Ontario, and Quebec have provided plenty of archaeological evidence to sort out the recorders' confusion about these and the smaller houses Ingram had seen elsewhere.[17]

Northern Iroquoian longhouses tended to be around three fathoms wide. Fathoms were adult male arm spans of about six feet (2 m). The houses had long, flat side walls that rose to around 10 feet (3 m). At that height, an arched roof was built to span the distance from the top of one side wall to the top of the opposite side wall. The top of the arch was about as high as the house was wide, a truly impressive architectural form.

The framework of a longhouse was made by setting and lashing poles together. Vertical poles for walls and interior supports were typically long, straight-rigid posts about four inches (10 cm) in diameter at their bases. The arched roof framework had thinner and more flexible members. Walls and roofs were both sheathed with panels of bark, typically American elm, that had been peeled from trees in the spring of the year in which a particular house was built or expanded. It was not unusual for a Northern Iroquoian longhouse to have at least 2,500 square feet (230 m²) of floor area, enough to accommodate 12 nuclear families, each averaging two adults and three children, a total of 60 people. Each interior compartment was about as long as it was wide and was separated from adjoining compartments by partition walls. Houses often had small storage rooms at each end of the longhouse, which also served to buffer the interior compartments from winter cold.

A senior woman presided over each longhouse, its compartments typically occupied by her sisters, daughters, their spouses, and children—what ethnologists call a matrilineage. The lengths of the houses varied according to the number of nuclear families that had to be accommodated in each of them. Many longhouses were in the range of six or eight compartments long, over 100 feet (30 m), but even longer ones have been found elsewhere in the region by archaeologists. Ingram said that the interior support posts were "pillars" about as big as the leg of a 15-year-old boy or slightly smaller. Some posts were as long as a man is tall, some twice that length.

Every longhouse had wide interior benches running along each side wall for nearly its entire length, interrupted only by compartment partitions. Each compartment bench was where a nuclear family sat, ate, and slept. Perhaps 10 feet (3 m) overhead was an attic floor for storage. The nuclear families of two women, usually sisters or cousins, faced each other across the aisle and shared the open interior fire between them. Smoke rose and exited through a smoke hole above each fire. Most of this is clear from archaeological evidence. The rest comes from early descriptions.[18]

The long interior benches prompted Ingram to describe them as "banquette" houses, a reference to the long benches against both of the outer walls. This in turn triggered confusion among those present at his interrogation. He did not intend to say that these were "banquet" or "banqueting" houses, but that is how Hakluyt and others heard it and how readers of Hakluyt's published version have read it since 1589.[19] Ingram also described the longhouses as having louvers on their tops, "like the louver of a hall in England." This was simply his way of describing the smoke holes and their coverings far above each of the fireplaces lined up along the center aisle of every longhouse. Finally, he said that the interior support posts on either side of the central longhouse aisle were decorated with quartz crystals, mica, and square sheets of native copper. When processed by his recorders and edited by Hakluyt these became solid square pillars made *of* crystal and silver. Longhouses thus morphed in the questioners' minds into pillared two-story English banquet halls constructed of crystal and silver, a description that would have astounded Ingram himself if he could have read the published version of his testimony.

Interior Iroquoian house posts were also decorated with carved masks, and there was often a single large totemic post set in a prominent location near the center of the house. The refilled post holes are known from archaeology, but none of these impressive wooden posts has survived intact.[20] Regrettably, the confusion about houses has provided more fodder for historians eager to discredit Ingram as a reliable source. Some link it to the Norumbega myth, which is discussed in Chapter 8.[21]

Ingram was also impressed by what the Susquehannocks told him about the beautiful quartz crystals they possessed and the fearsome people who controlled the source of these magical treasures. The Susquehannocks had recently relocated from northern to southern reaches of their river, at least partly because of the hostile Northern Iroquoian nations that lived even farther north in what is now New York State. Five of the distant Northern Iroquoian nations formed an alliance around this time, which today is often referred to as the Iroquois Confederacy, making them a formidable hostile power for those not included. Hodenosaunee (Longhouse People) is what they still call themselves. Of the five nations, the Mohawks were the easternmost and perhaps the most aggressive at the time. Despite also being themselves Northern Iroquoians, the Susquehannocks had little good to say about their Mohawk relatives to the north. However, the Mohawk Valley was not only home to their enemies but also the source of quartz crystals, a valued trade item.

The Susquehanna River has two main branches, one of which has its source in eastern New York, where a short portage connects with tributaries of the Mohawk River. The name "Mohawk" comes from what they were called by New England Algonquians, a name that translates as "man eaters." The Mohawks called themselves the Kanyenkehaka, "people of the place of the crystals."[22] The Mohawks traded these widely. It is likely that Ingram saw the attractive quartz crystals from Mohawk country and learned from the Susquehannocks that they had come from a marvelous source upstream far to the north. The magical qualities attributed to the naturally faceted crystals matched those of the marine shell beads that moved up the southern trails recently walked by Ingram. This must have attracted the interest of the itinerant traders that he, Browne, and Twide had become.[23] In Susquehannock eyes, the Mohawks were not only the source of valuable crystals but unfortunately were sometimes hostile cannibals as well. This was part of the Mohawks' reputation for savagery in their conflicts with other nations of the Northeast.

Ingram's mention of cannibals in this context is another example of the Elizabethan fascination with this topic. Unfortunately, Hakluyt later combined all such references of supposed cannibals, mixing this example with African ones. However, Ingram's references to cannibals in North America consistently point to the interior of the Northeast. The Susquehannocks of Balma had plenty of recent adverse experience with the Mohawks and probably other members of the Iroquois Confederacy. As often happens, the people of the place of the crystals were thus also bogeymen in the eyes of the Susquehannocks. Curiously, Ingram qualified his statement about Mohawk cannibals by saying there were "not many" of them.

Forty years later, John Smith of Jamestown fame would explore the Chesapeake Bay and go ashore at Port Deposit. Rapids prevented him from taking a boat farther upstream, but he learned of the same Northern Iroquoian people Ingram had visited. He was told that their town was two days' travel northward. It was Smith who would name the people "Sasquesahanocks," a version of which name would come to identify both the nation and their river. Imposing representatives of the Susquehannocks came down to the river's mouth to meet with Smith. The lure of European trade goods was too strong to keep them at home. They made a big impression on Smith, as they clearly had on Ingram four decades earlier.[24]

What Smith reported was consistent with both Ingram's earlier testimony and with the archaeological record. Smith added that the Susquehannocks spoke a very different language from the Eastern Algonquians and confirmed that they lived in large longhouses in a palisaded town. The Susquehannocks fortified their towns against their archenemies to the west, the Massawomeck people according to Smith. The exact identity of that nation is still debated by historians and archaeologists.[25]

> The Sasquesahanocks inhabit upon the chief spring of these 4 [rivers], two days journey higher than our barge could pass for rocks. Yet we prevailed with the interpreter to take with him another interpreter to persuade the Sasquesahanocks to come to visit us, for their language[s] are different. Three or four days we expected their return. Then 60 of these giantlike-people came down, with presents of venison, tobacco pipes, baskets, targets, bows and arrows. Five of their Werowances came boldly aboard us, to cross the bay for Tockwogh, leaving their men and canoes, the wind being so violent that they durst not pass.[26]
>
> These [people] are scarce known to Powhatan. They can make near 600 able men, and are palisaded in their towns to defend them from the Massawomekes their mortal enemies.[27]

John Smith's 1608 description of Susquehannock men claims that they were like giants. He was clearly impressed by the people and their town, as Ingram had been. Smith later provided a portrait of one of the men who came downstream to visit and trade with him (Figure 7.4).[28]

Ingram, Browne, and Twide learned more about the beliefs and religious practices among the Susquehannocks than anywhere else in North America. He said that they appeared to honor the sun, the moon, and the stars, which is consistent with the well-known Northern Iroquoian Thanksgiving Speech. Today, that long and heartfelt traditional speech still marks both the opening and the closing of major ceremonies in several Northern Iroquoian communities.[29]

The men encountered someone masked and dressed in the guise of what Ingram guessed was a black dog or a black calf. Ingram was convinced that this was a representation of the devil, which he said the Susquehannocks called "Collochio."

The Sasque=ahanougs are a Giant like peo= ple & thus a=tyred...

Figure 7.4. Susquehannock man from an illustration on John Smith's 1612 map. Public Domain via Wikimedia Commons. Detail from Map of Virginia by John Smith, 1612.

Where Ingram came up with this name is a puzzle. No known words that approximate "devil" in the Northern Iroquoian, Susquehannock, Mohawk, or Onondaga languages come even close to Collochio.[30] It might seem vaguely Spanish or Italian, but those languages provide no convincing source word either.[31] The word "Collochio" does not have any specific known meaning in the Susquehannock language, but it will come up again, this time as "Kalicho." This will reappear as the name of an Inuit man taken captive by Martin Frobisher on his 1577 voyage to the American Arctic (Chapter 11).

The Collochio entries indicate that the three Englishmen probably encountered a Northern Iroquoian curing ceremony at Balma. Ingram describes the costumed Collochio as someone masquerading as what appeared to him to be a creature with large eyes. The masked curer's performance was so terrifying to the Englishmen that they mistook its purpose, concluding that it was intended to execute rather than cure. When the sick person died, Ingram noted that burial was concluded quickly, and that the deceased was accompanied by food and implements, contributed by close friends.

Ingram also said that when Richard Browne saw the Collochio he shouted, "There is the devil," and immediately blessed himself in the name of the Father, the Son, and the Holy Ghost. Richard Twide then vehemently said, "I defy thee and all thy works." With that, Ingram said the performer skulked away and was not see again.

The apparition Ingram later called "Collochio" is consistent with later sources that describe Northern Iroquoian curing and religious practices. John Smith observed Susquehannock men wearing similar bearskin costumes in 1608.[32]

> Their attire is the skins of bears, and wools, some have cassocks made of bears' heads and skins, that a man's head goes through, the skins neck, and the ears of the bear fastened to his shoulders, the nose and teeth hanging down his breast, another bear's face split behind him, and at the end of the nose hung a paw, the half sleeves coming to the elbows were the necks of bears, and the arms through the mouth, with paws hanging at their noses. One had the head of a wolf hanging in a chain for a jewel.[33]

Champlain described the same sort of ceremony among the Northern Iroquoians of Canada in 1616, and Gabriel Sagard observed much the same thing during his 1623–1624 trip to Canada.[34] The Northern Iroquoian curing ceremony would later evolve into the elaborate False Face curing societies that became a major cultural theme. Northern Iroquoian False Face wooden masks developed along with elaborated curing ceremonies in the wake of devastating epidemics later in the seventeenth century. By that time the Northern Iroquoians had trade access to the iron knives, brass, and horsehair that were components of False Faces, or were used in their production.[35] When Ingram visited the Susquehannocks in 1569 these elaborations were still in the future. Costumes that looked like large black dogs or calves to Ingram must have been made from wolf or bear skins.

"Balma" was the name Ingram gave this town, but for linguistic reasons that name cannot be what any Northern Iroquoian speakers would have called it. Here again Ingram can be forgiven, for he was trying to remember a name that he had heard a dozen years earlier, one he had not heard accurately in the first place.[36] The Susquehannock language is poorly known apart from its being one of the Northern Iroquoian languages. Iroquoian utterances, which are typically longer than words but shorter than sentences, never begin with "B" or "P," nor do their languages use the "L" consonant. Neither does "Balma" appear to be a specific Eastern Algonquian word, which Ingram could have picked up from neighboring speakers of some Eastern Algonquian language. However, words in those languages often begin with "B" or "P," so it is possible that Ingram heard something he remembered as "Balma" from a speaker of one of the nearby Eastern Algonquian languages. Getting a name in one language from the speakers of another was a common way in which later European colonists came to identify American nations, as the Mohawk case has already demonstrated.[37]

In addition to a few place names, Ingram provided what he said was a short Susquehannock word list at the prompting of one of his questioners.

Collochio, devil
Gwando, a word of salutation
Garicona, king
Garrucona, lord
Tona, bread
Carmugnaz, privates
Kerucca, sun

The seven words all conform to the sounds of Northern Iroquoian languages but not to those of any Eastern Algonquian languages. Ingram spent a week at Balma, by far the longest stop made on the long walk. The native words that Ingram supplied via Hakluyt sound like Northern Iroquoian words, but mostly only in a general way. With one exception, they do not mean anything in particular.[38]

Two seventeenth-century Susquehannock word lists document 89 unique words and phrases for that language. These have been studied by linguists, confirming their Northern Iroquoian identity. The list is sufficient to show that the language was about equally related to Onondaga and Mohawk, both languages of the Iroquois Confederacy. Mithun has carried out comparisons with other related Northern Iroquoian languages as well.[39]

With one exception, the specific native words and their glosses listed by Ingram do not correspond to any of the 89 known Susquehannock words. *Kerucca,* "sun," is the notable exception to the uncertainties found in other words listed by Ingram. The Mohawk form for "sun" is *karáhkwa,* from the verb root *-rahkw-.* The Onondaga cognate is given as gaǽhgwa·ʔ. It is clear that these are cognates and that they all have the same meaning, "sun."[40] This last piece of definitive evidence stands like an exclamation point at the end of the Northern Iroquoian part of Ingram's long walk.

Resuming the Long Walk

While Ingram's testimony makes it clear that he spent a week in a Susquehannock town, it includes no information at all about what he saw on the next six legs of the long walk.[41] He must have passed into southern coastal Maine, but how he got there from Balma must be inferred from what is known about the regional topography, the network of trails through it, and the kinds of choices the three men had made up to this point. The coastal plain pinches out in New Jersey. Following trails along the fall line, which they had done for most of their journey, necessarily led them to choose trails taking them northeastward toward New York Bay. Beyond that, into southern New England, the topography would have prompted them to stay near the rocky coast.

Thus, after a week at Balma, the three Englishmen set off again, probably headed eastward to pick up a main trail along the fall line. As Ingram and the two other men moved on from Balma, they apparently stuck to trails that afforded them a wide berth to the land of crystals and alleged maneaters (Figure 7.2). Vague references to cannibals in the interior were probably voiced by Eastern Algonquians, just as the Susquehannocks had done, and it was the Eastern Algonquian trails the men used exclusively from now on. Even the Basque fishermen who frequented the same coast around this time picked up the demonization of the Northern Iroquoians in the interior, calling them Hilokoa, "the killer people" in Basque.[42] This is one possible origin for "Iroquois," the term later used for them by the French and other Europeans.

Ingram probably took the Great Miquas (Conestoga) Path, continuing eastward and striking the Delaware River at the mouth of the Schuylkill River. This was Shakamaxon, where Philadelphia now stands. This was a leg of 80 miles (129 km), and it would have taken them five days.[43]

From Shakamaxon they probably followed Falls Path northward along the Delaware River. They would have walked another 40 miles (64 km) to what is now Morrisville, Pennsylvania. By hiking up the west side of the Delaware River they would have found a good crossing just below the falls. This took another three days.

It is likely that after crossing the Delaware River at modern Trenton, they took the upper trail option along the Fall Line, a continuation of the natural boundary separating the highlands from the coastal plain that they had been following for months. This was the upper of the two alternative known trails connecting what the Dutch would later call the South River (the Delaware River) and New Amsterdam (New York).[44] The upper trail later became US Highway 1. Like the modern highways, the alternative trails converged south of the Raritan River and continued as one trail to the site of modern Elizabeth, New Jersey. The trail is now often referred to as the Assunpink Trail.[45] This option would have required a four-day hike of over 59 miles (95 km) of trail. At its end, they left the Coastal Plain behind them. This was where it pinched out, marking the beginning of the glaciated rocky coastline that stretches from Manhattan eastward.

Manhattan was 11 miles (18 km) farther away by dugout canoe. Manhattan was then a large island having a few indigenous settlements, lying at the mouth of a river that would later be named after Henry Hudson. Still later, in the early seventeenth century, the island became Dutch New Amsterdam. Ingram's trip across to the island could have taken all day. Perhaps this is the major crossing that Ingram said took 24 hours. A stop on Staten Island easily could have turned this into a day-long leg. There were probably only a few Delaware Indian villages on Manhattan Island, which the Dutch would later "purchase" for a few trinkets, from natives who had a very different sort of transaction in mind.[46] Ingram was still following a trail that would evolve into US Highway 1, and he would continue on that main trail through what is now Westchester County into southern New England. From then on, the trails became more rugged. As a consequence, they would have kept to the more coastal trails.

Following Giovanni da Verrazzano

New York Bay had been visited in 1524 by Giovanni da Verrazzano, whose story has already intersected with Ingram's. The primary purpose of the Verrazzano voyage that year was, of course, to discover a passage through or past the pesky obstacle of North America in order to get to China and the East Indies. This had been the objective of Columbus, Cabot, and many others as well, and it remained the single most important objective to northern Europeans decades later. The Portuguese had long since found a way around Africa to the East Indies, and some of Magellan's fleet had made it all the way around the world, although Magellan himself and much of the crew had died along the way. But neither of these time-consuming options was very satisfying. A quicker and safer route past the Americas was what lured Verrazzano and many others westward.[47]

Verrazzano had first struck the coast around the Outer Banks, as noted in passing in Chapter 6. He then continued northeastward along the coast, sailing too far offshore to discover the entrance to either Chesapeake Bay or Delaware Bay. Verrazzano did manage to find the narrows that now bear his name and thus the great harbor at modern New York City, but his boats did not get far enough in for him to find and name the main river that flows into it. That would eventually fall to Henry Hudson. Still, it was enough to get to the narrows and the site of the modern bridge that would be named for him.

Like the Delaware and the Hudson, the major rivers of New England tend to run north to south. That means that anyone seeking an east-west route was going to be best served by trails that took the most efficient coastal routes across the rugged landscape. These trails were well established in southern New England, and many of them are followed now by major highways, the least-cost routes being as obvious to modern engineers as they were to sixteenth-century hikers.

Southern New England Communities

By the time they got this far, Ingram, Browne, and Twide had passed through dozens of communities in which they had to have observed that tobacco smoking in pipes was well established. Hawkins had introduced smoking to

England after his second voyage, so it is probable that the three men were already comfortable with the practice and were prepared for the ritual importance of it in transactions with American Indians.

Tobacco and pipes were additional compact trade goods that they could have added to the sailors' trading stock, and it was increasingly valuable as they moved north through New England. Native tobacco, *Nicotiana rustica*, was a prehistoric introduction from South America. It had been carried northward, but the spread of tobacco as a cultigen was slowed by shorter growing seasons in the higher latitudes. It was strong stuff, associated with shamanism and curing, not mild like the *Nicotiana tabacum* strains that replaced it and today dominate the tobacco trade.

Figure 7.5 shows the density of the many communities and trails that existed in southern New England. Many of the native trails were later followed by colonial roads and remain in use today. The local Eastern Algonquians must have provided Ingram with some guidance through what otherwise would have been a confusing maze.

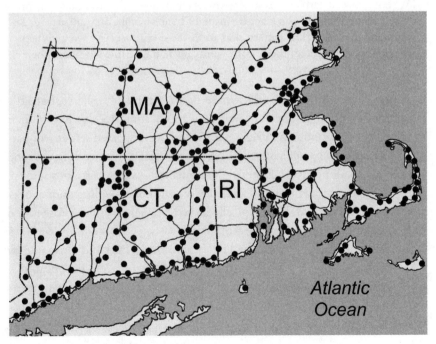

Figure 7.5. Native trails and communities of southern New England.

The trail eastward along the Connecticut coast was called the "Shore Path." As was the case across New Jersey, Ingram was probably still on what would become modern US Highway 1. This would have taken him from the Hudson River to Narragansett Bay, a distance of 190 miles (306 km). The eastern portion of it, from New London to Narragansett Bay, was known later as the Pequot Path, named after the Pequot nation that still lives in southern New England. The entire trail from New York to Boston would much later be named the Boston Post Road. This long leg across southern New England would have taken about 13 days.[48]

Giovanni da Verrazzano had also explored Narragansett Bay, Rhode Island, where he found the people to be friendly. Verrazzano and his men went for day-long excursions on well-traveled trails, through fields and open woodlands that he thought were as pleasant and suitable for cultivation as any he had ever seen. The fields were so fertile, so open and free of any obstacles or trees, that he judged any kind of seed would produce excellent crops. Verrazzano was also impressed by the plants and animals of the surrounding forest. He noted that native dugout canoes were sometimes big enough to carry a dozen men.

> When we went farther inland, we saw their houses, which are circular in shape, about 14 to 15 paces across, made of bent saplings; they are arranged without an architectural pattern, and are covered with cleverly worked mats of straw which protect them from wind and rain. . . . In each house there lives a father with a very large family, for in some we saw 25 to 30 people.[49]

Ingram and his companions must have had a similar experience, but little if anything Ingram testified to later appears to apply to this leg of their travel. Eastern Algonquian villages tended to have dispersed settlement patterns at this time, characteristically having wide spacing between houses and stretching out along rivers. Eastern Algonquian wigwams north of southern New England typically featured arched roofs with bent-sapling frameworks, as Verrazzano described. They typically lacked heavier posts like those found in Iroquoian longhouses (Figure 7.6).[50]

The bucolic landscape described by Verrazzano in 1524 and illustrated by Champlain in 1605 was surely what Ingram saw, before any European diseases disrupted the Indian communities he visited (Figure 7.7). Champlain's drawing of the land near Plymouth Harbor shows dispersed settlements, houses scattered among clearings filled by fields of maize and other crops.

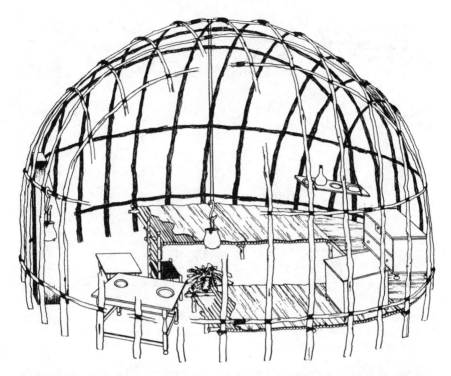

Figure 7.6. A typical Eastern Algonquian wigwam in the seventeenth century. Cambridge Press, *American Antiquity*. Sturtevant 1975:439.

This echoed what Verrazzano had seen and described about the land just to the south around Narragansett Bay in 1524.[51]

The same landscape would later be settled in 1620 by the English religious dissidents known as the Plymouth Pilgrims. However, what Verrazzano, Ingram, and Champlain had seen was profoundly changed by 1620. A terrible epidemic of uncertain type reduced the native population in the years just preceding the Pilgrims' arrival, opening Massachusetts Bay for almost unopposed colonization. Yet, although the population had been decimated, indigenous trails, fields, and some settlements all survived, and these were later described by the colonists.[52]

The first 1620 colonists ashore spent time exploring, robbing indigenous graves, and helping themselves to stocks of stored maize. Even this far north the trails were obvious. "After we had gone a while, we light[ed] upon a very broad beaten path, well nigh two feet broad."[53] These led them to

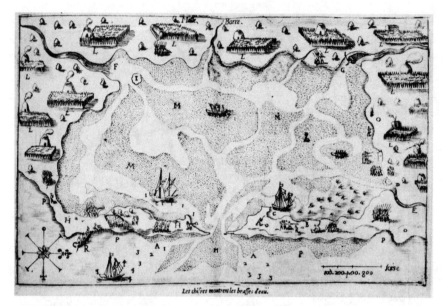

Figure 7.7. Champlain's 1605 map of Nauset Harbor. Wikimedia Commons. From H. H. Langton and W. F. Ganong, trans., The Works of Samuel de Champlain.

domed wigwams sheathed by mats and well furnished with cooking pots and implements. The trails also led to abandoned fields and the remains of houses left empty by the recent epidemic. The men were amazed to find dugout canoes left unattended on either side of a stream for the convenience of travelers, something Ingram and his partners had earlier encountered many times during the course of their long walk. They were also impressed that repeated firing of underbrush kept the woods open, such that a man could easily ride a horse through them. Open forest encouraged the deer population, on which the Indians depended for meat and hides. The girdling of trees opened up the canopy as well, allowing the natives to plant maize, beans, and squash, their staple crops.[54]

Ingram and his partners probably headed northeastward from Narragansett Bay on the most heavily used trail across peninsular New England. This would have been along the Winnicoek Trail to the Saco River of southern Maine, still followed by what is now US Highway 1. The distance was 165 miles (266 km), and it took them another 11 days.

However, Ingram and his companions were nearing the northern limit of where native agriculture could be reliably productive. When they reached Saco, they entered a new landscape, occupied by very different Eastern

Algonquian communities. It was the beginning of summer, and the weather was getting better. But it was also the season of black flies and mosquitos.

As they left agricultural communities behind, Ingram, Browne, and Twide almost certainly still stuck to a generally coastal route. Interior trails would have been more rugged, and the chances of misdirection would have been too great to risk. For the three Englishmen, from that point on, the other world once again changed in profound ways.

8

The Long Walk: Summer 1569

The Gulf of Maine

The overland legs of the spring 1569 segment of the walk from Bermuda Hundred to the Saco River would have required 53 travel days. In contrast, the Summer 1569 Saco River to Penobscot River segment of the long walk was a much shorter segment of six legs.[1] Ingram and his partners probably covered 204 miles on this segment (328 km). This would have taken 14 days of travel, with an allowance of five days of rest along the way. Three more travel legs were necessarily completed by birchbark canoe before their rescue (Figure 8.1). Those last three legs and their return to England are described in Chapter 9.

From Saco, the alternate trails became fewer, the main ones linking ever more distant villages over increasingly rough terrain. The physical environment changed for Ingram as they pushed northeastward through northern New England. The denser population of southern New England gave way to a much thinner population as they passed through what is now southwestern Maine. These more northerly Eastern Algonquian nations are now often referred to together as the Eastern Abenakis. The Englishmen had reached the part of the east coast where the growing season was too short to allow reliable farming. The forest changed, with spruce, fir, birch, and white cedar trees being much more common.

Ingram was impressed by the new forest environment he encountered north of Saco and the cultural differences of the more northerly Eastern Algonquian speakers he met there. "In the north part they are clothed with beasts' skins, the hairy side being next to their bodies in winter. There are in those parts plenty of wild beasts whose skins are most delicate and rare

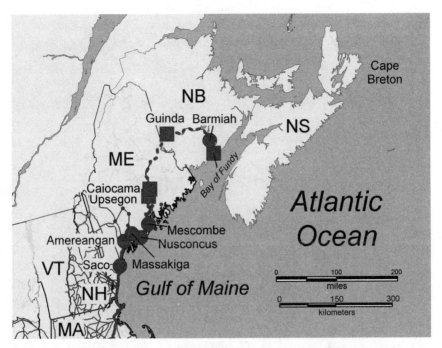

Figure 8.1. The junctions (•), waypoints (■), and probable legs of the fourth segment of Ingram's long walk, shown against a backdrop of known trails. The canoe route described in Chapter 10 is shown here as a dashed line. Figure by author.

furs." Ingram mentioned wolves, black bears, rabbits, and both red and gray foxes.

Although Ingram did not mention it specifically, the canoe birch species (*Betula papyrifera*) was particularly important here.[2] Ingram left familiar dugout canoes behind and entered a region where comparatively swift transportation in light birchbark canoes was easier and much more common. Instead of long overland trails, travelers from here northward more often traveled by canoe and hiked only over short portage trails connecting lakes and the tributaries of rivers. It was a faster means of travel, so long as Ingram and his partners could find people willing to transport them in exchange for the trade goods they still carried.

A trail map of northern New England shows the situation at a glance (Figure 8.2). Overland trails connecting communities were concentrated in southwestern Maine. The northeastern end of the vast network of North American trails came to an end in south-central Maine. The magnitude of this reality must have weighed increasingly on the men as they continued

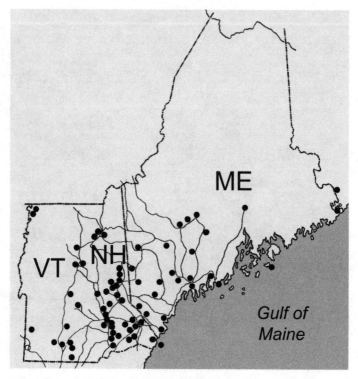

Figure 8.2. Northern New England trails and communities around 1614. Figure by author.

northeastward. It would have required a serious rethinking of how they were going to reach their goal, Cape Breton.[3]

The Testimony of Tisquantum

Records from the early seventeenth-century colony at Plymouth and various early English voyages provide information that also applies to the time of Ingram's long walk. A Wampanoag man later known as Tisquantum, "Squanto" to the English, was probably a teenager in 1605. He had been born in a Patuxet village, somewhere in the vicinity of present-day Plymouth, Massachusetts. Captain George Weymouth, who was exploring the New England coastline for Sir Ferdinando Gorges, owner of the Plymouth Company, captured Tisquantum and five other members of his tribe that year. He took them all with him back to England. There Tisquantum was taken in by Ferdinando Gorges, who taught him English and trained him as an interpreter.

John Smith explored Chesapeake Bay from Jamestown in 1608, as mentioned in the previous chapter. Ever the explorer, Smith also sailed from England to the Gulf of Maine in 1614, on which journey he named that section of the North American coast "New England." Smith took Tisquantum along on his 1614 expedition, intending to use the man to show him around and communicate with the locals. After nine years in England Tisquantum spoke excellent English as well as Wampanoag, his native Eastern Algonquian language.

Unfortunately, on his way back to Patuxet, Tisquantum was abducted again, this time by Thomas Hunt, Smith's insubordinate rogue lieutenant. Hunt was planning to sell fish, maize, and the captured people in Málaga, Spain. He transported Tisquantum and a number of other indigenous Americans he had kidnapped to Spain, where he tried to sell them into slavery for £20 apiece. Tisquantum persuaded sympathetic Spanish friars there to let him return to England.

In 1619, after a total of 14 years in England, Tisquantum finally returned to his homeland. He was again aboard John Smith's ship, having joined an exploratory expedition headed for the New England coast. This time, Smith's ship was captained by Thomas Dermer rather than by Smith. Smith had decided to stay in England, where he would remain until his death in 1631. At last, Tisquantum arrived home safely. He soon discovered that the Patuxets, as well as a majority of coastal New England tribes (mostly Wampanoags and Massachusetts), had been decimated the previous year by a terrible epidemic. He found himself regarded as a new leader of a devastated community. From their perspective he was a real-life survivor of a hero's quest through another world. When the Puritan pilgrims arrived to establish a colony the following year, Tisquantum would famously welcome them in perfect English.

During his two long stays in England, Tisquantum, and probably some of the others kidnapped by Weymouth, had been questioned about the people, villages, and trails of his homeland before the epidemics. This information was later published in two places, by John Smith and separately by Samuel Purchas, Richard Hakluyt's literary successor.[4] These two sources are very important for understanding the context of Ingram's walk into northern New England. When they are combined, the two accounts turn out to be remarkably consistent and complementary. To them can be added a few details from Champlain. Figure 8.3 shows a series of villages, at least some of which Ingram must have visited as he, Browne, and Twide made their way northeastward along the Maine coast.

The data from these sources provide an unusually complete description of Eastern Abenaki villages starting on the Saco River of southernmost Maine and extending to Indian Island on the Penobscot River. Unfortunately, the locations of eight villages cannot be determined with certainty. Consequently, they are not shown in Figure 8.3. Purchas even provided some travel times on trails linking the villages, which helps reconstruction of Ingram's progress on the last segment of his long walk. Ingram probably passed through only about half of the mapped villages, the others being off his main route.

Overall, the picture is one of thriving villages, having populations sometimes in the hundreds, despite being nonagricultural. Norumbega/Upsegon (modern Bangor) was where the leading man called Bashabes resided in 1605. Devastating epidemics had not yet reached New England when these data were recorded, so the records are relevant to any discussion of Ingram's visit in 1569. Even here in southwestern Maine, villages were linked by well-traveled overland trails. Indian Island, called Caiocama by Tisquantum,

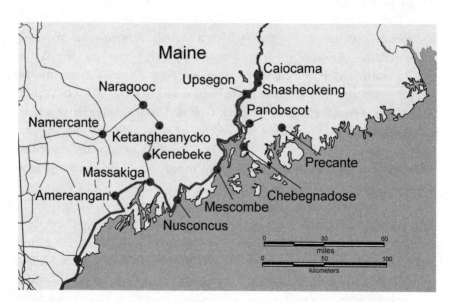

Figure 8.3. Fourteen Eastern Algonquian (Abenaki) communities reported by Tisquantum. The locations of eight more reported names (not shown) are uncertain. Figure by author.

is opposite modern Old Town. There, where the descendant Penobscot branch of the Eastern Abenaki people still live, the three sailors came to the end of the overland trail. From there northward and eastward the preferred way to travel was by water in swift birchbark canoes.[5]

John Smith described the 1614 situation well, albeit with his own renderings of place names. "The principal habitation northward we were at, was Penobscot. Southward along the Coast and up the Rivers we found Mecadacut, Segocket, Pemmaquid, Nusconcus, Kenebeck, Sagadahock, and Aumoughcawgen. . . . All these, I could perceive, differ little in language, fashion, or government: though most be Lords of themselves, yet they hold the Bashabes of Penobscot, the chief and greatest amongst them."[6]

Ingram's trek from the Saco River to the end of the trail took him a total of about two weeks. The first leg went 47 miles (76 km) from Saco to modern Lisbon Falls, a village named Amereangan as heard from Tisquantum by Purchas, and as Aumoughcawgen by Smith. This took three days. Two chiefs presided in that village, which had about 90 houses, each designed to accommodate an extended family. Tisquantum said that the village held about 260 men, which converts to a total population of 1,040 using a standard multiplier based on an assumed fraction of 25 percent men per community.[7]

The next leg took them from Amereangan, 22 miles (35 km) or one day of travel to Massakiga at modern Dresden. It was a small village, having only eight houses and 40 men, which converts to a population of 160 people. Villages like this were common this far north of the limits of reliable agriculture, but they were not occupied all year round. They were all but abandoned in summer, when families dispersed to the seashore. They were mostly abandoned again in winter, when people dispersed to northern interior family hunting territories.[8]

It was another two-day walk from Massakiga to Nusconcus (now spelled Muscongus) along an indirect shore route. It was a 27-mile (43-km) leg along a well-traveled but rocky trail.

A long three-day walk would have taken the men to Mescombe, modern Camden, on Penobscot Bay. There might have been other small villages in this part of Maine, and the route to Mescombe might have followed alternative trails and overnight stays in two of them. However, the three sailors were not likely to have taken detours if they could avoid them. The leg from Nusconcus to Mescombe was 40 miles (64 km) long. Mescombe was a seaside village that had about 50 houses, and a population of about 320 people.

Giovanni da Verrazzano had encountered hostile people somewhere along this last stretch of coastal trail 45 years earlier in 1524. Perhaps these indigenous people were then still smarting from some unpleasant experience with still-earlier European explorers. Verrazzano's description of them is revealing.

> The people were quite different from the others, for while the previous ones had been courteous in manner, these were full of crudity and vices, and were so barbarous that we could never make any communication with them, however many signs we made to them. They were clothed in skins of bear, lynx, sea-wolf and other animals. As far as we could judge from several visits to their houses, we think they live on game, fish, and several fruits which are a species of root which the earth produces itself [ground nuts]. They have no pulse, and we saw no sign of cultivation, nor would the land be suitable for producing any fruit or grain on account of its sterility. . . . Against their wishes, we penetrated two or three leagues inland with xxv armed men, and when we disembarked on the shore, they shot at us with their bows and uttered loud cries before fleeing into the woods. We did not find anything of great value in this land, except for the vast forest and some hills which could contain some metal: for we saw many natives with . . . beads of copper in their ears.[9]

Verrazzano's rebuff caused his cartographer brother, Gerolamo, to refer to that portion of the continent as the Land of Bad People (*Terra Onde di Maila Gente*). Perhaps the fact that these were successful hunter-gatherers living beyond the limits of productive agriculture had something to do with their hostility. Like the nomadic people of northern Mexico, they might simply have been less accustomed to encounters with traveling strangers.[10] However, Verrazano's description of his own behavior is probably sufficient explanation. Whatever had been the case in Verrazzano's time, there is no evidence that Ingram and his companions encountered any unfriendliness almost a half century later.

At Mescombe, modern Camden, Ingram finally saw Penobscot Bay, a broad body of water that might be the one Ingram described as "so large that they could scarce cross the same in 24 hours." Ingram and his partners probably took the advice of locals and did not try to cross it. Instead, they most likely would have been advised to follow the trail along the west side of the bay four days northward to the village of Norumbega on the site of modern Bangor, a distance of 56 miles (90 km). Forty years later, Norumbega would be called Upsegon by Tisquantum, who claimed it had 60 houses and as many as 1,000 people living there at least part of the year.

Ingram remarked that they hiked along the first half of that leg for two days.[11]

Had they made their long walk four decades later, the three sailors would have encountered Bashabes at Norumbega/Upsegon. By that time, this would be the man to whom all other chief men of the Eastern Abenaki people deferred, as Smith noted. After he kidnapped the group of people that included Tisquantum, George Waymouth also noted that they all regarded Bashabes as the most influential man in the region.[12]

It was an easy one-day walk 12 miles (19 km) upstream to the end of the trail, the Penobscot settlement on Indian Island, a place Ingram called Saganas. Decades later, Tisquantum and others of Purchas's informants said it was called "Caiocama."

Here Ingram and his companions had to decide what their next move would be. It was the end of the long walk because the overland trail route ended abruptly at Saganas/Caiocama. But they were still 450 air miles (725 km) from their goal at Cape Breton (Figure 8.1). The English sailors knew that English ships from Bristol frequented the waters off Cape Breton, but they might not have known that by then French and Basque fishing vessels occasionally stopped on the Maine coast as well. Fishermen sometimes came ashore there to dry fish and to trade with local people. In exchange for iron tools, beads, mirrors, and other portable goods, the locals provided food, furs, and other products of the sea and forest. Beaver pelts brought particularly good prices back in Europe, meeting the growing popularity of beaver felt hats, and this eventually grew into the lucrative beaver fur trade of the following century.[13] Keeping Cape Breton as their intended destination had to hold out the strongest possibility of rescue.

Ingram was in the land of boreal forest, a place for travel by canoe and deep winters, and he knew it. It was still summer, but autumn would bring cooler days and colder nights. He was impressed by the Eastern Abenaki clothing, shelters, and other adaptations to current and expected conditions.

The Norumbega Diversion

Ingram had at last reached the land of the Norumbega myth, which would drive the ambitions and plans for English exploration and colonization through the next decade and beyond. Like so many myths, "Norumbega" first appeared as a minor mention. It began with Verrazzano's 1524 voyage.

His brother, Gerolamo, produced a 1528 map of the American coast-line based on his journal and oral accounts. On this map, the coast from North Carolina to Maine bristles with names assigned by Giovanni as he sailed by. The fanciful name *Le tre figlie di Navarra,* (The three daughters of Navarre) labels the big islands in Penobscot Bay, with the label "Oranbega" identifying the Penobscot River. This was the name that got the attention of other cartographers. It was the first appearance of the place name that would morph into "Norumbega" over the following decades and acquire all sorts of embellishments to prejudice the interest of Ingram's 1582 interrogators.[14]

Esteban Gómez (1483–1538) had been a Portuguese explorer in the employ of the king of Spain in 1524. He had sailed in search of a northwest passage around North America in September of that year. He explored the Gulf of Maine as part of this expedition, sailing from northeast to southwest, the reverse of Verrazzano's earlier route that same year.[15] Gómez discovered a very wide and deep river to which he gave the name Rio de los Gamos, which is generally agreed by historians to have been the Penobscot River. Gómez described the landscape, forest, and plants as well as some pyrites he thought were gold. Gómez clearly went some distance up the Penobscot, but how far is difficult to estimate. Perhaps it does not matter, because his name for the river did not stick.[16] The historian William F. Ganong once speculated that "Oranbega" might have originated by way of some kind of combination of poor writing and poor eyesight from the Spanish "Gran Baya." He thought Estaban Gómez might have first used this name for Penobscot Bay.[17] This is just another example of the long history of speculation about Norumbega and the myth it spawned.

Just a few months before Gómez visited the Penobscot River, Verrazzano had been unable to get closer than a rope's length from Eastern Abenakis not far away on the same coast. In contrast, Gómez came away with 50 captives. Just how they were captured is unknown. Somehow, Gómez was more successful than Verrazzano in approaching the people. He hauled his captives back to Spain, but in his case the Spanish king was so appalled at the idea of their random enslavement that the people were set free when Gómez arrived in Seville.[18]

Figure 8.4 is a detail from the Dauphin map, which was drawn around 1543. This map shows discoveries reported by Cartier for his three voyages in the years just preceding that date. Notice that the tight array of rivers feeding the Gulf of Maine includes Penobscot Bay, which is above an inverted

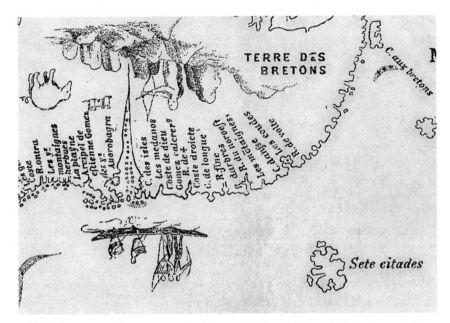

Figure 8.4. Detail from the Dauphin Map of Canada, ca. 1543. Alamy J7RRTP. Dauphin Map ca. 1543 detail.

canoe-load of people. The Penobscot River was labeled "Auorobagra," which approximates "Norumbega." The label was also supplied with an inverted symbol for a city. The Bay of Fundy was missing, leading users of the map to imagine that Cape Breton, shown here as a coastal island (C. aux Bretons), was in much easier reach than was actually the case.[19]

Jean Alfonse provides another example of an attribution that reinforced the Norumbega myth. Alfonse was a well-known pilot in the employ of Jean-François de la Roque de Roberval. In 1542–1543, Alfonse served as pilot of a French attempt to colonize Canada, based on Cartier's explorations. The colony failed, but Alfonse was able to provide information in 1545, which included his own sketch map of rivers feeding the Gulf of Maine. Alfonse referred to the Penobscot River as "Norenbegue."[20]

Mercator's popular map of 1569 (Figure 8.5) completed the establishment of the myth of "Norombega" as an impressive city. Mercator followed the precedents found on the Dauphin map and others of the period. However, Mercator also added the illustration of a towered city and expanded the same name to identify the large region drained by the Penobscot River. In this case, Mercator labeled the river the "Rio Grande." John Dee, Richard Hakluyt's predecessor, had a 1580 copy of the Mercator map. That is how

Figure 8.5. Detail of Mercator's 1569 map, showing mythical Norumbega in what is now Maine. Public Domain via Wikimedia Commons. Detail from Mercator's 1569 map.

Norumbega became a focus of Dee's advocacy for his proposed expansion of what he had named the "British Empire."

Norumbega was also on the mind of George Peckham, who was present at Ingram's interrogation and whose intent was to promote colonization in America. He was supported in this effort by Humphrey Gilbert, whose interests in the fabled Northwest Passage and colonization of the American east coast drove much of the discussion when Ingram was brought in for questioning in 1582.

In 1580, Gilbert sent his man John Walker to America with explicit orders to explore the "River of Norumbega." Walker returned with little to report, but he was at Ingram's interrogation two years later. Walker made the most of what he had found on the Penobscot River when Ingram was questioned, and he apparently had some influence on the conversations.

Ingram provided a list of seven towns he passed through, including Balma, along with information about how these and others were spaced out along the route of his long walk. The five towns that can be located and mapped indicate that he listed them in chronological order. Somehow that order was not lost in the course of Hakluyt's editing. Gunda and Ochala were apparently two large towns he encountered along earlier segments of his trek from Mexico. Balma was the Susquehannock town discussed in Chapter 7. Ingram dutifully named "Bega" as one of the cities he had visited, and he supported Walker's claim to have stolen a large number of ox (moose) hides there. [Norum]Bega, Barmiah, and Guinda can all be identified as later waypoints on his list, as described in Chapter 9. Apart from Norumbega, none of the town names Ingram mentioned can be associated with any of the many imaginative place names that adorn various maps produced earlier in the sixteenth century.[21]

Ingram reinforced the Norumbega myth by describing towns that his questioners thought they heard were a mile to a mile and a half in size. This no doubt conjured up large towns in their minds, but these were misconceptions. Ingram had described the Northern Iroquoian town of Balma as stretching a mile and a half along the Susquehanna River, while Norumbega stretched three-quarters of a mile along the Penobscot River. His estimate was probably correct for Balma's palisaded longhouse village, along with its associated fields and field houses. Despite the fact that it was a seasonal community of hunter-gatherers, the community he saw on the Penobscot River easily could have been an unpalisaded scattering of houses stretching for more than a half mile along the shore. While his estimates were technically accurate, Ingram should have known that his interrogators would have been imagining the dense English towns they were familiar with, not dispersed scatterings of field houses or wigwams. The power of myth is that it selectively reinforces what the listener wants to hear; it is the opposite of critical thinking.

Tisquantum was kidnapped in 1605, 23 years after Ingram's interrogation. The names he provided for the towns included none that sounded even remotely like Norumbega. John Smith and Samuel Purchas did not mention Norumbega either, and they might not have even asked Tisquantum about it. It is clear that by 1605 the myth of Norumbega had faded from English thinking.

Fannie Hardy Eckstorm (1865–1946), was a prodigious Maine historian and linguist, and contemporary of the ethnologist Frank Speck. Both were active in the first half of the twentieth century. Eckstorm examined multiple versions of hundreds of native place names along coastal Maine. Of the villages listed by Ingram, Eckstorm cited only Norumbega, first noting that it could be a word from the Penobscot language, and then dismissing it as mythical. She was familiar with Hakluyt and Purchas, but like them both she paid little or no attention to Ingram. She regarded the place names reported in the earliest English sources to be "the despair of historians," and so they still remain. Modern Penobscots can only guess that "Norumbega" might have meant something like "where the river is wide" in their language.[22] Today the myth is only an interesting curiosity for scholars.

The Fateful Choice

Ingram, Browne, and Twide faced a difficult decision at the beginning of
the autumn of 1569. Everywhere north or east of Saganas/Caiocama was
largely trackless forest. A network of trails and roads would not penetrate
northern and eastern Maine until the heyday of nineteenth-century lumbering. The three men were at the end of the trail but still far from their
goal, Cape Breton.

To make any progress in that direction they had to choose from three options. The first was to bushwhack their own path northeastward through the
forest. Another option was to go back down to the sea, along the east shore
of the Penobscot River and Bay, and look for a way eastward, either by
coastal trail or by canoe. Their third option was to accept the apparent help-
fulness of the people at Saganas/Caiocama and be transported to the next
big river by way of birchbark canoes, along a well-known interior route.

9

The Return: Autumn 1569

The Penobscot village Ingram called Saganas and Tisquantum later called Caiocama was at the end of Ingram's long walk, but it was not the end of his journey. This was at the community on what is now called Indian Island, at Old Town, Maine. Here the Englishmen faced a set of three options.

The Overland Option

Without a map, a compass, or any clear idea about where they were going, bushwhacking eastward through the boreal forest would have been a foolish choice. It is likely that the Penobscot people discouraged it strongly. It is just as likely that Ingram and his partners did not give it much thought. They wisely looked past this option to consider more reasonable solutions. For this, Ingram's lack of information made him dependent on the Penobscots for advice and help. The records of previous expeditions by Europeans reveal how little any of them knew about the realities of travel in this region, and there is no reason to believe that Ingram knew even that much.

The Coastal Option

Maps of the era foreshortened the distance from the Penobscot to Cape Breton and left out the Bay of Fundy altogether (Figure 8.4). Had Ingram and his partners been misled by this simplistic notion, they might have been tempted to return downriver and press on eastward along the trackless rocky coast. They were probably very lucky to not have had that false information available, but they still imagined that they were closer to Cape Breton than was actually the case.

Coastal people known as the Etchimens and Mi'kmaqs paddled the waters east of Penobscot Bay in large seagoing birchbark canoes, and the men might conceivably have been able to persuade some of these natives to carry them eastward toward Cape Breton. However, taking advantage of this coastal alternative would have required the men to initially reverse their course by going back south along the east bank of the Penobscot River toward the Gulf of Maine. There were a few Eastern Abenaki communities just east of the Penobscot, and there were probably trails connecting them (Figure 9.1). There was a chance that they could have found waterborne coastal transport, but it would have carried them up the cul-de-sac of the Bay of Fundy and led to further adventures that Ingram certainly would have mentioned had he experienced them. The waterborne coastal option probably would have also required the men to first spend the winter at Saganas/Caiocama.[1]

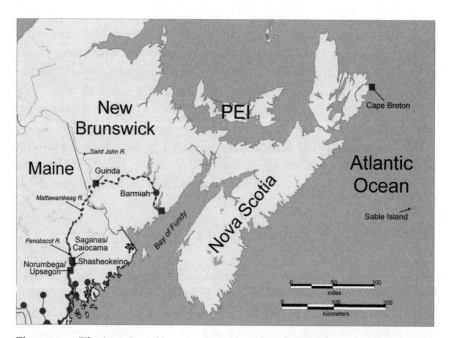

Figure 9.1. The junctions (•), waypoints (■), and probable last legs of Ingram's long walk, shown against a backdrop of known rivers. The canoe route is shown as a dashed line. Figure by author.

Another coastal option that has to be considered is that the town at the end of the trail was actually the place Ingram called Guinda and thus "the most northerly part that this examinate was at."[2] Guinda was the place where the people made a drawing of a ship and indicated to the three men that it was currently at the mouth of the river.[3] By 1568, the Gulf of Maine was being visited every year by French ships and probably some ships from other European ports as well, so this option is a reasonable one.[4] However, there is too much intervening detail to allow this possibility to be taken seriously.

There is little doubt that [Norum]Bega refers to the Penobscot Bay and the Penobscot River, as well as to the imaginary city that John Walker and so many others expected to find there. Ingram's Saganas is probably the trail terminus that Tisquantum later called Caiocama. Ingram said that Guinda was the farthest north he reached. The fact that Guinda, not Barmiah, was the last listed shows that the last two are in reversed chronological order. The reason for this is clarified by Ingram when he mentions Barmiah a second time, indicating that Barmiah was in fact downstream from Guinda and much closer to the Bay of Fundy.[5] Thus Ingram, Browne, and Twide must have traveled northeast from Saganas to Guinda, the farthest north point they reached, then went southward from there, past Barmiah, and to rescue on the coast.

It is thus most likely that Ingram's rescue occurred at the mouth of the St. John River, on the Bay of Fundy.[6] Once at the mouth of the St. John, Ingram took his French rescuers the short distance back up the river to Barmiah so they could do some trading. This makes it possible to define Guinda and the mouth of the St. John on the Bay of Fundy as the last two high-probability waypoints on Ingram's journey (Figure 9.1).

Traveling through the Interior

The only remaining possibility is that the men went by way of birchbark canoe on smaller interior streams and portages between the Penobscot and the St. John Rivers, along routes well known to and frequently traveled by the people of the region, both then and later. The question thus becomes where was Guinda and how did Ingram and his partners get there?

In 1569, it was much easier to travel by swift birchbark canoes than by other means. Penobscot craftsmen had long ago mastered their design, construction, and use. Trails eastward existed, but only as short portages (carries) between lakes and streams. Pressing on by canoe was their best option, one that probably seemed like the only rational option to the Englishmen.[7]

The specific route can be reconstructed based on evidence from later recorded accounts of canoe routes taken by people resident in the region. Reports from three such sources are particularly informative. They all consistently point to the most likely route as three brief digressions reveal.

Joseph Treat, a surveyor for the new-at-that-time state of Maine,[8] set out from Indian Island (Saganas/Caiocama) in late September 1820, with a famous Penobscot leader, John Neptune, as his guide.[9] They paddled up the Penobscot to the junction near Millinocket where the west and east branches of the river join. Treat took a long, meandering route, many days longer than necessary. It was the kind of route that was favored by explorers like Treat, who was charged with getting a detailed impression of the state's northern forest. It was not his intention to get to a distant destination quickly. Because he took a long, circuitous route, it was November before Treat reached Meductic, New Brunswick, from the north. By this time the weather was cold, and a speedy return to Indian Island was important. They set off November 9, westward up a tributary of the St. John, and across portages to the upper Mattawamkeag River. The nights were bitterly cold and there were heavy snowfalls. From Meductic to where the Mattawamkeag joined the Penobscot they encountered no people. The men struggled to protect their fragile birchbark canoes from rocks in low water and thickening ice on the streams. Once on the Penobscot River again, they paddled quickly and safely downstream to Indian Island. Treat reached Bangor (Norumbega/Upsegon) on November 20. Even with icy conditions, they made the most direct route from Meductic to Indian Island in only 11 days.[10] This is the most likely route taken by Ingram, although in the opposite direction, going from Indian Island to Meductic, Ingram's Guinda.

Henry David Thoreau's accounts of his canoe travel in northern Maine add certainty and travel time to what is already clear from Treat's report. Thoreau included details that have allowed reconstruction of the distances and times. Joseph Polis, Thoreau's Penobscot guide in 1857, was an extraordinary man and a frequent traveler of the same route as that taken by Treat almost four decades earlier. According to Thoreau, after they explored streams and lakes in northern Maine, Joe Polis proposed taking a different route home. This involved following Treat's roundabout route, to Meductic. From there, Polis proposed taking the short way back to Indian Island, using the same route as John Neptune and Joseph Treat had taken in the late autumn of 1820.[11]

Travel speeds varied, being slower when they were paddling upstream than when they were moving downstream with the current. Fortunately, Thoreau's 1857 journal allows the computation of the average daily distance he traveled in a birchbark canoe guided by the experienced Joseph Polis. This was 22.5 miles per day over a sample of nine days.

Frank Speck was an early twentieth-century ethnologist who wrote about the Penobscot people after spending much time with them. At the time, Penobscot culture was still oriented to life in the interior of Maine, and long-distance travel by canoe was common. Speck described the canoe route often used by Penobscots to travel from Indian Island to Meductic, the principal Maliseet town on the St. John River and very probably the place that Ingram called Guinda.[12]

Ingram, Browne, and Twide probably traveled with Penobscot guides in two or three birchbark canoes, each capable of carrying up to three men. Assuming no unusual problems, the party could have completed the trip to Meductic in six days. But it was the autumn of 1569, and Ingram's party might have encountered strong head currents, low water, ice, or some of the other hazards faced by Treat in 1820. Treat had required 11 days to make the journey, much of it with the river current, but through dangerous icy conditions. Thoreau did not face the same cold-weather hazards. From Thoreau's detailed evidence, it is reasonable to conclude that Ingram probably took nine days to reach Guinda (Meductic) from Saganas.

Somewhere along that leg of their journey, their guide told Ingram that there was a threat of cannibals in the region.[13] This is the third of three places in which Ingram is reported to have mentioned cannibals. The first instance pertained to Africa, where maneaters were identified by their filed teeth (Chapter 3). The second instance was in connection with the prolonged stop at Balma, where the Susquehannocks said there were cannibals far to the north (Chapter 7). This was a clear reference to the Mohawks, who had a reputation for ritual cannibalism all across what are now New York and New England. The third reference to cannibals specifies northern Maine, through which Mohawks conducted lethal raids during the coming colonial era. Once again, the threat of maneating bogeymen pointed toward the interior forest of the Northeast.

Later accounts in colonial times of Abenaki conflicts with Mohawks shed light on the matter. The Penobscots on Indian Island still remember the

Mohawk attacks of 1638 to 1655. In 1853, Thoreau also picked up on traditions about a battle between Maine Penobscots and the Mohawks near Moosehead Lake.[14] It is fragmentary, but it is likely that Ingram provided evidence of the traditional enmity between Mohawks and Penobscots, and that it went back at least to the middle of the sixteenth century.

Rescue on the Bay of Fundy

Guinda (Meductic) is 138 miles (222 km) up the St. John River from the Bay of Fundy. It was at Guinda that the Maliseet people told Ingram that there was a French ship at the mouth of the St. John River. The three Englishmen were shown sketches of ships. It is unlikely that much time was wasted arranging for canoe transportation down the St. John River. They set out with the current on the relatively broad and straight river, making good time over the 138-mile (222-km) run to the Bay of Fundy.

While paddling downstream to the Bay of Fundy, Ingram passed a settlement he called Barmiah, which he said was about 20 miles (32 km) upstream from the river's mouth. The entire downstream run on the river could have taken as much as eight days, but certainly no more than that. They probably stopped for the last night at Barmiah. The final 20 miles to the bay would have taken only one more day. There they found the French ship *Gargarine*. They probably had spent 244 travel days between Tampico and this spot on the Bay of Fundy.[15] English relations with the French were still cordial, and there were no problems arranging for their passage back to Europe in exchange for their service as extra sailors.

Had they come to the mouth of the St. John River by a coastal land or sea route, Ingram would not have known about Barmiah and could not have guided Captain Champaigne there in order to facilitate trade with the Maliseets. But the three men did take the Frenchman back upstream to Barmiah, where he benefited from their experience with trading. Champaigne obtained furs and some large leaves that he imagined might make a good red dye. It was autumn, and bright red leaves a foot wide and three feet long could only have been the large compound leaves of the staghorn sumac (*Rhus typhina*), which is bright red in autumn. Champaigne must have been disappointed to discover later that while the fuzzy red fruits of the sumac could be made to produce black ink, the beautiful fall leaves did not yield red dye. The doubt expressed by Ingram was borne out.

Champaigne also saw mica, or rock containing it, and bought a good quantity of it thinking it was silver. In this he made the same mistake as Ingram and others had made. It was not silver ore, of course, and it must have been another subject of disappointment when Champaigne arrived home.

Richard Browne had a huge shell bead that he had found in a canoe during the long walk. Browne thought it was a pearl and he gave it to Champaigne in further consideration of the rescue. The later discovery that it was actually a shell bead might have given the captain yet another reason to regret rescuing the Englishmen.

Ingram at Newfoundland

As usual, Ingram talked about the things that stood out most vividly in his memories of his rescue. Once again, these were not the personalities and their interactions that typically engage the interests of historians, but observations of the exotic natural world that Ingram was passing through.[16]

Ingram saw a walrus, possibly on one of the ice floes that came south as far as Newfoundland during the Little Ice Age. He might also have seen one brought in by hunters while the *Gargarine* was anchored at Newfoundland. He described it as "a monstrous beast twice as big as a horse and in every proportion like unto a horse saving they be small toward the hinder legs like a greyhound. They are like unto a horse . . . saving these beasts have two teeth or horns of a foot long growing straight out of or by their nostrils." This is a reasonably good description of a walrus (*Odobenus rosmarus*; Figure 9.2).[17]

While at Newfoundland, Ingram also saw feral sheep that had been released to reproduce in the wild. "There is also a great plenty of another kind of great sheep which carry a kind of coarse wool red as blood, whose horns are very crooked and sharp. This sheep is very good meat, although the flesh is very red. They are exceedingly fat and by nature loath to rise when they are lain, which is always from five o'clock at night until five in the morning. All that time you may easily kill them. But after they are up on foot they are very wild and do not rest in one place. They live together in herds of 500, more or less as it happens, a thousand in some, a hundred in others, more or less. These red sheep are most about the Bay of St. Mary's, or thereabouts" (Figure 9.3).

Figure 9.2. An adult walrus. Public Domain via Wikimedia Commons.

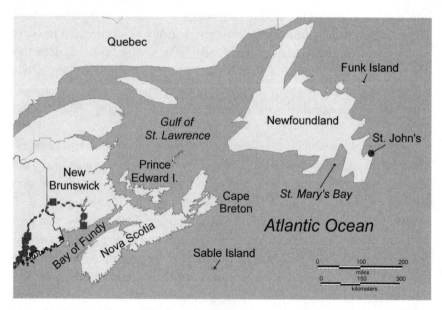

Figure 9.3. Key stops on the return voyage aboard the *Gargarine*. Exact route unknown. Figure by author.

This description of red-fleshed sheep was mentioned briefly in Chapter 7. Spanish references to Chesapeake Bay as St. Mary's Bay led Ingram's interrogators and virtually all later historians to conclude that Ingram saw the sheep there. However, Ingram was referring to the St. Mary's Bay on southeastern Newfoundland. There are several sixteenth-century maps of the region relating to the earlier voyages of explorers like Cartier, Roberval, and Alfonse. They all show a St. Mary's Bay just southwest of St. John's on Newfoundland's Avalon Peninsula. The bay is still known by that name.[18] It is clear that this was the bay Ingram mentioned twice, because Edward Hayes's account of Gilbert's last voyage reports that in 1583 there was grass near St. John's that allowed the rapid reproduction of feral sheep. These had been introduced by English merchants in order to provide an easy source of fresh mutton.[19] It would have been a very good place for the *Gargarine* to stock up on food and water, and the fact that Ingram mentioned both the bay and the sheep indicates that they almost certainly did. They could also have found meat on Sable Island, but there is no evidence that they took that detour. Sable Island comes up again in Chapter 11.[20]

Ingram appears also to have seen St. Elmo's Fire while off St. Mary's Bay.[21] He referred to the phenomenon as "fire dragons." This is a weather phenomenon that sometimes appeared on sailing ships at sea during thunderstorms. When it occurred, corona discharges were visible at the ends of masts and spars, as shown in Figure 9.4. It was considered a good omen, a sign of the protective presence of the sailors' patron saint Elmo.

After taking on food and departing Newfoundland, the *Gargarine* apparently also stopped at Funk Island rookery to stock up on great auk (*Pinguinus impennis*) meat for the return voyage. This was a common practice of ships departing for Europe from Newfoundland. Ingram described the birds as being as big as geese. They nested on the island rookery, but spent much of their time at sea, where their evolved wings made them excellent divers but flightless. The birds were very fat and the sailors found their meat to be unusually flavorful. The northern birds could be herded like sheep on Funk Island and easily caught.

Great auks were eventually driven to extinction by European sailors (Figure 9.5). Ingram provided the first reference to these birds as "penguins," which is preserved in the bird's scientific name. This was probably at the prompting of George Peckham at Ingram's interrogation. "Penguin" was subsequently extended to the southern hemisphere to cover the 17 flightless seagoing species of the *Spheniscidae* family. As will become clear in

Figure 9.4. St. Elmo's Fire on the masts and spars of a
sailing ship. Public Domain via Wikimedia Commons.

Chapter 10, it is possible to attribute this extension to David Ingram, and
many lexicographers do.

The *Gargarine* came within sight of Lizard Point near the southwest tip
of England after only 20 days of sailing.[22] Captain Champaigne did not stop
to set the English sailors ashore, but continued on to Le Havre. From there
Ingram, Browne, and Twide found passage back across the English Channel
to England. Ingram later remained in touch with some of the French sailors
he met on the *Gargarine*. They lived in Honfluer, and he had contact with
them as late as 1579.

Coming Home

The exact date of their arrival in England is not recorded, but it was around
the time the decade of the 1560s passed and the 1570s began. It is likely

Figure 9.5. The great auk. Public Domain via Wikimedia Commons.

that the men landed at Plymouth, and the news of their safe arrival home spread quickly. They had been given up for dead over a year earlier, and their sudden appearance had an immediate effect that probably surpassed their expectations. An astonished John Hawkins met with all three men, and gave them each a substantial reward. There is no information to suggest that they were also greeted by Francis Drake, but that too could have occurred. Drake had escaped from the battle at San Juan de Ulua, and he arrived back in England before Hawkins. If Hawkins thought Drake had deserted him, there is no unambiguous record of it. However much the return of Hawkins and Drake might have been characterized by disappointment and recriminations, the astonishing return of Ingram and his friends long after the gloomy failure of Hawkins's third voyage provided an unexpected epilogue that everyone could cheer about.[23]

Ingram, Browne, and Twide went back to work in their ordinary world. Ingram and Browne continued to sign on ships as ordinary sailors, albeit famous ones in their profession. Richard Twide went to work in John Sherewood's house at Ratcliffe, and died there around 1579. Indeed, both Browne and Twide were dead by the time of Ingram's 1582 interrogation. This circumstance has been a convenient excuse for many of Ingram's detractors to call him a travel liar, a man inclined to spin tall tales with no fear of contradiction. However, Ingram swore that everything he said was true, and that he was willing to sail to America again to demonstrate it.

Hawkins was still alive when Hakluyt published his confused version of Ingram's testimony in *The Principall Navigations* in 1589. Hawkins might even have been involved in Ingram's 1582 interrogation, and he could have provided checks of at least some of what Ingram said in his testimony. There is nothing to indicate that Hawkins challenged anything contained in the section that Hakluyt represented as "The Relation of David Ingram of Barking." Hawkins or anyone else might have later objected privately to all or parts of the badly scrambled version produced by Hakluyt, perhaps contributing to Hakluyt's later decision to drop the account from the 1598–1600 edition of the *Principall Navigations*. However, this gets ahead of Ingram's story, which continued on a new path through the 1570s.

10

Ingram in the 1570s

A measure of fame must have followed David Ingram, Richard Browne, and Richard Twide before they each had to return to the demands of making a living. We do not know the nature of the rewards given to them by Hawkins, but it might have been enough for the men to enjoy an extended period of recuperation.

Ingram was still an ordinary sailor of limited means and ability, intelligent but uneducated. A dozen years would pass between Ingram's return home and his interrogation by Francis Walsingham. That event, late in the summer of 1582 would bring him new and more enduring recognition. What he did during the 12 years between 1570 and 1582 is revealed only indirectly by the surviving documents. Despite the paucity of direct evidence, remarks Ingram made in his interrogation allow some inferences regarding his life during the decade of the 1570s.

John Hawkins did not go to sea again in this decade, but Francis Drake did, and there is evidence that Ingram was with Drake, at least in the later years of the decade. Instead of slaving, Hawkins decided to put his disastrous third voyage behind him and hire others to carry out his family's more dangerous ventures. He then turned to politics and the affairs of the Elizabethan court.

John Hawkins's New Career

The 10 hostages Hawkins had given to the Spanish at San Juan de Ulua in 1568 received generous treatment from their captors following the battle. This was partly because they had been noncombatants and partly because at least one of them was Catholic. All 10 were sent back to Spain, and at least three of them were still alive in 1570. One of the three was George Fitzwilliams, Hawkins's assistant, who had secretly gone to Catholic church services in the Canary Islands back in 1567 (Chapter 2). Fitzwilliams was a gentleman who had been a faithful agent for Hawkins in the weeks leading up to the departure of the ill-fated slaving expedition. He eventually secured his release by the Spanish, at least partly because he was seen as having influence with Hawkins. He reported in with Hawkins upon his return to England. Fitzwilliams's stated goal was to work with Hawkins to find a way to get the government to secure the release of the remaining English hostages who had remained captives after San Juan de Ulua and were still being held in Spain. But there was more to it than that.

Fitzwilliams went back to Spain with some proposals in March 1571. However, at the same time, Roberto Ridolfi, an Italian double agent, was traveling from Elizabeth's court to the Continent with his own secret proposals for her adversaries. What has since been called the Ridolfi Plot was an effort to get the Spanish to help depose Elizabeth and replace her on the throne with Mary Stuart, Queen of Scots. Elizabeth's secretary of state, William Cecil, whom Elizabeth had just recently made Lord Burghley, found out about the plot. In fact, Burghley might have cooked it up himself in the first place, hoping to embarrass the Spanish. It was a ridiculous plan, one that called in part for the Spanish recruitment of John Hawkins as an agent. That part of the effort was carried forward by none other than George Fitzwilliams, when he reached Madrid. Hawkins was indeed involved in all this double dealing, playing both sides until he could predict the eventual winner. Once it became clear that the plot had been foiled, Hawkins was content to leave Fitzwilliams confined in the Tower of London and wash his own hands of the matter. For her part, the eventual sad fate of Mary, Queen of Scots, was sealed.[1]

Hawkins survived the fallout from the Ridolfi Plot and began working to build a new role in the English government. In 1571, both he and Humphrey Gilbert went to Parliament as representatives from Plymouth. The two men also cooperated on some business in the Netherlands. By 1572, Hawkins had managed to rescue the surviving English hostages being held by the Spanish and bring them home from Seville. He soon hired them to carry out another slaving expedition for him.

Things became more complicated when Hawkins was randomly stabbed by a madman on a street in London. Hawkins nearly died, but then he surprisingly recovered. Persisting suspicions regarding his role in the Ridolfi

Plot diminished after the attack, but they did not completely disappear. After his recovery, Hawkins arranged for still more privateering ventures by others but stayed close to home himself.

Hawkins perceived a new way to advance his career and accordingly wrote to Lord Burghley. He suggested that there was too much graft in the operations of the Navy Board, which oversaw the construction and maintenance of the Royal Navy. The queen agreed that Hawkins should be put on the Navy Board and charged with reducing expenses and seeing to the proper redesign, new construction, and maintenance of fighting ships. The queen elevated Burghley to the office of Lord High Treasurer, and replaced him as her secretary of state with a pair of men, Francis Walsingham and Thomas Smith. When Smith retired three years later, Walsingham's role expanded, and he became the sole occupant of the post. This set Walsingham up for his historic role as the queen's spymaster.

Hawkins continued to push economy and innovation in the shipyards, and at the same time he continued to carry on with his private ventures. He grew ever closer to both Burghley and Walsingham during the later 1570s. Because of Hawkins, by the time the British Navy faced the Spanish Armada in 1588, England would have a world-class navy. Another major figure in the years leading up to that momentous confrontation would be Francis Drake.[2]

Francis Drake's Voyages, 1570–1575

Drake's ship, the *Judith*, was one of the two ships to escape from the battle of San Juan de Ulua in 1568. Drake took the *Judith* back to England, and apparently suffered no negative consequences when John Hawkins limped home on the *Minion* a short time later. For his part, Drake had concluded after the battle that Hawkins and everyone else had been lost, and there was nothing else to do but sail home with his crew. If Hawkins concluded that Drake had deserted him at San Juan de Ulua, there is no record of it beyond innuendo in Hawkins's subsequent report. "So with the Minion only and the Judith (a small bark of fifty tons) we escaped, which bark the same night forsook us in our great miseries."[3]

Drake returned to the Caribbean multiple times in the early 1570s. It is worth considering whether Ingram's observations in that same region all derived from Hawkins's third voyage or if some of them came from a later voyage with Drake prior to Ingram's 1582 interrogation. It is unlikely that Ingram sailed from Plymouth with either Drake or Hawkins at the beginning of the 1570s. That is because he had just returned from his long walk, and his home was in Barking, very near London. If and when he went back to work as an ordinary sailor, it is likely he would have sailed out of London or Medway on the lower Thames. Nevertheless, it is possible that Ingram sailed with Drake or someone else out of Plymouth early in the 1570s. Thus, the major voyages of the decade must be examined to adequately assess both Ingram's probable career choices and Drake's rise to fame.

Drake's 1570 and 1571 Voyages

Drake harbored a deep and enduring resentment of the Spanish after the disaster at San Juan de Ulua, and he looked for ways to take revenge. Through this decade he became a national celebrity in England and a villain to the Spanish. He was known in Spain as El Draque, which approximated the Latin *draco*, "the dragon." There is some evidence that he took two small ships, the *Dragon* and the *Swan*, on a reconnoitering voyage back to the Caribbean in 1570, and did so again in 1571, this time with just the *Swan*.

Drake was interested in intercepting Spanish treasure on poorly guarded trails inland from the town of Nombre de Dios on the Isthmus of Panama. Spanish treasure ships brought gold and silver from Peru, unloaded it on the Pacific side of Panama, transported it through the rain forest on mules, and reloaded it on ships again at Nombre de Dios on the Caribbean side of the isthmus. Drake reasoned that he could secretly march inland, intercept the mule caravan, seize the treasure, and bypass the Spanish garrison. He reasoned he could escape with his booty back to his own ships on the Caribbean coast without being caught. It was an audacious plan. It was also the sort of thing that the Spanish regarded as so improbable that they took no measures to guard against it.[4] As they had just returned from a year of hardship and uncertainty in America, it is unlikely that Ingram or either of his two companions would have signed up to sail with Drake so soon.

Drake's pirating was much more lucrative than Hawkins's slaving, and other Plymouth entrepreneurs quickly adopted it. The queen's admiral William Wynter, whose nephew John captained a ship in another of Drake's expeditions later in the decade, sent three well-armed ships to the Caribbean later in 1571. They captured a ship off Jamaica and unsuccessfully attacked St. Augustine, Florida. Two, perhaps four, more ships from

Plymouth and nearby ports made their own attempts at raiding for treasure in 1572. Meanwhile, Drake's star was rising, and investors, including the Hawkins family, decided to support Drake financially.[5]

Drake's 1572 Voyage

Francis Drake sailed from Plymouth, again with two ships in May 1572. The ships were the *Pasco* and the *Swan*, the latter captained by his brother John Drake. Francis Drake had a total of 73 men and boys, of whom all but one or two were under 30 years of age. Unfortunately, once again crew rosters for Drake's voyages are nearly nonexistent. These anonymous young men were attracted by the possibility of sharing in Drake's profits and also by the prospect of profiting from trading privately with locals on the side. David Ingram would have just barely made the age cut. Again, there is no evidence that he signed on, but the voyage set the scene for later exploits by Drake and various others, including Ingram.

Drake headed for a section of coast near the port of Nombre de Dios, on the Caribbean coast of modern Panama. There he found evidence of a recent visit by Captain John Garret, a friend and another Plymouth pirate. As Drake stopped to assemble his pinnaces, Captain James Raunse of the Isle of Wight showed up with his own prizes and joined Drake's enterprise. John Oxnam of Plymouth would make his own attempt at fame and fortune as a pirate a year later, and there must have been still others unrecorded doing the same thing around this time. This was clearly a time of much activity by both English and French pirates in the Caribbean. Piracy was a popular and lucrative business.[6]

Drake captured two frigates that had come out from Nombre de Dios. Some Cimarrons (Sp. *Cimarrones*) were aboard the frigates. These were men of African descent whose families had escaped slavery and had formed independent communities in the Panamanian forests. Drake knew and trusted such men from his previous experience with Hawkins. The Cimarrons told Drake what the Spanish were up to, impressing him as intelligent potential allies. He treated them accordingly, thanking them and releasing them to go home.

The Spanish residents of Nombre de Dios were already on guard, fearing attacks from the Cimarrons as well as from pirates. Drake attacked the Spanish colonists there with his customary enthusiasm, his men finding two great stacks of treasure, one of them gold and the other of silver bullion. A

Cimarron named Diego helped Drake with information on Spanish forces and their deployments. Drake was so impressed by Diego that he hired the African man as a special assistant, an arrangement that lasted for many years.

Drake was wounded by a musket ball to his leg in the midst of this effort. Against his objections, his men carried him back to the boats and there followed a general retreat before any of the treasure could be secured. Many other men were also wounded, and one man had been killed. The Spanish sent an emissary to find out why someone as notorious as Drake would have retreated before having seized any treasure. The leg wound was Drake's explanation. After the emissary left, Diego came forward to suggest that a new attack with Cimarron assistance might succeed. While Drake's brother and others reconnoitered the forest, the English newcomer James Raunse changed his mind about working with Drake, deciding to leave for more promising opportunities as an independent pirate. After this defection, Drake decided to give up on Nombre de Dios and attempt an attack on Cartagena instead (Figure 4.1). He reached his new target in the middle of August. There they seized Spanish ships, including one large vessel.

Drake then decided to consolidate his command. This involved secretly arranging for the *Swan*, his brother's ship, to be scuttled. This was done, and the *Swan* sank on August 15. A crestfallen John Drake never had a clue as to the cause. For the next two months, and with the help of Cimarrons, Francis Drake burnished his reputation by raiding along the Spanish Main, setting up secret storage depots here and there in case he needed supplies in a hurry. All of this led to a sporadic running battle in early November that involved Drake's men and his Cimarron allies against Spanish colonists and their native allies. The indigenous men used poisoned arrows, as Ingram had observed in 1568.

John Drake was killed while trying to board a Spanish frigate. Another brother, Joseph Drake, died of disease. Despite these personal losses, Drake resolved to take his men and, with the assistance of a force of Cimarrons, use trails through the forest to cross over to the Pacific side of the isthmus. His intent was to finally carry out his initial plan to intercept the mule train carrying treasure being transported from the Pacific to the Caribbean side of Panama. They were eventually successful, seizing 15 tons of silver that they then buried near the Caribbean coast, to be picked up later. The feat would inspire many later yarns about buried pirate treasure.

Drake's piracy took a long time to play out. His expedition eventually sailed for home, arriving in Plymouth on August 9, 1573. They had been

gone for well over a year, causing enough havoc to satisfy Drake's lust for revenge against the Spanish. But it had been at the cost of the lives of his two
brothers. Nevertheless, Drake returned to England a wealthy man. There his
celebrity status equaled his notoriety in the Spanish Caribbean.

Despite Drake's success and fame, Spain and England were moving toward some sort of mutual accommodation. Consequently, members of the
English government advised Drake to lower his pirate profile in the months
leading up to the conclusion of diplomatic efforts to avert war. Drake com-
plied, to the extent that almost nothing is known of what he was doing for
nearly two years after his triumphant return to Plymouth.

Drake's 1575 Voyage

When Drake at last returned to public life, it was to assist Queen Elizabeth
in the tawdry effort to take Ireland by conquest. Robert Devereux, the 1st
Earl of Essex, was one of Elizabeth's confidants and a rising star. In early
1575, Essex recruited Drake to help him in the effort to expand English
control across Ireland. At the time, England's toehold on Ireland was Dublin
and three contiguous counties. The border of this enclave was called the
"Pale." Beyond the Pale, on the comparatively vast majority of the island,
lived Irish people who were stubbornly resistant to English influence and
the prospect of English rule.[7]

Essex had the use of two Spanish ships that Drake had brought home
from the Caribbean as prizes. Drake also volunteered his personal services
as captain, along with two of his own ships, one of which was the *Falcon*.
Essex gave Drake the task of using this little fleet to attack Rathlin Island,
which lies off the north coast of Antrim, a stepping-stone between Ireland
and Scotland. The operation ended with the massacre of Irish locals by the
English attackers. Drake's biographer argues that his participation in this
awful finale was out of character for Drake and that there is no evidence
that he condoned it.[8]

There is no direct evidence regarding what David Ingram was doing
during this time, but the odds are that he was not with Drake anytime during the four years that El Draque was raiding in the Caribbean or attacking
Ireland. Ingram was more likely working on less dangerous voyages operating out of London. So too might have been Richard Browne, one of the
two men who had been with him on his long walk. His other companion,
Richard Twide, might already have opted for less dangerous work inland,

possibly already in the house of John Sherewook of Ratcliffe. It was there that Twide died around 1579. Before again picking up the threads of David Ingram's and Francis Drake's shared story, the side story of Martin Frobisher deserves examination.

Martin Frobisher's Arctic Voyages

Ingram somehow gained firsthand knowledge of both walruses and polar bears by the time of his 1582 interrogation. The simplest explanation is that Ingram's knowledge of the Arctic could have been acquired either on his return trip 12 years earlier on the French ship *Gargarine* or later from friends who had served under Frobisher. However, Ingram was consistently adamant about his truthfulness, and there are few if any examples of him depending on secondhand information. There were occasionally walruses near Newfoundland at the time. White (polar) bears brought in by hunters could also have been seen at Newfoundland. However, it is also possible that Ingram saw these not on a stop in Newfoundland after his long walk in 1569 but while sailing with Martin Frobisher in the latter 1570s. Of course, it is remotely possible that he knew about these animals not from his direct experience but from shipmates who told stories of their own travels. In any case, the question prompts a brief examination of the Frobisher expeditions with Ingram in mind.

Martin Frobisher sailed from London to the American Arctic three times in the years 1576–1578. Frobisher was a large, quiet man possessing remarkable physical strength. He was not a courtier skilled in ways to flatter the queen, but his steady leadership would eventually make him a key player in the defeat of the Spanish Armada. Neither was he much of a writer, and he left that mostly to others. Both he and they spelled his name with the creative anarchy that was customary in English documents at the time. "Frobisher" appears in at least 41 different spellings in the documents. Most important among the documents were the accounts written by George Best, who was an officer on two of Frobisher's three voyages to the Arctic.[9]

Like many others in the 1570s, Frobisher was caught up in the quest for a northwest passage around North America, the fabled equivalent to the Strait of Magellan far to the south. There was no evidence that such a strait existed, but hope and a sense of geographic symmetry persuaded men like

Frobisher and Humphrey Gilbert to believe that there should be. Frobisher was the first Englishman to attempt to find it.

Frobisher had approached the Privy Council for support in 1574 and was politely referred to the Muscovy Company, a consortium of merchants pursuing the search for a passage north of Russia and Siberia, eastward toward Asian markets. The company held exclusive rights to the search, and in 1576 it granted Frobisher a license to explore the northwest option on the American side of the Atlantic. This was in the opposite direction of the route the company had initially hoped to find.

Michael Lok was a director of the Muscovy Company, and his fastidious records have survived. They preserve much detail about Frobisher's efforts. Frobisher had enough funding to acquire the use of three barks, the *Gabriel*, the *Michael*, and an unnamed pinnace. Under him were two masters, Owen Gryffyn on the *Michael* and Christopher Hall aboard the *Gabriel*. The three ships had crews totaling only 32 men and boys.

Martin Frobisher assembled this miniature fleet at Blackwall, just east of London and a scant four miles from Ingram's home in Barking. Ingram could have signed on. They left on June 7, 1576, but did not get far before the pinnace lost its bowsprit in a collision with incoming traffic. They put in to Greenwich for repairs. The stop allowed Frobisher to be received by the queen in her summer palace nearby.

After setting out once again, they soon had to take refuge, this time at Harwich. Finally, 11 days after leaving Blackwall they were at last able to sail with favorable winds northward. They reached the Orkney Islands on June 26, 1576. Frobisher pressed on toward Greenland, doing his best to navigate with the brass instruments then available but ill-served by a new map drawn by William Burough. The map confusingly displayed some fictitious North Atlantic islands copied from a 1558 map.

The unnamed pinnace was lost with its crew of four in a storm, but Frobisher pressed on. Then the *Michael* and the *Gabriel* became separated, and Owen Gryffyn, master of the *Michael*, decided to give up. He sailed the *Michael* safely home, there to disappear from the sailing profession. Meanwhile Frobisher pushed on, thinking the *Michael*, like the pinnace, had also been lost. He was at this point down to one small damaged ship with 18 officers and men.

The *Gabriel* passed the southern tip of Greenland and entered the Labrador Sea (Figure 10.1). On July 28 he sighted Resolution Island, which he dutifully named "Queens Foreland." Just beyond was the southern tip

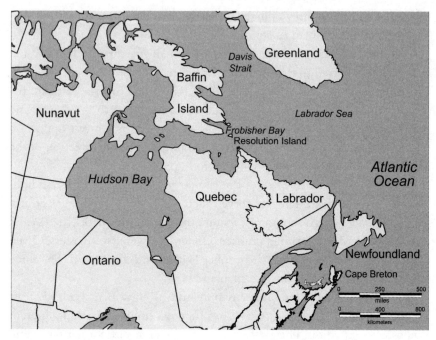

Figure 10.1. Key locations mentioned in connection with the Frobisher expeditions. Figure by author.

of the much bigger Baffin Island. Here, the southern part of Baffin Island was split by a deep bay, which Frobisher hoped was a strait that would take him through the much-hoped-for northwest passage, a strait to match that of Magellan at the other end of the Americas. It proved to be a dead end that is still known as Frobisher Bay. That seems sadly appropriate given the outcome of Frobisher's career in the Arctic.

There were treacherous icebergs, rocky shoals, and contrary currents in these seas, and everyone regretted the loss of the pinnace and the *Michael*. However, the ship's master, Christopher Hall, took the ship's boat through the hazards. He found a tiny island on the north side of the false strait and went ashore. One of the souvenirs they picked up there was a heavy black rock that seemed to hold some metallurgical promise.

Frobisher later encountered Inuit men in kayaks. Using sign language, Frobisher thought the natives were trying to tell him that there was open water up the presumed strait, and that they would lead the Englishmen there. It turned out otherwise. Five men were sent in the ship's longboat to explore ashore, but they were captured by the Inuits. Counting himself,

Frobisher was down to 13 men and boys. Frobisher managed to seize one of the Inuits, but he had to give up on exchanging the man for the crewmen he had lost. Beset by ice and contrary winds, Frobisher was unable to explore the strait he had named after himself any further. He sailed for home with a reduced crew and a morose Inuit man on August 26, 1576.

Frobisher arrived safely back in London. The Inuit man he had captured was suicidal and sick. He died within days of their arrival. He was not the first American to be kidnapped and brought back to Europe as a specimen, and he would not be the last. He died too soon to be painted by a portrait artist. At least his death spared him the indignity of being displayed around London as a curiosity.

The usually meticulous Michael Lok did not provide a crew roster for the 1576 voyage, so there is no way to confirm or exclude Ingram's presence. If David Ingram was on Frobisher's crew, he could easily have seen both walruses and polar bears, if probably at a safe distance. However, the French ship that rescued Ingram and his comrades stopped at Newfoundland, which could have allowed Ingram to gain some knowledge of them. The Newfoundland option remains more likely because it is the simpler of the two hypotheses.[10]

Frobisher's 1577 Voyage

In London, assayers looked hard for gold in Hall's black rock, but found none. The search for gold in the samples then morphed into a search for an assayer who would give them the result they wanted. Eventually a man who claimed to be an assayer said that he had found a little gold in the rock. This news generated a rush of new interest in and funding for a return voyage to the Arctic by Frobisher in 1577. In March, the Cathay Company was formed on the model of the Levant and Muscovy Companies. Exclusive rights in the American Arctic were granted, and Michael Lok was appointed governor of the enterprise. Queen Elizabeth contributed money and the loan of a much larger ship to accompany the *Michael* and the *Gabriel*. Frobisher prepared for the new expedition with a new title: High Admiral of Cathay. This time he would sail with a total of 240 men. There were three ships in the new fleet, the tall ship *Aid* carrying two pinnaces for close-in work.[11]

George Best sailed with Frobisher as a lieutenant on this second expedition. Best provides our most useful early accounts of all three voyages. His account of the second voyage includes a description of silent trade with the Inuits of Baffin Island. Their familiarity with silent trade has been considered by many later historians to be evidence of prior trading between the Baffin Inuits and other European boats. However, many experienced sailors like David Ingram were familiar with silent trade from Africa, and he had used it in North America. It was probably a common practice almost everywhere at the time.[12]

Frobisher put his crews to work digging up what he thought was gold ore and loading as much of it as they could into the ships. He also spent time trying to recover the five men who had disappeared the year before. The Inuits knew that Europeans could communicate by writing on paper. Accordingly, at one point they accepted a letter from Frobisher and he thought they indicated that they would deliver it to the five men they had captured in 1576, then bring back a reply.

Meanwhile, Frobisher's crew captured another Inuit man. Frobisher lured him to midships with a bell, then seized him, lifting him bodily, kayak and all, into the ship. It was one of Frobisher's feats of strength. They later also kidnapped a woman with a child, thinking to use the three as exchange for the five missing men. Instead of delivering the captured men or bringing back some message, the Inuits returned in force and attempted to lure the English into a trap. This led to a brief standoff. Frobisher retained the three captives, but the missing Englishmen were still unaccounted for.

By this time the season was getting late and ice was forming around the ships at night. Frobisher had to give up his search for the missing crewmen. In late August, Frobisher sailed for home once again, but this time with heavy cargos of what was thought to be gold ore, and three Inuit captives, but without the five lost crewmen. Once home, Frobisher rushed to inform the queen of his success, and she was suitably pleased. The supposed gold ore was offloaded and securely stored.

The evidence seems to indicate that Ingram probably did not sail with Frobisher on either of his initial two voyages.[13] However, there is another tantalizing piece of evidence, the name of the Inuit man. That Ingram knew it keeps open the possibility of some connection.

The Inuit Captives

The three Inuits kidnapped by Frobisher in 1577 make Frobisher's explorations relevant to understanding Ingram's experiences in North America in the previous decade. The Inuit man captured in 1576 had soon died of one of the

Figure 10.2. The Inuit man Kalicho (Collochio).
Watercolor drawing by John White. Public
Domain via Wikimedia Commons. John White ca.
1577. Kalicho.

common illnesses of England to which Americans then had no resistance. There
are no known images of that man. Although the three Inuits Frobisher brought
back to England in 1577 also soon died, they lived long enough to be paraded
in London, and for John White to paint their portraits. John White was the same
artist who later did so much to illustrate the people of northern Florida and
coastal North Carolina (Chapters 5 and 6). The man was called Kalicho (Figure
10.2). The woman and child were Amaq and Nutaaq (Figure 10.3).[14]

White's paintings are so detailed and lifelike that, given the few days the
Inuits lived in England, some historians have concluded that White was
probably with Frobisher on his second voyage and was working on the
paintings even before the return trip.[15] There were 134 officers and men on
the 1577 voyage, but there is no clear evidence that John White was one of
them and no compelling reason to infer it. White would have had enough
time to paint them in England, if only just barely.[16]

Figure 10.3. The Inuit woman and child, Amaq and Nutaaq. Watercolor drawing by John White. Public Domain via Wikimedia Commons. John White ca. 1577. Arnaq and her daughter Nutaaq.

The primary importance of the Inuits to Ingram's story is found in the man's name: "Kalicho." This is rendered in typically Elizabethan style in several spellings, including "Collochio." The significance of this name is that it appears in four of David Ingram's statements that are part of a set of five related to his experiences at a town he called "Balma" (Chapter 7). It is difficult to believe that the masked curer Ingram called Collochio and the Inuit name Collochio are identical because of mere coincidence. It also is difficult to understand how Ingram would have known the name of the Inuit man if he had not been a crew member on one of Frobisher's ships. This increases the possibility that Ingram was a crewman on Frobisher's second voyage. They were home by late September, and Francis Drake's new fleet, which Ingram later joined, did not leave until December. Thus, the timing of the two voyages does not exclude the possibility that he was on both voyages.

We know the Inuit's name from other sources, so it is also possible that Ingram simply used the name in his responses about North America for purposes of storytelling embroidery. One of those sources could have been the artist, John White, himself. Another possibility is that Hakluyt supplied the name gratuitously while editing Ingram's testimony.

Gold fever heated up after the return of Frobisher's 1577 fleet and its load of ore. Many people, from Elizabeth down the hierarchy of precedence, thought that easy wealth was at hand. Consequently, there was plenty of funding available for a third voyage. By May 31, 1578, Frobisher had 15 ships and over 400 men ready to sail from Harwich, the *Aid* being the flagship once again. This time, in addition to the names of officers, gentlemen, soldiers, and laborers, Michael Lok provided lists of mariners and others for several of the ships.[17]

Lok's records include a list naming a total of 177 mariners, miners, and other skilled men, many of whom were expected to establish a colony and stay behind on Baffin Island over the coming winter. David Ingram's name is not among them, nor should it be. As mentioned above, the evidence indicates that Ingram was aboard the *Elizabeth*, one of the ships of Francis Drake's expedition that had already left in December 1577.

Frobisher's planned attempt at colonization was lunacy under the circumstances.[18] As it turned out, everyone in the expedition eventually realized that wintering that far north was an insane idea. No one was left behind when the expedition sailed for home. They set out in August and reached England by October. On their return, they learned that the ore brought back on the second and third voyages was all worthless. The Cathay Company went bankrupt, and Michael Lok was financially ruined. Frobisher was temporarily sidelined, and the thread of David Ingram's story rejoined the more certain one of Francis Drake.

Drake's Voyage of 1577–1580

Whether or not Ingram took advantage of opportunities to sail with Drake in the early 1570s, he was with the first stages of the Drake expedition that ended up going around the world. Having established his reputation as El Draque, the scourge of Spanish interests in the Caribbean, Drake sailed again in 1577–1580. This time he first led a fleet to the Strait of Magellan, subsequently completing his voyage around the world in the *Golden Hind* (Figure 10.4).

There is evidence in his testimony that Ingram was on one of the ships that set out from England on Drake's historic voyage. David Ingram and Richard

Figure 10.4. The *Golden Hind.* Alamy 2A600R1.

Browne both went down the Thames and out to sea on the new ship *Elizabeth*, a vessel of 80 tons, with John Wynter as captain, in the autumn of 1577. Wynter was the son of George Wynter, and of a family long engaged in English naval affairs. The ship was built and berthed near Ingram's home in the town of Barking, the proximity having been a prerequisite for his known prior sailings.

The *Elizabeth* sailed from London to Plymouth to join a small fleet commanded by Francis Drake. Drake sailed on the *Pelican*, a ship of 120 tons, and they were accompanied by the 30-ton *Marigold* and a 50-ton flyboat. Between them they carried 164 men. Drake had with him an ambitious nobleman named Thomas Doughty, with whom he would later clash. After a false start, Drake's little fleet of three ships left Plymouth on December 13, 1577.

Drake's cover story was that they were headed for the Mediterranean. But it soon became apparent that he had other unmentioned plans, a deception that angered many of his men. They sailed to the northwest coast of Africa, where they made contact with "Moors" on the shore. Drake sent some men in a boat to the shore, but warned them not to get out of their boat. One did, and he was immediately seized and carried off. He was never seen again. The fleet then sailed westward to the Portuguese Cape Verde Islands. There John Wynter and Thomas Doughty took men ashore to find provisions. They found plenty of grapes, gourds, melons, and coconuts. They tried to take some cattle and goats, but the animals were so wild that the men could catch only a few kids. They also discovered that the Portuguese had salted the wells there in order to deny the English fresh water.

Drake later seized a Portuguese merchant ship, near the Cape Verde Islands. This last ship, the *Santa Maria*, he renamed *Mary*, probably after his wife, and put it under the command of Thomas Doughty. Her previous captain, Nuño da Silva, was retained as a pilot. The fleet then sailed southwest, crossed the equator, and coasted toward South America to the mouth of Rio de la Plata, which they reached in April.

They continued southward, reaching what is now southern Argentina in May. They went ashore there, encountering and eventually trading for food with about 30 indigenous people, probably Tehuelches. There Drake decided to break up their little flyboat for firewood. In June they landed at San Julian where an encounter with hostile people led to a couple more deaths of crew members. More complicated disputes then arose between Drake and Thomas Doughty. Drake, who was infected by Puritan sanctimony, accused Doughty of mutiny, treason, and witchcraft. The upshot was that Doughty was beheaded in early July. This gave Doughty the dubious distinction of being the first Englishman, a gentleman at that, to be executed for witchcraft.[19]

The little fleet spent the southern hemisphere winter there until August 1578. Then it set out for the Strait of Magellan. Nobody on board, not even Nuño da Silva, had ever been in these waters before. Drake rallied enthusiasm by saluting the queen, conducting a commemorative religious service, and renaming his flagship the *Golden Hind*. This was in honor of Drake's patron, Sir Christopher Halton, whose crest was a golden hind (female red deer).

While waiting for a favorable northeast wind, men went ashore to bludgeon flightless penguins so they would have fresh meat on the arduous journey ahead. Two chroniclers describe the birds in detail but without calling them "penguins." One of them, Edward Cliffe, reported that they saw many large birds "whose flesh is not far unlike a fat goose here in England. They have no wings, but short pinions, which serve their turn in swimming. Their color is somewhat black, mixed with white spots under their belly and about their neck. They walk so upright, that a far off man would take them to be like children [toddlers]."[20]

In his own account, Drake wrote, "In these Islands we found great relief and plenty of good victuals, for infinite were the number of fowl, which the Welsh men named Penguin."[21] Thus, Ingram and Drake both later said that "penguin" was a Welsh term meaning "white head." Both were referring to the 1577–1580 voyage, but it is not clear which of them learned it from the other. It may be that neither of them thought much about it until after Ingram's 1582 interrogation, at which George Peckham would be so eager to find a Welsh link with the Americas. Nobody seemed to mind that both the northern great auks and all 17 species of southern penguins had black heads with variable white markings, not white heads.

Ingram was probably one of the few men aboard the *Elizabeth* having had experience with both bird families that were being called "penguins." There is no evidence that Ingram himself had any Welsh ancestry. Penguins might not have been of much interest to anyone until 1582 and the decade following (Chapter 11).

Everyone had observed an eclipse of the moon at around sundown on September 15, 1577. They later found out that the same eclipse had been observed in London at one in the morning of September 16. Navigators still lacked the chronometers necessary to determine longitude, but in this case simultaneous observations of the eclipse led to calculations that allowed Drake's navigators to later conclude that they had been at about 90° west longitude from the prime meridian in Greenwich. They were actually at about 68° west, but theirs was not a bad approximation by sixteenth-century standards.

The *Golden Hind* and the *Elizabeth* made it through the 300-mile strait in two weeks, but then they got separated. Behind them, the *Marigold* sank with all hands in a storm. John Wynter put the *Elizabeth* into a sheltered sound, where the ship waited for three weeks, everyone hoping to make contact with the *Golden Hind*. That never happened.

During the long, futile wait for the *Golden Hind*, many men became sick with scurvy and other illnesses related to poor food. Wynter sent men ashore to look for food and medicine. They came back with a load of penguins and what is still called Wynter's bark (Spanish and French *canelo*), from the thick-barked species of the cinnamon tree (*Drimys winteri*) that dominates the coastal evergreen forest of Tierra del Fuego. The meat and bark tea revived Wynter's crew of 140 men.[22]

Wynter's men had probably been directed to the bark by local people. The bark contains vitamin C and was a good remedy for the scurvy Drake's men were suffering. In 1582, Ingram would testify that Wynter brought some of the bark home. Specimen plants were apparently also brought back by Wynter. These grew well in England, and two centuries later Wynter's bark sustained Captain James Cook and his crew in the South Pacific.

The sailors also observed the people of Tierra del Fuego, while spending time on shore in May.

> In the meanwhile there came about 30 of the country people down to the sea side: and when they were within 100 paces of our men, they set themselves in array very orderly, casting their company into the form of a ring, every man having his bow and arrows, who when they had picked a staff on the ground, with certain glasses, beads, and other trifles returned back. Then the country people came and took them and afterward approached nearer to our men, showing themselves very pleasant, insomuch that Mr. Wynter danced with them.[23]

Wynter sailed the *Elizabeth* back through the Strait of Magellan to the Atlantic. In November 1578 he incorrectly decided that like the *Marigold*, the *Golden Hind* must have been lost. The *Elizabeth* headed for home. Meanwhile, Drake would continue his famous voyage around the world in a lone ship (Figure 10.5).

In 1582, Ingram told his interrogators that Richard Browne had been killed aboard the *Elizabeth* about five years before. If Ingram's estimate were truly precise, that would put Browne's death near the beginning of the voyage rather than near the end of it. However, the context shows that Ingram's comment was approximate with respect to timing. Browne was killed late, not early, in the voyage. An important point was that Ingram specified that Browne had been killed "in" the *Elizabeth*, not in Africa or in South America.

There appears to be no other source that references Browne by name in connection with the loss of lives on the *Elizabeth*, so familiarity with his death must have been based on Ingram's personal knowledge. The *Elizabeth* had suffered the loss of at least one man on the coast of West Africa, and a few were killed by people while ashore in South America. However, Ingram said that Browne died on board, and not on one of the earlier trips ashore where men were lost. This makes it most likely that Browne was the man who had his brains dashed out by a spinning capstan on the return voyage. This accident was later described by an independent source, Edward Cliffe. Only now can it be said with reasonable certainty that the man who was accidentally killed was Browne.

Figure 10.5. Francis Drake. Alamy D98942.

Here also our ship was in great danger, by the means of a strong current, which had almost cast us upon the shore before we were aware, insomuch that we were constrained to anchor in the open sea, and broke our cable and lost an anchor, and presently let fall another anchor; in weighing whereof our men were sore spoiled. For the capstan ran about so violently with the rising of the ship in the sea, that it threw the men from the bars, and broke out the brains of one man: one other had his leg broken, and diverse others were sore hurt.[24]

A ship's capstan was used to raise and lower anchors (Figure 10.6). The anchor line was tied to the narrow center waist (drum) of the capstan. Sailors inserted bars into the square holes in the top to turn the capstan clockwise to winch (weigh) the anchor up from the sea floor. A heavy anchor required a capstan with more men and more and longer poles for greater leverage. Small ratchets at the base of the capstan prevented it from spinning out of control should the men lose their footing on a wet deck. In Browne's case, the primary anchor had been lost, and another anchor was being lowered

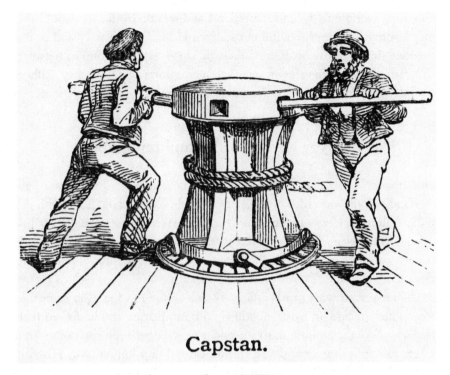

Capstan.

Figure 10.6. A traditional capstan. Alamy HHEDM9.

to replace it. Turning the capstan counterclockwise to lower the anchor required disengagement of the ratchets. It was probably then that a sudden
upward lurch of the ship made the weight of the anchor spin the capstan
out of control. Men lost their footing and their grips. One of the bars of the
spinning capstan struck Browne in the head and killed him.

While the *Elizabeth* sailed home directly, Drake sailed around the world
in the *Golden Hind*, returning home in 1580. It was a feat unduplicated since
Ferdinand Magellan's expedition had completed its own circumnavigation
in 1522. Drake captured the Spanish galleon *Nuestra Señora de la Concepcion*
while crossing the Pacific, seizing a huge treasure, half of which he presented to Elizabeth when he returned to Plymouth Harbor the following
year. She was delighted to be able to pay off her annual national debt, and
Drake's reputation with her and with the public rose accordingly. Such
men were valued in a time when moral clarity did not encumber international business. Hawkins, Drake, and other adventurers who sailed with
the consent and backing of Elizabeth I made the English competitive in the

emerging worldwide race for fame, land, and wealth. Both men would also play leading roles in the building of a formidable English navy and in the eventual defeat of the Spanish Armada (Chapter 11). The contrast between that remarkable achievement and the failed efforts of Humphrey Gilbert that played out over some of the same months could not be more stark.

The 1577 Voyage of Humphrey Gilbert

Humphrey Gilbert had been interested in the search for a northwest passage and colonization of North America for almost 20 years. Trade with the indigenous people was an attraction, but Gilbert's experience in the English conquest of Ireland convinced him that permanent colonization of North America also was a good idea. How better to prey on Spanish shipping than from bases on the east coast of North America?

Gilbert served with brutal efficiency as a colonel in the 1569 campaign to conquer Ireland. In battle, he killed without quarter, and he forced Irish leaders who were coming in to surrender to walk between rows of severed heads. His appalling atrocities in Ireland earned him knighthood. His violent and perverted nature also included a penchant for young boys, which later contributed to his demise.[25] Gilbert returned to England in 1570, married, and served alongside John Hawkins as a member of Parliament for a few years. He later served in the military in the Netherlands, but that episode did not add luster to his reputation (Figure 10.7).

The mythical city of Norumbega on the Penobscot River in what is now Maine was well established in English consciousness and ambition by the time Humphrey Gilbert got excited about colonizing America. This, along with the persisting interest in finding a northwest passage, became his new obsessions. In 1577, Queen Elizabeth granted Gilbert a patent to undertake American colonization a year later in 1578. Gilbert accordingly left on his first American expedition that year. With him were his much younger half-brother Walter Ralegh and several other relatives. The fleet of seven ships left Plymouth for North America, but they encountered storms that forced them back. Ralegh's ship made it the farthest, but overall the expedition was an expensive failure. Gilbert stopped in an Irish port on the way home, where he engaged in a bit of murderous mayhem that was becoming his signature.[26] However, Gilbert's reputation as a seaman suffered because of the voyage's failure. Nevertheless, he somehow managed to

Figure 10.7. Humphrey Gilbert. Alamy FJRD2P.

survive financially. In the 1580s he would revive his colonizing enterprise with the help of Francis Walsingham and David Ingram.

The End of the Decade

In 1579, Hawkins was still working hard to shed persisting suspicions that he had been a duplicitous participant in the Ridolfi Plot. His break came when he took charge of naval contracts that year. It was his big chance to at last wash away the faded stain that lingered on his reputation. He still had enemies on the Navy Board, but his attention to cost reductions, careful inspections, and innovative ship design served both the queen and Hawkins himself well. By this time, Hawkins was working directly with the Privy Council.

The *Elizabeth* came home to London in June 1579, and David Ingram returned again to his ordinary world. Queen Elizabeth questioned John

Wynter closely, trying to determine whether Drake had indeed gone down in the Pacific or was still alive somewhere. As the decade ended, Wynter found himself beset by blame for various reasons. He had participated in the illegal seizure of the Portuguese ship *Santa Maria*. He had been foreman of the jury that had condemned Thomas Doughty (a gentleman!) to death aboard the *Golden Hind*. He might have deserted his commander, Francis Drake. By September 1580, when Drake returned from his circumnavigation of the globe, Wynter was in prison and awaiting trial.

The events of the 1570s remain hazy with respect to David Ingram. Only a few events seem certain to have involved him. Some others are possible, but they range from probable to unlikely. Still other events had to have been considered but have been discarded without mention after evaluation. Ingram was still in his 30s as the decade closed. It is likely that his celebrity had gradually faded through the course of years following his return. However, he was still known to key people as the only survivor of the long walk in America. This would revive his reputation in the early years of the next decade.

II

Ingram in the 1580s

As the new decade dawned, David Ingram had been home for six months, following his service in Drake's fleet, under John Wynter on the *Elizabeth*. It was the decade in which English sea power rose to a level that would enable Great Britain to fight off the Spanish Armada. This would establish British naval dominance that would endure for three centuries. Ingram was nearly 40 years old in 1580, experienced and still young enough to work as an ordinary seaman. We can only surmise what his life was like over the next two years. What we do know is that the well-known people who were major figures in Ingram's life were fully engaged in the events that would define the history of the decade. Ingram was usually an anonymous participant in those events, emerging from the background from time to time.

The activities of Francis Drake, Richard Hakluyt, Humphrey Gilbert, and George Peckham provide the context in which Francis Walsingham arranged for the examination of David Ingram, still the only living Englishman with substantial experience of traveling through America. Walsingham's talent for eliciting information from compliant sources and evaluating that information for the benefit of the queen and country was what mattered most in 1582. It was the kind of evidence-based effort that bright, young, scientific men like Galileo and Francis Bacon, then both still in their middle 20s, would have appreciated. But so too did political opportunists.

This was also the story of entwined political and commercial machinations. Powerful people, and others who aspired to become powerful, did their best to bend information from the past to promote the objectives of the present. Those who were good at it knew that selective use of history and minor dishonesty were usually less risky than outright lying. This chapter explores the events of a momentous decade in English history, and it follows the thread of David Ingram's story through his final years as a minor celebrity.

Francis Drake at Home

Francis Drake completed his circumnavigation of the world when he sailed the *Golden Hind* into Plymouth harbor in September 1580. The treasure he had taken from the Spanish galleon *Nuestra Señora de la Concepcion* brought great riches. With that, a man of modest origins became an even bigger celebrity, soon to become an English folk hero.

Neither Queen Elizabeth nor King Philip was ready for war quite yet, but both England and Spain were inching toward their eventual conflict. The Catholic pope had sent an expedition to try to wrest Ireland away from English control in 1578. King Philip of Spain was furious with Drake, and he demanded compensation for Spanish losses in the Pacific. Such moves exacerbated relations and pushed the two kingdoms closer to war.

When he arrived home, Drake discovered that John Wynter was confined in the Tower of London. This was at least partly because Wynter had turned back at the Strait of Magellan and returned home. Wynter's decision had left Drake on the *Golden Hind* to sail around the world alone. However, Drake appears to have thought that Wynter was not guilty of deserting him and the expedition. At the time, Wynter had reasonably concluded that the *Golden Hind* had been lost.

Wynter came from an influential family, presided over by his uncle, William Wynter. Drake's fame was also secure. These connections worked in John Wynter's favor. Drake interceded, and Wynter was released from prison. Wynter would later serve under his uncle on the *Vanguard*, one of the bigger ships in the great fleet that would fight off the Spanish Armada in 1588. Today John Wynter is still perhaps best remembered for the medicinal bark named after him, which Ingram later mentioned at his interrogation.[1]

Spanish treasure had enriched both Drake and his queen. He was seen more and more frequently in her company. Drake acquired Buckland Abbey, a former monastery just north of Plymouth. From there he managed a new business built on various investments, including speculation in real estate.

In April 1581, Drake brought the *Golden Hind* from Plymouth to London, where it was put on display.[2] At a banquet following the ship's arrival, Elizabeth arranged for Drake to be knighted, and he became Sir Francis.

This was a rare honor in the Elizabethan world, and it was rarer still that knighthood would be bestowed on a man of Drake's modest origins. But with knighthood, the pirate was transformed into a gentleman, complete with a coat of arms. This transformation also enabled Drake to become a member of Parliament.

At this time Drake also met with Walsingham, Hawkins, William Wynter, and some other influential men. They developed a plan to send an expedition to the Azores under Drake's command. The Azores were a Portuguese possession, but Portugal had recently become part of Spain when young Portuguese king Sebastian died without a clear successor.

Sebastian had been killed in battle in 1578, at the age of 24. As usually happens in such uncertain situations, a series of pretenders claimed the throne. Philip II of Spain took advantage of the confusion and annexed Portugal, which would remain under Spanish rule for the next six decades. Elizabeth sought to take her own advantage of the situation by sending Drake to lead the expedition to the Azores in support of António, prior of Crato, one of the handful of pretenders to the Portuguese throne. The deal fell apart because of financial and political difficulties, but its failure did no damage to Drake's reputation.

Francis Drake and his wife, Mary, had no children. Drake had lost two brothers, John and Joseph, on his 1572 voyage to the Caribbean. Perhaps because of these losses, Drake regarded his much younger cousin, another John Drake, like a son. Regrettably, Francis lost both his cousin John and his wife, Mary, in 1582. The younger John was captured and imprisoned by the Spanish on a minor voyage to South America. Mary died at home, apparently of natural causes. Drake soldiered on despite all these losses. He continued in Parliament until 1585, in which year he remarried. His service against the Spanish Armada was only three years in the future.

Richard Hakluyt's Ambitions

As mentioned in Chapter 1, Richard Hakluyt was younger than Francis Walsingham, but they had known each other for several years by 1580. Around then, Hakluyt wrote a pamphlet in which he recommended the English seizure of the Strait of Magellan. He wrote it either at Walsingham's request or as a means to get the powerful man's attention. Hakluyt was probably present at Ingram's 1582 interrogation, but John Dee, a leading advocate for

English colonization of America, appears not to have been invited. Hakluyt was already well along in gathering material relating to English explorations up to that time, and he was replacing Dee as the Champaigne of British settlement. One way or another, Hakluyt compiled the Tanner manuscript, and he would use it as the source for the "The Relation of David Ingram of Barking" in his encyclopedic publication seven years later.[3] Hakluyt had a good start on compiling this, his 1589 *Principall Navigations*, and the rest of the decade provided him with much more information.

In 1583, a few months after Ingram's interrogation, Walsingham sent Hakluyt to France. Walsingham had selected him to serve as chaplain and secretary to Edward Stafford, the English ambassador to the French court in Paris. Walsingham's intent was that Hakluyt should spend his time collecting information on Spanish and French activities, with special attention to anything having to do with English plans for American colonization. Walsingham almost certainly also expected Hakluyt, as his agent, to keep him informed regarding Stafford's activities. Walsingham and Stafford were rivals, and Walsingham would have expected intelligence from that quarter as well.[4]

Hakluyt proved to be very good at his job, which enabled him to simultaneously supply Walsingham with valuable intelligence and to fill out his own collection of documents relevant to his publishing project. In 1584 he wrote a separate manuscript entitled *A Discourse Concerning Western Planting* while he was on a visit home. This was written for Queen Elizabeth, with a copy to Walsingham. It turned out to be part sermon and part practical guide for the establishment of English colonies in America. The document reveals that Hakluyt valued evidence, but that he used it selectively to advance his objectives. He was, after all, trained as a preacher, not a historian.[5]

With the writing of the *Discourse*, Hakluyt took over the cause previously promoted by John Dee. Hakluyt asserted that the North American coast from 38° to 58° north latitude was legitimately claimed by neither Spain nor France and was thus ripe for English colonization. He concluded, "If England cry out and affirm, that there is so many in all trades that one cannot live for another, as in all places they do, this Norumbega (if it be thought so good) offers the remedy."[6] The fabled Norumbega was still luring adventurers at this time.

One of Hakluyt's fact-finding excursions in France was his trip to visit with Étienne Bellenger, who had recently returned from an exploratory trip to the Gulf of Maine and the Penobscot River, the supposed site of

Norumbega. Bellenger had information on the Penobscot River that supplemented what Hakluyt had already learned from Ingram and John Walker. Bellenger lived in Rouen, a city at the height of tide on the Seine, just inland from Le Havre. There was a colony of English merchants there too, from which Hakluyt could also get useful information.[7]

Unfortunately for Hakluyt, by the time he returned permanently to England in 1588, the first grand experiment in Elizabethan empire building would be over.[8] Hakluyt subsequently used his Oxford background and the time afforded by a generous sinecure to finish assembling and editing his *Principall Navigations*, which he would dedicate effusively to his friend Francis Walsingham when it was published in 1589.[9] All this would happen at the end of the 1580s. For present purposes, it is appropriate to return to 1580 in order to follow the thread of another major player of the decade.

Humphrey Gilbert's Ambitions

Despite his repeated setbacks, Humphrey Gilbert was still pushing forward with his designs on America in 1580. Trade with the native inhabitants was an attraction, and so was the prospect of preying on Spanish shipping from American bases. However, Gilbert's experience in the English war of conquest in Ireland was leading him to decide that permanent colonization of the east coast of North America might be an even better idea. In 1577–1578, Queen Elizabeth had granted Gilbert a patent to pursue such settlement the following year. His resulting expedition had been an expensive failure, as was mentioned in Chapter 10.

Gilbert was in financial difficulty after the failed expedition, but he was still obsessed with the idea of colonizing America. He set off again in the *Squirrel*, perhaps the only ship he had left, in March 1580. He hired Simon Fernandes as the ship's master, a man who had been master of Ralegh's ship in the previous expedition and who was sometimes also in the employ of Francis Walsingham. This time Gilbert made it across the Atlantic, apparently landing briefly in New England. One of the men with Gilbert was John Walker. They did not linger long on the American coast, and the *Squirrel* was back in England after only three months and once again with little to show for Gilbert's efforts.[10]

Gilbert then sent John Walker out to explore the American coast around 44° north latitude again, apparently later in 1580. Finding Norumbega was an important objective of this voyage. Walker found Penobscot Bay and sailed up the river to the vicinity of modern Bangor. He went ashore and pilfered about 300 dried moose hides from an Eastern Abenaki community before hurrying back to England. This was the big news that later prompted question 7 at Ingram's Interrogation: "Item whether he saw a beast far exceeding an ox in bigness."[11]

John Walker was as impressed by Penobscot Bay as Ingram had been a decade earlier in 1569. Walker guessed that it was about 20 miles wide. A waterfall had prevented him from getting any farther north than modern Bangor on the river. Where Esteban Gómez had earlier thought he had found gold, Walker imagined he had found a silver mine "not far from the river side about 9 leagues from the mouth thereof."[12] This was, of course, nothing more than mica of the sort that had also fooled both Gómez and David Ingram.

Humphrey Gilbert was still lobbying Walsingham for support, mainly to establish a colonial base for raiding Spanish treasure fleets.[13] But he also still thought there had to be a northwest passage around North America. Frobisher, he reasoned, had not gone far enough to find it. Almost nobody but Gilbert himself thought he could do better. Gradually the idea of British colonization on the American coast prevailed because that was what other men preferred. The fabled northwest passage accordingly began fading from Gilbert's objectives and English ambitions more generally.

Gilbert's 1577 license was good for six years, and it was close to expiring when Gilbert finally raised sufficient funds from Catholic investors to pursue his objective to colonize northeastern North America. Catholics were repressed in England but loath to migrate to the European continent. Catholic Ireland did not suit them any better because that island was undergoing its own subjugation to Protestant English rule. Thus, Gilbert's proposals to colonize Newfoundland and the American east coast seemed more than a little inviting to them. Gilbert's plan was to seize 9 million acres of land around the river of Norumbega and parcel it out to his investors. The colony would be under Elizabeth's sovereignty but at a safe distance from England, in the thinking of the investors.

Gilbert was probably 45 years old in 1582, only a few years older than David Ingram. Gilbert and George Peckham signed agreements in June of that year to cooperate in the establishment of an English colony somewhere between Florida and Cape Breton. These were followed by supplementary agreements, some involving Walsingham and Thomas Gerrard, to work out the obligations and benefits of what would later turn out to be Gilbert's final disastrous project. Picking up the threads of that story requires a return to David Ingram's testimony.[14]

Ingram's 1582 Interrogation Revisited

Walsingham and the other men present to interrogate Ingram had only the most limited prior knowledge of America on which to base their evaluation of the new evidence they were hoping to elicit from their unlikely source. All of the emerging discussion of colonization drew the attention of George Peckham, who consulted with John Dee regarding the legality of colonizing Norumbega. Peckham, a Catholic, was primarily interested in finding a destination for English Catholic colonists who were searching for a sanctuary from political and religious persecution. He still thought Norumbega seemed like a good place to try it.

In addition to accounts of English exploration, Richard Hakluyt was also acquiring translations of Cartier's earlier voyages to the St. Lawrence and Verrazzano's exploration of the east coast. Hakluyt had used these sources to compile his 1578 notes on colonization, which included a list of plants, animals, minerals, and other resources of America.[15] That list, and probably Hakluyt himself, were present at David Ingram's interrogation.

Recall that Miles Phillips was probably in attendance at the interrogation as well. He had elected to be marooned with Ingram and the hundred or so others at Tampico in 1568, but he had then decided to go with those who turned themselves in to the colonial Spanish. Phillips had eventually escaped and made his own way back to England, reaching London by February 1582. Phillips and David Ingram somehow found each other soon thereafter. It is likely that Phillips heard about Ingram's own miraculous return a dozen years earlier, and tracked him down through the network of mariners living around London.[16] The two shared memories of their experiences, questioning each other to fill in a more comprehensive understanding of the history and consequences of Hawkins's disastrous third slaving voyage. What little they could reconstruct together was not encouraging. In his own published account, Phillips said, "Ingram since hath often told me . . . that of the company that went Northward, there is yet lacking, and not certainly heard of, the number of three and twenty men."[17] That number, nearly two dozen men who were never heard from again, did not include Ingram, Twide, and Browne.

Phillips was educated and able to vouch for what Ingram said so far as what had happened before they parted company in October 1568. For what happened to Ingram after that, Phillips was as dependent on Ingram's testimony as anyone else in attendance. Humphrey Gilbert was apparently not there for all of the proceedings, but he was probably present at least part of the time. However, Gilbert's man, John Walker, was almost certainly there throughout, and it is clear that he interacted with Ingram.[18]

John Hawkins was in London at the time and either he or Phillips could have contradicted Ingram had he perceived the need to do so. However, there is no evidence that he did. For his part, George Peckham saw Ingram as useful, if perhaps imperfect, for his purposes. They were all clearly confused by Ingram's testimony but mindful that if they used it cleverly, it positioned them well in the eyes of investors, particularly Queen Elizabeth.

George Peckham's Ploys

George Peckham published his *True report of late discoveries* in late 1583, a year after Ingram's interrogation. It was a polemic designed to advance the idea of colonization of North America. David Quinn's reprinting of the Peckham report runs 45 pages.[19] The first two chapters contain lengthy justifications for English colonization of America based on biblical passages. This involved the selective use of those passages to justify Peckham's political agenda. The third chapter had the same purpose, but there Peckham used a mix of real and invented recent history to make his case. His chapters 5–7 argued that colonization would be profitable for the English, beneficial for the native Americans, and unlikely to be difficult. Peckham, like all promoters, played down potential difficulties and deployed rhetorical ploys to advance his cause.

Peckham's Welsh Ploy

George Peckham's questions for Ingram were intended to elicit evidence he could manipulate to support John Dee's argument that Elizabeth had sovereignty in North America by right of prior discovery. Dee had previously argued that America had been discovered by the Welsh in the twelfth century.

He did this so Elizabeth I could claim sovereignty over the continent by way of Welsh ancestry in the Tudor line. The supposed key link was to Welsh Prince Madoc, who, according to Dee, had earned the right of discovery by being the first European prince to travel to America. Thus, Dee's conception of a British Empire was a political ploy ready-made for Peckham's use. It was like many other political abuses of history devised before and since.[20]

The supposed Madoc connection is why Dee had argued for a British Empire rather than an English Empire. After all, the Welsh were British, not Anglo-Saxons. Successive invasions by waves of Romans, Angles, and Saxons pushed the original British into the peninsular portion of the island now known as Wales. Multiple minor Welsh kingdoms subsequently contended for local dominance there. A handful of dynastic lines competed in a long-term process that occasionally produced a single overlord, but rarely anything like political unity. Welsh language and culture survived, even thrived, but political unity eluded the Welsh people most of the time. The last sovereign prince of Wales was Llywelyn ap Gruffydd of Gwynedd, who became a vassal of English king Edward I late in the thirteenth century.

It should not be surprising that the subsequent creeping Anglicization of Wales prompted linguistic and literary revivalism among the Welsh. Tudor kings even promoted it, and by the second half of the sixteenth century there were publications of well-established Welsh myths that men like Dee and Peckham could exploit for their own purposes. The story of Madoc was a classic one in which a Welsh prince led an expedition across the Atlantic, went through various trials, and returned triumphant. It was another version of the hero's quest that storytellers have always treasured.

Dee used this obscure Welsh folktale to claim that the Tudors generally and Elizabeth in particular represented the return of King Arthur that had been predicted by the sorcerer Merlin. Thus, the Tudor monarchs were descendant sovereigns not just of England but all of Great Britain. The next step was to use the Madoc legend to claim that British precedence in America had been established by him in 1170. It was all nonsense, but it was also a brilliant political ploy, and it took root quickly.[21] Hakluyt repeated the Madoc legend in his 1584 *Discourse on Western Planting*. Hakluyt had also picked up the thread of the Norumbega myth from Dee.

Peckham used all of this as part of his argument in favor of colonization, and he probed Ingram for additional evidence during the interrogation. He seized upon Ingram's reference to "a red Berrie like a pescodd called guyathos," which Ingram had encountered in Texas.[22] Peckham changed the spelling to *gwynethes* in order to make it sound Welsh. However, even then the possible connections with Welsh should not have been encouraging. Gwynedd was the dynastic name of the last independent Welsh prince. However, *gwynethes* is now seen mainly as a female given name, Gwyneth. Its deliberate corruption by Peckham includes the addition of an English plural to make it approximate *guyathos*. Without the English plural Gwyneth means "white" or "fair," which has little to do with why someone might use it to name an exotic red berry. Peckham also picked one of six random American Indian words listed by Ingram near the end of his interrogation as supposed additional evidence. Peckham claimed that Ingram's *gwando*, a corrupted salutation from an unidentified language, was cognate with Welsh *gwrando* (listen). [23]

Peckham also latched on to Ingram's description of penguins. The flightless bird that Ingram described and named could have been either the great auk or the magellanic penguin. Both were called "penguins" by English sailors by 1582. The great auk was later driven to extinction by sailors who routinely stopped to gather them at their rookery on Funk Island off Newfoundland. [24] The *Gargarine*, with Ingram, Browne, and Twide aboard, probably stopped there to stock up its supply of fresh meat on its way home to France. Ingram later also saw southern penguins around the Strait of Magellan when he sailed with Wynter in 1578. In both cases, a major problem with Ingram's folk etymology for "penguin" is that he asserted that it derived from the Welsh word for white head. This was no doubt partly at Peckham's prompting. However, neither the great auk nor any penguin species have white heads. The great auk had a distinctive white patch on its face, but like southern penguins its head was in fact mostly black. It seems likely that if it identified anything, "white head" referred to the guano-coated island rookery of great auks rather than the birds nesting on it. In Peckham's account "Pengwyn" appears as the name both of an island and of a bird. [25]

Peckham also got Ingram to say that there were other unspecified words of Welsh origin worth noting. Peckham's effort to use folk etymology as linguistic evidence is a game that can be played with any two languages, whether they are related or not. If one allows for liberal variation in pronunciation, spelling, and meaning, possible (but very unlikely) cognates can always be found. Trained linguists know that only broad systematic similarities indicate common language origins, and that the evolution of subtle phonetics must be well understood. Furthermore, clear historical explanations must be found to support the identification of random loan-words or simple coincidences. Little of this is possible with a short list of utterances picked up by someone like Ingram, who had remembered hearing them for the first time in an unfamiliar language. That is why most linguists have made no serious effort to identify any of the 14 words Ingram apparently recalled from memories that were already over a dozen years old in 1582. Ingram and his companions probably encountered at least two dozen languages belonging to at least eight North American Indian language families during their long walk. All but one of the words Ingram said he remembered could have come from any of them. The only convincing word is *kerucca*, "sun." That word is convincing only because Ingram heard it in the Northern Iroquoian town he called Balma, because he reported its meaning, and because the word has clear cognates with the same meaning in other surviving languages of the Northern Iroquoian language family (Chapter 7).[26]

The Welsh legend might never have emerged from its folkloric origins had the Elizabethans not thought they needed it for political justification. The Norse sagas, which put Scandinavian explorers in Iceland, Greenland, and Newfoundland a couple centuries earlier than the imaginary Welsh explorers, and which enjoy both some archaeological and documentary support, were not mentioned at all in 1582. This is understandable because the justification by way of the partial conquest of England by the Norse and Danes around the same time left no strong genealogical links for a Tudor queen to exploit.[27]

Peckham's Mexican Ploy

Having used Ingram to make his case for the Welsh discovery of North America, Peckham also found what he promoted as additional support for the idea in a letter written by Hernán Cortés to King Carlos I (Charles I) of Spain in 1520. Cortés quoted the young Aztec emperor Moctezuma II as saying that his people had come from a distant land. The Aztec story of their migration from a mythical Aztlan was well established by then, as it still is today. Peckham found it convenient for his purposes to identify that origin as Welsh. Peckham then produced what he said was a translation of the first part of Moctezuma's speech (Figure 11.1). According to Peckham, it reads:

Figure 11.1. Moctezuma meeting with Cortés. Malinche is to the right. Wikimedia Commons/ RG de Tlaxcala 257 recto.

My kinsmen, friends, and servants, you do well know that eighteen years I have been your king, as my fathers and grandfathers were, and always I have been unto you a loving prince, and you unto me good and obedient subjects, and so I hope you will remain unto me all the days of my life. You ought to have in remembrance, that either you have heard of [from] your fathers, or else our divines have instructed you that we are not naturally of this country, not yet our kingdom is durable, because our forefathers came from a far country, and their king and captain who brought them hither, returned again to his natural country, saying, that he would send such as should rule and govern us, if by chance he himself returned not, etc.[28]

Peckham either made up most of that supposed quote himself, or he copied it from someone who did. According to Cortés, Moctezuma actually began his longer speech with the following words, shown here as translated from Nahuatl to Spanish for Cortés by his Aztec translator Malinche and Gerónimo de Aguilar. Aguilar was a Spanish sailor who learned a Mayan language in Yucatan after having been marooned there years earlier. Malinche was a native woman who spoke both that language and Nahuatl, the language of the Aztecs. Between them they enabled communication between Cortés and Moctezuma:

> *Muchos días ha que por nuestras escripturas tenemos de nuestros antepasados noticia que yo ni todos los que en esta tierra habitamos no somos naturales de ella sino extranjeros, y venidos a ella de partes muy extrañas; y tenemos asimismo que a estas partes trajo nuestra generación un señor cuyos vasallos todos eran, el cual se volvió a su naturaleza, y después tornó a venir dende en mucho tiempo.*[29]

An English translation has been published, which is revised slightly here for clarity.

> For a long time we have known from our writings of our ancestors that neither I nor any that inhabit this land are natives of it, but rather foreigners, and that we come here from very foreign places. We also know that our nation was led to these parts by a lord to whom all were vassals, who returned to his native land, and then he stayed there a long time.[30]

Peckham's inventive elaboration on this passage is extraordinary. Peckham also added some gratuitous advice on self-government that is not found in the original. This was presumably to bring the passage into line with the belief that Madoc returned to Wales from Mexico with wonderful stories, the gift of first discovery for a future queen, and no intention to return to America. In fact, in 1520 Moctezuma rambled on about how the Aztec lord stayed away from Aztlan for so long that when he returned to where he had come from things had changed so much that the community would no longer consider letting him resume his leadership role there. This is the standard Aztec origin legend that is known from many sources. Aztlan was in or near the northern Mexican domain of the Chichimecs, the people who gave Ingram and the other marooned sailors such a hard time in October 1568.

The conclusion to be drawn is that Peckham was not very concerned with the truth of what he was writing, so long as it promoted his agenda.

Either he did not anticipate that later readers would be able to check the accuracy of his report, or he did not care that they might.[31]

Peckham Hires Ingram

Peckham made further use of Ingram after the interrogation was over. At least part of what he said he learned from Ingram came from separate visits after the interrogation, one of which occurred when he sent Ingram to see John Dee. On November 1, 1582, two months after the interrogation, Peckham sent a man named Clement with Ingram to John Dee's residence in Mortlake, a western suburb of London.[32]

At the end of his interrogation, Ingram had sworn that his testimony was true, and he was willing to prove it by sailing with Gilbert on the proposed colonizing expedition. Ingram had specifically told Peckham that he wanted to be employed on a future expedition to America.[33] George Peckham's report was published late in 1583, by which time Gilbert's final journey to Newfoundland had ended in his disappearance at sea. Peckham's report indicates that Ingram did, in fact, sail with Gilbert earlier in that year, and that Ingram had survived Gilbert's final disaster.

Gilbert's Last Voyage

With Peckham's creative politics as context, the subsequent English efforts to carry out the colonization of North America can now be better understood. Humphrey Gilbert's half-brother, Walter Ralegh, returned from his military service in Ireland in 1583. He was not needed there any longer. By that time, Gilbert had resumed his efforts to find backing for American colonization. Elizabeth initially stopped him, probably because Gilbert had a bad reputation as a naval commander and she did not wish to waste more money on him.

However, despite his many failures, Gilbert still possessed some powers of persuasion. His use of John Walker to search for Norumbega, and his use of the ox hide story to influence Walsingham's list of questions for Ingram are examples. However, compared to Peckham's ploys, this was not an impressive effort. Nevertheless, Gilbert eventually managed to get the backing from Elizabeth that he needed for the voyage, possibly because he took on Walter Ralegh as a partner. They left on Gilbert's colonizing trip to America on June 11, 1583. Gilbert had five vessels, including his own *Squirrel*, the *Swallow*, the *Delight*, a new *Golden Hind*, and Walter Ralegh's bark *Raleigh*. Ralegh's scientific advisor, Thomas Harriot, had helped design the sleek new bark. The ships held a total of 260 men, including many craftsmen and plenty of trade goods, but they failed to take adequate provisions for the voyage. David Ingram was on the crew of one of the ships, probably on the *Golden Hind*. This was not the *Golden Hind* that Francis Drake had sailed around the world but a newer one named in honor of Drake's ship.

The *Raleigh* soon ran into difficulties and turned back to Plymouth, probably at the demand of its disgruntled crew. The other four ships made it to Newfoundland, where Gilbert attempted to dominate the polyglot fishermen there and claim the island in the queen's name. It then became apparent that Gilbert had no funds with which to purchase the provisions he needed to continue, so he left the *Swallow* behind as compensation. The remaining three ships headed for Sable Island to stock up on fresh pork and beef from the feral herds there. The *Delight* was wrecked and lost with most of its men there. That left only the *Golden Hind* and the *Squirrel*.

The *Squirrel*, with Gilbert aboard, also later disappeared, but not necessarily with all its crew.[34] The only surviving account of the loss of Gilbert and the *Squirrel* was written by Edward Hayes, master of the *Golden Hind*. It reads like a story contrived to cover up a more serious series of events. When he wrote it, Hayes was probably reacting to rumors that Gilbert had been murdered. He mentioned that Gilbert had beaten a cabin boy, apparently something consistent with both Gilbert's appalling violent streak and his penchant for young boys. Hayes makes no mention of the *Squirrel*'s crew, which most historians have presumed were also lost. However, Hayes's other accounts suggest that he would not have failed to mention the loss of the *Squirrel*'s crew if it had occurred. It is possible, perhaps likely, that the crew was taken aboard the *Golden Hind* and the hapless Gilbert was set adrift alone on the little *Squirrel*. Hayes said Gilbert was last seen sitting alone in the stern of the *Squirrel*, reading a book.[35]

Regardless of which ship Ingram was on at the beginning of the expedition, Peckham said that he survived to return home on the *Golden Hind*. This is the last explicit mention of David Ingram in the historical record.[36] At this time (1583) Ingram was still in his early 40s, and his history up to then was that of a durable survivor. Circumstantial evidence suggests that he might have survived for another decade, perhaps longer. During this time Gilbert's fatal efforts in colonization were pushed forward by his half-brother, Walter Ralegh.

Walter Ralegh and Colonization

David Ingram's story now turns to the longer-term consequences of his interrogation, in the events of the later 1580s. Those events unfolded in part as a consequence of Ingram's testimony. In turn, those same events confirmed the truth of much of what Ingram had to say about North America. Walter Ralegh was by this time at the center of the attempted colonization of the region Ingram had passed through early in 1569.

Ralegh, Humphrey Gilbert's much younger half-brother, is one of the great personalities of Elizabethan history. He was a man of many parts, some of them contradictory. Because of that many biographers have found him difficult to portray accurately. He was capable of brutality, but not to the appalling depths to which his half-brother Gilbert descended. Unlike Gilbert, Ralegh admired and valued what he could learn from other cultures. He was also a more successful courtier, and he became Elizabeth's favorite while he was still young. Nevertheless, he eventually found himself confined to the Tower of London for three extended incarcerations.

Ralegh had gone to France in 1569 to serve with the Huguenots in the French religious civil wars. From there he went to Ireland to help in the English conquest of that island. It was the beginning of Ralegh's run as Elizabeth's favorite. Alan Gallay argues that Ralegh also would not have become a colonizer in the absence of Gilbert's lead. Both half-brothers benefited from their mother's connections, as she was the niece of Queen Elizabeth's governess.[37]

Walsingham had sent Ralegh as a captain to Ireland at the end of the 1570s. This was Ralegh's first significant military appointment. From it he learned the techniques of military suppression and came to appreciate the nature of the Irish landscape, a large piece of which he would soon own. For his success in that brutal war, Elizabeth rewarded him with an immense estate in Munster. This Ralegh referred to as a "plantation," a term that signified that the sovereign granting it had a secure claim to do so. Thus, it was in Ralegh's mind different from a "colony," which would have signified a settlement on territory for which royal sovereignty had not yet been established. Here was the fine distinction that explained the elaborate arguments developed by Dee and others in order to claim Tudor sovereignty over Ireland and America. The distinction later enabled Ralegh to argue that the establishment of plantations in America did not amount to conquest, which would have run against his preferences for accommodation with American Indian nations.[38]

When Ralegh returned from Ireland in 1583, Elizabeth granted him a residence known as Durham House in London. From there he would direct the next steps in American colonization that had been left undone by Gilbert. This complicated story played out through the course of the 1580s, ending with the disappearance of the Lost Colony on Roanoke Island.

Thomas Harriot

Thomas Harriot was only in his early 20s in 1582, but he was probably one of the "diverse others of good judgement and credit" who attended the interrogation of David Ingram. Harriot was a young man of modest origins who had gained admission to Oxford in 1577 and graduated in 1580. He was a polymath astronomer, an ethnographer, a linguist, and an applied mathematician with practical interests in navigation.

The last of Harriot's interests, navigation, was an application of vital interest to Walter Ralegh. It was Ralegh's interest in navigation that had caused him to become associated with Harriot in the first place. It is not known how Harriot managed such a major move or when he met Walter Ralegh, but they might have been introduced by Richard Hakluyt. Harriot moved into Ralegh's Durham House in the winter of 1583–1584. At Ralegh's request, Harriot trained Ralegh's navigators in techniques to determine their positions at sea with the available navigational instruments and the tables he had prepared.

Harriot was a remarkable man, a contemporary of Galileo, Bacon, and other early scientists. He would have later been just as famous as they became had he worked harder to publish his work. All the scientists of the late sixteenth century were benefiting from the rediscovery of long-suppressed works of Greeks like Democritus, Epicurus, and Hipparchus as well as the more recent example of Leonardo da Vinci's evidence-based research. Because he did not publish much, Harriot's role in the revival of science has only recently come to be widely appreciated.[39]

Walter Ralegh's 1584 Expedition

Ralegh inherited the colonizing patent from Humphrey Gilbert, and he wanted to make use of it. He had to hurry, because the patent was set to expire in 1584. However, George Peckham and others were also involved as partners, and that complicated and delayed matters. They failed to colonize before the patent expired, and it accordingly lapsed. Peckham, John Dee, and other investors petitioned for an extension in order to take it over, but this request was rejected by Queen Elizabeth. Instead, she granted a new patent, this time to her current favorite, Walter Ralegh.[40]

In April 1584, only a month after he received the new patent, Ralegh sent out two small ships to do what Gilbert had not succeeded in doing before he was lost at sea. One ship, the *Bark Raleigh*, was captained by Philip Amadas and piloted by Simon Fernandes. The other ship was captained by Arthur Barlowe. David Ingram and Thomas Harriot both might have been aboard one of the ships, but there are no records to confirm it.

Amadas and Barlowe followed Columbus's long southern route, then steered north, reaching land on the Carolina Outer Banks at about 36° north latitude. This was the very stretch of American coast that Dee, Hakluyt, and others had persuaded Queen Elizabeth to colonize. Amadas and Barlowe landed at Roanoke Island and established a camp on shore. It was not a good place for a larger permanent colony, but they thought it would serve as a beachhead from which to search for a more suitable location.

They were well received by the local Carolina Algonquians. Like Ingram before them, the men discovered that the people were eager to trade, and that the customary procedure involved the pretense of gift exchange. This was fortunate, because Ralegh had instructed Amadas and Barlowe to seek the cooperation of the Algonquians in the intended establishment of a permanent plantation. At the same time, the Englishmen appear not to have understood that all the effusive amity was diplomatic protocol to the Carolina Algonquians, not an indication of their alliance with, let alone subordination to, Queen Elizabeth. The notion of sovereignty by a remote queen would have meant nothing to the indigenous leaders. Although language and culture were shared more broadly, the town or village was what mattered politically to the Carolina Algonquians.[41]

The American tradition was that friendship was a mutual matter, which had to be constantly renewed and maintained if it was not to fall apart. The currency of that maintenance was repeated generosity with gifts. This led to an enthusiastic exchange of English and American goods. Amadas and Barlowe were also able to explore the surrounding countryside and to gain a better understanding of the land and places suitable for settlement.

Trade and diplomacy were so successful that the Englishmen persuaded two local leading men to come aboard and sail back to England with them. One of these was Wanchese, from Roanoke Island. The other was Manteo, from the island called Croatoan (now Hatteras Island) to the south. Both communities were on Pamlico Sound. On the expedition's arrival back in London, Ralegh installed Manteo and Wanchese in luxurious accommodations in Durham House. There they would interact with Harriot, Ralegh, and their network of friends.

Ralegh requested Harriot to prepare for the next voyage by working with Manteo and Wanchese in Durham House and to learn as much as he could of their language and culture. Ralegh arranged for the two men to dress in elegant taffeta and to be entertained around town. Thomas Harriot worked to render their Eastern Algonquian language into writing. To accomplish this, he invented his own phonetic alphabet, anticipating the international phonetic alphabet that would be developed by linguists centuries later.[42]

The information Harriot gathered from Manteo and Wanchese supplemented the information that had been provided by David Ingram in his testimony two years earlier. Harriot's research confirmed many of Ingram's observations. At the same time, Ralegh, Hakluyt, and Harriot were all reading the works of Bartolomé de las Casas, the Spanish priest who argued convincingly that American Indians should be treated with respect, humanity, and freedom. As laudable as it was, the argument was not extended to Africans, who remained too valuable as slave labor to be accorded the same rights. For his part, Ralegh ordered that future colonial enterprises under his authority had to treat Americans humanely.[43]

Walter Ralegh's 1585 Roanoke Expedition

Even before the two small ships had departed early in 1584, Ralegh was already preparing a second, larger expedition for the following year. Spanish spies got wind of both Ralegh's plans and a separate anticipated voyage by Francis Drake, with predictable results. Spanish diplomats did their best to discourage both projects.

Queen Elizabeth ignored Spanish resistance and instead knighted Ralegh. During the ceremony she proclaimed that the American lands Ralegh would settle were to be called "Virginia," in her honor. Hakluyt and Walsingham, having their own intelligence network, picked up on the Spanish reactions and kept both the queen and Ralegh informed. The result was that Ralegh planned the 1585 colonizing expedition as secretly as possible. Queen Elizabeth decided to not allow Ralegh himself to go along on this hazardous follow-up voyage. Instead, she chose his older cousin, Richard Grenville, to establish and supply a proper plantation.[44]

There were about 600 men aboard the five ships and two pinnaces. If the *Elizabeth* was the same ship that Ingram served on under John Wynter in Francis Drake's 1577 fleet, the likelihood is that he was aboard in 1585 too.[45] Ingram had said that the *Elizabeth* was owned by Mr. Cockins of London in 1577. The ship was rated at 80 tons. Thomas Cavendish's *Elizabeth* was rated at 50 tons in 1585. These displacements were both rough estimates at the time, so the difference does not necessarily force a conclusion that they were two different ships. However, there could have been several English ships named after the queen around this time. Consequently, although it is possible, it is not certainly known that David Ingram was employed on this venture.[46]

Ralegh had arranged for both Thomas Harriot and the artist John White to be part of the expedition. Manteo and Wanchese went along as well, returning home after nearly a year in England. Harriot had been working with Manteo and Wanchese to learn as much as he could about their language and culture. The two men were expected to assist in negotiating with their relatives in Virginia. Harriot's assignment on this new voyage was to continue his linguistic research and to make whatever additional ethnological observations he could. White was there to illustrate it all.

The fleet left Plymouth in early April 1585, with Simon Fernandes serving as the pilot. They departed in seven ships, stopping first at Puerto Rico.[47] From there the ships dispersed in a complex series of separate adventures in the Caribbean. The *Tiger* was damaged and nearly lost before most of the ships managed to reunite at Roanoke Island in August. It was not an auspicious beginning, but Grenville sent one ship back to England to report their safe arrival. Grenville was charged with building a fort, constructing housing, and planting fields. However, for these tasks he had a mix of sailors, soldiers of fortune, and gentleman adventurers. These men had few of the needed inclinations or skills to carry out their assignment. In addition, many provisions carried by the *Tiger* had been lost, and Grenville would have had to depend on friendly Algonquians for food.

For their parts, the local people were astonished by the English lack of planning and preparation. Women were the highly regarded primary food producers in their own communities. To them the proper role for men was hunting, and the cultivation of crops was in the women's domain. They assumed that the same was true in England. The English colonists had showed up with no women at all, and no men willing to take up what the Algonquians thought of as women's work. The oversight mystified them. The real problem was that the English had brought along no experienced farmers of any kind.

After a silver cup was stolen, Grenville conducted a punitive raid to show the locals who was boss. He carried out the sacking and burning of an entire Algonquian village. Relations naturally deteriorated after that. Ralph Lane was officially an English military commander under Grenville's overall command. The two had a falling out, and this led to even more organizational problems.

Grenville had overall command, but Lane had been appointed to oversee the colony. Grenville disliked both Lane and Francis Drake, which would later put the whole enterprise at risk. After the fort was constructed, Grenville was happy to sail back to England in September, saying that he would be back by Easter with supplies. However, Grenville had left only about a hundred men behind, a sixth of the original company. On the way home, Grenville pirated a Spanish ship, which at least paid for the costs of the expedition.

Grenville left Lane in charge, and he left John White and Thomas Harriot to continue conducting their anthropological research. While the fate of the larger effort was at considerable risk, Harriot and White's part of it went well. So, for the moment, did trading. Ralph Lane and Thomas Harriot both noted that they occasionally found small pearls in freshwater mussels they were eating. One of the men in the company, who was skilled at working with pearls, reportedly acquired some of them in trade with the local people. He selected the best pearls, then drilled and strung them as a gift intended for the queen. Lane also reported that a leader named Menatonon gave him a string of what he called pearls, but his description of them clearly indicates that in this case they were shell beads.[48]

John White

Recall that John White was the artist who had painted the three Inuits who were brought back from the Arctic by Frobisher in the previous decade. The Inuit man was called Kalicho (Collochio) in 1577. This appears to be the same name that Ingram used for the masked curer he, Browne, and Twide had encountered in the Northern Iroquoian town of Balma in 1569 (Chapter 7). This is tenuous evidence, but it suggests that there might have been some prior connection between White, Harriot, and Ingram.

White painted remarkably accurate images of Eastern Woodlands Indians while he was at Roanoke Island just as he had with the Inuits. These illustrations also supported earlier descriptions provided by David Ingram and later ones by English colonists such as Ralph Lane and John Smith.[49] Both Harriot and White were very skilled, but like the other gentlemen, neither of them had the kinds of practical skills the larger colonizing effort needed to thrive.

White was about 45 years old in 1585. He and the French artist Jacques le Moyne (then 52) were friends, the latter having moved to England in 1581. Le Moyne had been the artist in residence at the short-lived French outpost of Fort Caroline in Florida back in 1564 (Chapter 6). He was a Protestant, and he found his new home in London to be more congenial than France. The two artists each drew on the other's work. Regrettably, their drawings and watercolors were regarded as dispensable at the time, mere prototypes for the more permanent commercial engravings that would be based on them. Several of White's watercolors from America survive today, but Le Moyne's originals do not. This is regrettable because Le Moyne's paintings were apparently more detailed and more accurate than any of their copies. White's copies of Le Moyne's watercolors of two Timucua people depicted (Figures 6.5 and 6.6) suggest that Le Moyne was the more accomplished of the two artists, making the loss of so many of his other paintings all the more tragic.[50]

As soon as they made land at Roanoke, White began using Manteo and Wanchese to introduce him to the local people.[51] It is likely that White was seeing America for the first time.[52] Things initially went well for White and Harriot. White sketched and painted watercolors of the villages and the inhabitants of Roanoke and nearby villages. They are still the best illustrations we have of these people before the destructive effects of Old World diseases reached them. At the same time, Harriot learned still more of the local Algonquian language and culture. Both men were successful, but not all of the results of their anthropology would make it home.

Like Le Moyne and other European artists of the time, White had difficulties drawing native Americans. The stylized postures and facial representations that were then standard in European portraiture sometimes failed to
convey those of Americans. Despite these fundamental problems, White's
portraits depict the Carolina Algonquians in informative ways that could
not have been captured by Harriot's ethnographic descriptions alone. [53]

David Ingram's knowledge of what was now called Virginia had already
informed the organizers and financers of the expedition. Possible links
between Ingram and John White have already been mentioned. Whether
Ingram was a crewman on the *Elizabeth* or one of the other ships is unknown. However, if he was there, he would have been of use to both Harriot
and White.

The End of the Expedition

Some of the sailors had been sick on the outbound voyage. This was the
probable source of illness that afflicted one of the nearby native communities. Harriot reported that the Algonquians attributed the illness to a solar
eclipse and the appearance of a comet just before the outbreak. Harriot was
probably stretching a bit to illustrate the superstitions of the local people. [54]

There were too many strong-willed gentlemen and not enough laborers or farmers in the new colony. This led to internal strife, and their
Algonquian neighbors became weary of the English settlers' dependence on
them for food. Lane, like Grenville, made bad relations with the Algonquians
worse with his soldier's sense of proper conflict resolution. There was a
complicated series of alliances and conflicts between the colonists and the
Algonquians that played out over the winter months. Easter came and went
without Grenville's promised return with supplies. Violence between Lane's
settlers and the Algonquians increased, and soon the English were facing
starvation. Things were near collapse by the spring of 1586, but the hapless
colonists were about to be rescued by Francis Drake.

Francis Drake's 1585 Voyage

Elizabeth decided to support Dutch rebels who were resisting
Spanish rule in the Netherlands, and this finally put England at war
with Spain. Walsingham and the queen ordered Francis Drake to lead an

expedition to carry out a preemptive strike on the Cape Verde islands and then sail on to attack Spanish colonies in the Caribbean, with 29 ships and 1,800 soldiers. Drake's plan was to intercept and seize Spanish treasure wherever he could from ships headed back to Spain. Whether David Ingram sailed with him is unknown.

The 134-leaf manuscript in the Morgan Library known as the Drake Manuscript was mentioned in Chapter 4. Most of the watercolor paintings in the manuscript cannot be associated with specific locations. However, one is labeled *Hinde de Loranbec* (Indian of Roanoke). This is a plausible identification (Figure 11.2).[55]

Drake, the man the Spanish still called El Draque, sailed in September 1585. He carried out destructive raids on Santo Domingo and Cartagena. Drake was not much interested in colonization, but he was still effective in recruiting allies from the Cimarron communities of escaped African slaves

HINDE·DE·LORANBEC·

Figure 11.2. Depiction of an Algonquian man of Loranbec (Roanoke) hunting birds. Drake Manuscript, folio 90, 264. The Morgan Library & Museum, MA 3900. Bequest of Clara S. Peck, 1983.

who dwelled at safe distances from the settlements of their former Spanish masters. Drake, like Ralegh, did not view people of African descent as natural slaves, nor did he think that only Africans should be enslaved. Unlike Hawkins, he and Ralegh were both equal-opportunity slavers. Accordingly, Drake successfully allied himself with the Cimarrons, people he genuinely respected and admired.[56] Drake ravaged Spanish outposts and sought to destroy Havana as a fitting end to his efforts. In the end, Havana looked too formidable to take, so Drake headed around Florida and then northward toward Ralegh's Roanoke colony. Along the way he stopped to attack the Spanish colony at St. Augustine. He left the nearby Timucua communities alone, preferring to spare them because they too were potential allies.

After destroying what he could of St. Augustine, Drake sailed north to Roanoke Island. He reached it in early June 1586. There he found despondent colonists and still no sign of Richard Grenville. Grenville had long since gone back to England for supplies, and Ralph Lane thought there was no prospect of a timely return. Roanoke Island was proving to be no more viable for the English than St. Augustine was for the Spanish. Drake arrived just in time to aid in a chaotic evacuation of the failing Roanoke colony.

When Drake sailed in, a ship that had been left for Lane's use, the *Francis*, already had many colonists aboard it. Their intention was to at last find a more suitable site for a colony northward, somewhere in Chesapeake Bay. However, a storm came up and the ship quickly made for England instead. That left only Drake's ships and some remaining colonists. Several of Drake's ships broke anchor in the same storm, forcing them to head out to sea. Thomas Harriot, John White, and all the remaining English colonists decided to take Drake up on his offer to convey them back to England.

The weather was bad. Drake was not inclined to wait for a small number of men who happened to be away from camp, but he took all the rest of the men and their baggage aboard. Manteo and another native man named Towaye went with them as well. Drake's men, who had been at sea for 10 months, took issue with the amount of new baggage, and they threw much of it overboard to lighten the ship. This included much of Harriot's and White's work, along with their books and the freshwater pearl necklace that had been intended as a gift for Queen Elizabeth.[57]

Ironically, a supply ship from England arrived within days of Drake's departure from Roanoke Island, and it found the colony empty and abandoned. The unlucky men who had been away when Drake came and went were still unaccounted for. In addition, Drake had come to Roanoke Island with African slaves and European slaves he had rescued from the Spanish in the Caribbean. These people were also not accounted for afterward. There is nothing to indicate that Drake took them back to England on his already overloaded ships. It is likely that both missing groups were taken in by local Algonquian communities. It was the beginning of the long process through which immigrants become Americans.

Two weeks after Drake's departure for home, Grenville also arrived back at Roanoke with more supplies, having been delayed in his return because of the irresistible attraction of pirating detours. The colony was still abandoned. Grenville then also decided to return home, leaving 16 hapless men who had come with him to man the shrunken colony and ensure the survival of Ralegh's claim to ownership. Still missing were the Englishmen who had been away and the Africans Drake had probably left behind. Grenville went, home and none of the marooned people were ever seen again by English eyes.[58]

Thomas Harriot and John White returned to England with Drake, intending to arrange for more supplies to be sent to Roanoke Island. Harriot published *A Briefe and true report of the new found land of Virginia* the following year, but without illustrations. Harriot apparently wrote this under Ralegh's supervision while living with him on his huge estate in Ireland. A folio edition, which included engravings based on White's watercolors, would be produced by Theodor de Bry, four years later in 1590. Both men were careful and accurate in their work. It is telling that Harriot, always the scientist, did not attempt to titillate his readers with tales of exotic adventures.[59] The book confirmed much of what David Ingram had reported in 1582.

Harriot and White, North America's first genuine ethnographers, managed to salvage enough of their materials to produce maps, paintings, and descriptions of the Carolina Algonquians, but the rest of Ralegh's enterprise seemed all but unsalvageable. Nevertheless, at the urging of Hakluyt, Harriot, and White, Ralegh decided to try again. After hearing and reading Harriot's observations, particularly those regarding silk production, Ralegh was still impressed with the commercial possibilities of silk and vineyards in North America.

Meanwhile, Francis Walsingham and his agents were unraveling a conspiracy called the Babington plot. This was another scheme to assassinate Elizabeth and replace her on the throne with Mary, Queen of Scots. Walsingham got Elizabeth to agree to Mary's execution, because Mary had been judged complicit in the plot. Elizabeth was of two minds, and she did not want the execution to occur without her explicit final approval. However, it was carried out at Walsingham's instigation in 1587. These events accelerated the certainty of a wider war with Spain.

Ralegh's 1587 Expedition

In January 1587, Ralegh approved a charter for a new "City of Raleigh." He realized that it had been a mistake to try to establish a colony using military men like Grenville and Lane, rather than a civilian governor and complete families having the skills that could establish the farming and trades necessary to create a self-sustaining plantation. To that end, he recruited suitable farming families. Astonishingly, he also appointed the artist John White as governor. White was a talented artist and an apparently personable colleague, but he lacked experience as an administrator. Ralegh had moved from one extreme to the other in his selection of a leader.

About 115 people were recruited for the revived venture, including White's pregnant daughter, Eleanor, and her husband, Ananias Dare. This time there were just a few gentlemen and no soldiers in the company. The colonists were mostly middle-class families. They all sailed to America along with Manteo and Towaye. They might have succeeded, but the effort was doomed.

White was given three vessels. The *Lion*, White's flagship, had the contrary Simon Fernandes as its master and pilot. The other two vessels were a flyboat and a pinnace. The tiny fleet left London in early May 1587 and reached Hatteras in late July. Leaving the *Lion* at Hatteras, White took their pinnace to Roanoke Island to meet up with the men who had been left there the year before. He anticipated recruiting them to join his intended new colony, to be established somewhere to the north in Chesapeake Bay. Not surprisingly, there was only a skeleton and few other traces of the lost men.

Once White was off the *Lion*, Fernandes and some others decided to leave all the colonists at Roanoke Island. Like it or not, the colonists found themselves compelled to disembark on this demonstrably unpromising place rather than seek a new and better location. Ralegh's intent had been that they would establish the "Citty of Raleigh" on better land to the north in Chesapeake Bay. However, White had no option but to agree to stay at Roanoke Island, and Fernandes set off on the *Lion*, apparently to pursue another round of piracy against the Spanish.

White sent a delegation to Croatoan with Manteo in order to reestab-
lish friendly relations. This succeeded, but for the arrangement to last, the
colony needed substantial additional supplies from England. The colonists
persuaded John White to return to England with what was left of the little
fleet to arrange for a shipment of relief supplies. In August, after the birth
of his granddaughter, aptly named Virginia Dare, Governor White left the
Roanoke colony for the return trip. He would never see any of the colonists again.

After a difficult voyage, White arrived back in London in early November
1587. By this time, rumors were flying that the Spanish were preparing a
huge armada to attack and invade England. Every English ship was em-
bargoed in anticipation of the expected naval battles. During the winter,
Richard Grenville was given a waiver allowing him to attack the Spanish
in the Caribbean, and White was to be allowed to accompany him with a
supply ship for Roanoke. But this plan was canceled in March while the
ships were still waiting in port for favorable sailing weather. Later that year,
White was able to get permission to take two smaller supply ships that were
unsuited for military service to Roanoke. However, these were attacked and
looted by French pirates, forcing White to turn back to England. He was
lucky to get home alive. John White would not get a chance to try again
until 1590, over two years later, after the coming naval war with Spain.

The Spanish Armada

While the Roanoke tragedy was playing out, John Hawkins had done
much to prepare the queen's navy for the looming war with Spain. He very
much wanted a naval command and lobbied hard for it. His chance came
in August 1586. He took command of a modest fleet of five royal warships,
plus 10 armed merchant ships and some pinnaces. He took this fleet first to
the Canary Islands, and then on to the Azores. They captured some Spanish
ships, but the fleet was broken up by a storm. The scattered ships limped
back to England, and the voyage was regarded as a failure by everyone but
Hawkins. The fading taint of the Ridolfi Plot also still quietly dogged him.[60]
Fortunately for Hawkins, the ominous prospect of a major naval conflict
kept him professionally alive.

No one saw the coming of war more clearly than John Hawkins and
Francis Drake. Drake received a new commission in March 1587. Elizabeth

assigned four warships to him. London merchants provided another dozen ships, some of them substantial. Including the warships, there were two dozen vessels holding 3,000 men under Drake's command. Drake's fleet was an impressive force that included fast, new, and renovated vessels. Drake's orders were to disrupt Spanish shipping, attack them in their ports, and capture as many treasure ships as possible. If the Spanish Armada had already left to attack England, he was to attack and delay it. However, the Armada was still in port.

Drake sailed his fleet quickly to Cadiz in southwestern Spain and surprised a crammed port of unsuspecting and unprepared Spanish ships early on April 19. Drake led a furious and virtually uncontested attack, inflicting heavy damage. He later claimed to have sunk 39 ships, but some Spanish sources put the number as low as 25. Either way it was a major victory for Drake.

Drake's fleet spent the next month prowling the Iberian coast between Lisbon and Cadiz, intercepting shipping and seizing ships and supplies. From there it went to the Azores, where it took more prizes. These included the San Felipe, an East India ship owned by Spain's King Philip II. Drake was back in Plymouth by late June. The voyage had been both a military and a financial success. Drake had forced the Spanish Armada to put off sailing until the following year.[61]

There is no direct evidence that David Ingram was one of the 3,000 men on the ships of Drake's 1587 fleet, and there is no compelling evidence to infer that he was. But the Armada had been delayed only a year, and confronting it in 1588 would prove to be a much bigger undertaking, requiring all available hands on English decks. That makes it likely that Ingram was involved.

The Spanish Armada finally sailed for England in the summer of 1588. There were 73 fighting ships, supported by over 50 supply ships. Together, they carried 2,400 guns and nearly 30,000 sailors and soldiers. They made for the English Channel, and the first sea battle took place off Plymouth on July 21.[62] The English shipping embargo maximized the number of ships and men available to hold off invasion. In the end, 197 ships and 15,925 men were sent out to confront the Armada. It was to be a colossal confrontation by the standards of the Elizabethan age.[63]

The demand for almost 16,000 English sailors meant that a man with David Ingram's ability and experience was very likely to be among those committed to the effort. He was 46 years old, no longer young by the standards of the time, but a decade younger than Hawkins and a couple years younger than Drake, both of whom were fully engaged. The royal warships were mostly anchored at Medway, convenient to Ingram's home in Barking. From there, most sailed to Plymouth where they would pick up support vessels and be deployed in positions to intercept the Armada. Unfortunately, crew rosters have not survived, and nearly all the ordinary seamen are anonymous today. It is speculative, but if he was alive and fit for duty, Ingram was probably among them.

If Ingram served in the battles against the Spanish Armada, he probably would have enlisted under a senior officer who knew him, including Hawkins, Drake, and Wynter. These and others were aboard the *Vanguard*, *Revenge*, *Victory*, *Triumph*, and *Swallow*. These five carried a total of 1,560 anonymous men, around 10 percent of all those who manned the 197 ships in the great fleet.

The English fleet was commanded by Admiral Charles Howard.[64] In June, Howard took three squadrons out from Plymouth to try to intercept the Armada before it reached the English Channel. He put two of them under the command of Drake and Hawkins, on the *Revenge* and the *Victory*, respectively.[65] He kept the third under his own command aboard the *Ark Royal*. However, it was too late. The Armada had already advanced too far north. The English fleet returned to Plymouth, where contrary winds pinned them down, even as the Armada appeared off the Lizard. They would have to fight it out in the English Channel.

The English had many more ships than the Spanish, but only about half as many men. This was because the Spanish had bigger vessels, and because they were transporting a large number of soldiers to carry out the planned invasion of the British Isles. Apart from Marines, the English had no reason to take many soldiers into the naval battles that played out in late July.

The campaign unfolded as a series of six naval battles, moving eastward up the English Channel (Figure 11.3). The faster English ships engaged the larger Spanish ships at distances that did not allow the Spanish to grapple and attempt boarding. The more maneuverable English ships could more easily tack upwind and gain the weather gauge. The lumbering transports carrying Spanish soldiers could not coordinate sufficiently with the naval support they needed to carry out the intended invasion.

The running sea battle began off Plymouth on July 21, according to the Old Style Calendar still used in England.[66] Three days on, Howard reorganized his fleet into four divisions, giving it improved coordination. Frobisher

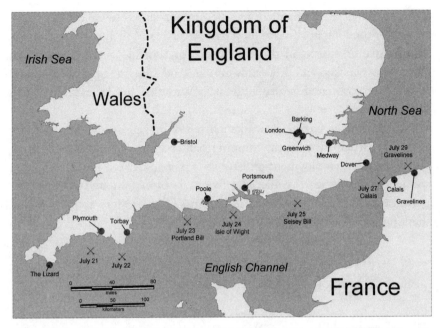

Figure 11.3. Sea battles against the Spanish Armada in the English Channel, 1588. Figure by author.

was given a divisional command and assigned shoreward. Drake was assigned to the seaward, where his mobility and spontaneous aggression would be most effective. The divisions under Howard and Hawkins covered the center.

A big problem for both fleets was that no effective method of signaling had yet been developed for naval vessels in 1588. The result was that captains were tactically left to their own initiatives much of the time. In the end, this worked better for the English than it did for the Spanish.

Howard held a council of war on the morning of July 28. He used the occasion to knight both Hawkins and Frobisher. The Spanish fleet was by then anchored off Calais, France. The Spanish marine and land forces were trying to find a way to carry out their mission, the invasion of England. The English commanders decided to launch eight fire ships on a freshening west wind, toward the tightly packed Armada. They loaded eight merchant ships with explosives, one of the ships being Drake's own *Thomas*. None of them damaged any Spanish ship, but they caused such a commotion that the Armada dispersed. By July 30, the Spanish commander, the Duke of Medina-Sidonia, decided to return to Calais if he could, or alternatively to sail around the British Isles and back to Spain if the winds were unfavorable.

The latter alternative prevailed, and the Armada set out to sail back to Spain by way of the long northward loop. The Armada was then struck by a huge North Atlantic storm off the west coasts of Scotland and Ireland. Many ships were wrecked and thousands of men died. Only 67 Spanish ships and fewer than 10,000 men returned to Spain. With that, the Armada sailed into history.

No subsequent voyages placed such heavy demands on English sailors. Ingram's participation in the running battles of 1588 is itself speculative, and subsequent employment on later voyages requires too much additional speculation to be worthwhile. The five years from 1583 to 1588 were the period in which the story of David Ingram's life faded into anonymity, and the long journey of his soiled reputation began.

Search for the Lost Roanoke Colony

The queen would not allow Walter Ralegh to send adequate supplies or rescue ships to Roanoke Island while a Spanish invasion of England remained a threat. John White finally sailed one last time to find the Lost Colony in 1590, reaching Roanoke Island around his granddaughter's third birthday. The place was dismantled and deserted. Only the word "Croatoan," carved on a post, gave a clue as to the colonist's fate. The relief party accordingly then decided to sail southward across Pamlico South to Croatoan, Manteo's hometown, on what is now Hatteras Island, to find out more. It was only 60 miles (100 km) away. However, one of the ships snapped its anchor cable, and they then decided that it was too dangerous to do anything but sail home to England. The fate of the Lost Colony has been a topic of interest ever since.[67]

The people of the lost Roanoke colony of the 1580s probably joined the other English and African people abandoned to their fates in America, melding into local Algonquian communities. In 1587, White had talked about the Roanoke colonists' intention to move "50 miles further up into the maine of Virginia."[68] Perhaps that was what had initially happened to them. Perhaps they made it to Croatoan, as their carved message had suggested. In any case, it might not have been a rapid process. This research problem is ripe for coordinated study by ethnohistorians, archaeologists, and biological anthropologists. Current archaeological research by the First

Colony Foundation suggests that at least some of the marooned colonists and Africans moved inland and established settlements near Algonquian communities.[69]

John White gave up the search for the lost Roanoke colonists, which included his own daughter and grandaughter, and retired from England to Ireland in 1593. Ralegh continued the search in a desultory way, but to no effect. The failure of Ralegh's Roanoke venture led Ralegh to return to his vast plantation in Munster, the Irish estate Elizabeth had granted him.[70] This ended English attempts to colonize North America until after the death of Elizabeth I in 1603.[71] Ralegh turned his thoughts to the exploration of northern South America, and Thomas Harriot helped him with the anticipated navigational problems of such a venture.

While all of that was playing out, Harriot was also pulling together his surviving notes. He continued his scientific work at Durham House, but he had no interest in the political life of the royal court. That was Ralegh's domain, where he continued to enjoy the queen's support. Two decades after Ingram's long walk, Harriot wrote an account describing the native crops and farming practices of the region around the Outer Banks. Harriot was largely correct in identifying the central importance of maize, beans, and squash, but he went on to identify many other roots, fruits, and game animals that contributed to the diet. He included cassava in his report, which no other source indicates was cultivated this far north. This shows that Harriot was gathering such information from a variety of sources in the later 1580s, just as Gilbert and others had done at the time of Ingram's interrogation. Not all of it was correct. However, apart from the rare cassava error, Harriot's work was mostly accurate.

Harriot had published his pamphlet entitled *A Brief and True Report of the New Found Land of Virginia* in 1588. Two years later he published a folio edition of it containing 28 engravings by Theodor de Bry that were derived from John White's surviving watercolors.[72] The folio appeared in four languages. The text and the images confirmed much of what David Ingram had said during his interrogation eight years earlier. These two editions are the only works of Harriot to be published in his lifetime, which explains why it has taken centuries for his scientific contributions to be fully appreciated.[73]

Theodor de Bry used the paintings of both White and Le Moyne as sources for most of his engravings.[74] In many cases the original sketches and watercolors were lost. Fortunately, more than 60 of White's drawings have survived, but only one of Le Moyne's originals remains. Those that are related to the Roanoke voyages were sorted out centuries later by David Quinn.[75]

Harriot later sold the Irish abbey Ralegh had given him. He then took up a sinecure on the estate of the Earl of Northumberland, west of London. He remained friends with Ralegh, but he was at a safe distance in 1603, when Elizabeth died and Ralegh's fortunes spiraled downward. Harriot's later work was productive. He used a telescope to map the moon months before Galileo did, but as with so many of his other accomplishments, Harriot failed to publish the results of his findings. He died in July 1621.

George Peckham had provided the last known mention of David Ingram in 1583. It is uncertain whether Ingram was still alive when Harriot and White confirmed many of his observations. Ingram had been only about 40 when he was interrogated, but probably so had been his long walk companions Richard Browne and Richard Twide, and both of them had been dead for years. Perhaps Ingram had been on one of the ships that took on the Spanish Armada, perhaps not. Perhaps like an old soldier he faded into comfortable old age, with a kind family surrounding him, perhaps not. Perhaps some lost document will be discovered and it will shed new light on the final years of David Ingram, perhaps not. In 1589, Richard Hakluyt published "The Relation of Dauid Ingram of Barking" as part of his *Principall Navigations*, a clumsy misrepresentation of Ingram's story that would condemn an ordinary man to infamy for four centuries.

12

Ingram's Legacy

There is no record to indicate that John Hawkins, Miles Phillips, or anyone else in a position to know better objected to anything Richard Hakluyt published in his *Principall Navigations* in 1589.[1] Ingram's supposed relation was sandwiched between the accounts of Hawkins and Phillips in that publication. These were accounts that the two men had written themselves, accounts that Hakluyt had compiled but had not edited in any substantial way.

Hawkins lived until 1595, Drake lived until 1596, and Phillips was probably still living as well in 1589. They were probably all in a position to check Hakluyt's editing of Ingram's testimony as easily as they could review their own accounts in the publication after it was printed. Whether Hakluyt asked any of them to proof their contributions before sending them to the printer is unknown. *The Relation of David Ingram of Barking* was a chaotic mess, and at least some of its early readers should have spotted a few of Hakluyt's many editing errors. However, there is no surviving evidence to indicate that they did so.

During the course of the 1590s, something happened that caused Hakluyt to leave his version of Ingram's *Relation* out of his 1598–1600 second edition of the *Principall Navigations*. Perhaps unrecorded criticisms of the relation caused Hakluyt to devalue Ingram's testimony. Perhaps one or more of the men in a position to know better pointed out the many problems with Hakluyt's version of Ingram's testimony. Perhaps Hakluyt realized that the *Relation* was a mess because of his own inept editing. With Hawkins and Drake gone, and with Phillips and Ingram nearing 60 years of age, if they were in fact still living, Hakluyt would have been able to simply and silently drop the embarrassing "Relation of David Ingram" from the second edition without much risk.

Ingram's legacy deserves more credit than it has customarily received over the last four centuries. However, like Hakluyt, he did not leave an unblemished record. Ingram was at once a mariner, a slaver, a natural historian, and a survivor. Not everything he did in his life was admirable. However, it has been worth considering his whole record, as fragmentary as it is. In doing so, it has been necessary to address not just the admirable but also the repugnant portions of his legacy.

Ingram's Legacy as a Slaver

David Ingram lived in a violent time, when the standards of today did not apply. Some may choose to judge him by the standards of his own time, while others will not. Either way, there is no denying the history of the Elizabethan Age, and our moral judgments about what went on in that context should not be allowed to cloud our understanding of it. Whether or not we forgive Ingram for his participation in the emerging slave trade, his journey through what Columbus called the "other world" provided information that would not otherwise be available. It is up to each reader to decide whether Ingram's legacy as a slaver is adequately balanced by his legacy as a sympathetic observer of the people he encountered in Africa and in the Americas.

Ingram played the hand he was dealt by the lottery of life in a highly stratified and sometimes violent society. He took advantage of the limited opportunities that the time and place of his birth offered. In doing so, he made himself complicit in the despicable business of enslaving innocent people, transporting them like livestock, and selling them at a huge profit. But he also had experiences and made observations that are of value for understanding the world in the 1560s.

Ingram was not the compulsive travel liar he has been made out to be, but it is inescapable that his legacy was stained by his participation in slaving. It seems unlikely that he ever agonized much about it. We do well to remember that anything anyone does seems like a good idea at the time to that person. That is true even when wiser or better-informed minds then or later conclude that it was not a good idea at all. Most people should be able to recognize their own errors in thoughtful retrospect, but it appears unlikely that John Hawkins, his investors, his competitors, or his employees were ever much burdened by remorse in the wake of their careers as slavers.

Race-based slavery, horrendous by any measure, was too lucrative to resist until three more centuries had passed. Many American Indians escaped
enslavement, but many did not, and some even participated in it by keeping
slaves themselves. Obvious physical differences between people of European
origins and people of sub-Saharan African origins typically made it easy for
anyone to tell them apart at a glance. This operationalized the facile notion
that Africans were the not-quite-fully-human descendants of Noah's son
Ham, a biblical argument that condemned them to permanent subservi-
ence, at least for the time being.

The ideological underpinnings of race-based slavery began to erode
slowly almost as soon as they were deployed. Latin American colonists
found to their dismay that people of European, American, and African descent could reproduce across the supposed boundaries of imagined racial
categories as easily as they could within those categories. To deal with this
perceived problem, Latin Americans undertook to define human breeds,
based on various crossings and back-crossings of the basic *Español(a)*, *Indio(a)*,
and *Negro(a)* categories. These were elaborately illustrated by the famous
Casta paintings of Spanish colonial America. Various kinds of recombin-
ations produced a plethora of more specific breed names as time passed.
Predictably, the effort largely collapsed of its own weight after only three
generations. Too many categories to manage had been generated. Only a
few terms, such as *mestizo*, remain in use today, and these are typically used
in self-identification.[2]

In North America, things were eventually made simpler by rigid definition. A person was either black or white. Only blacks could be slaves, and
it was a heritable condition. However, a few of them and their descendants
were emancipated even early on. Black slavery was still legal in one form or
another in all 13 of the colonies that created the United States in 1776. In
1787 Congress specified that for tax purposes, a slave was valued at three-
fifths of a free citizen. At the same time, whether or not anyone was deemed
to be black was a matter of assignment, not necessarily self-identification,
particularly in the South. The bar was set high for white identification, and
it remained so well into the twentieth century.

Abolitionist sentiment grew rapidly in the early nineteenth century,
leading to general emancipation in the North and deepening geographic
division between free states and slave states. The American Civil War was all
about slavery, despite many later efforts to reframe the narrative as a conflict over states' rights. The war led to the abolition of slavery, but racism

endured, and it remains with us to this day. David Ingram participated in the beginnings of the legacy of racism that still afflicts us.

Ingram's Legacy as an Observer

At the same time he was engaged in slaving, David Ingram displayed empathy and appreciation for all the peoples he encountered, much as Ralegh, Drake, Harriot, and White did a bit later. Ingram took an ethnographer's delight in learning about the peoples and the natural history of the other world of Africa, the Caribbean, and North America. Sympathy and admiration come through in his testimony. He never expressed contempt, not even with regard to supposed cannibals, to whom he nevertheless gave a wide berth. His interactions with American Indians in particular appear to have been generally positive. He could not have completed his long walk had they been otherwise. The evidence is particularly clear from that experience because the long walk took the largest fraction of his time over the two and a half years of his odyssey to and through the other world.

Ingram told his story as well as he could, but he was ill-served by his betters. Walsingham, Peckham, and Gilbert selectively used what Ingram told them for their own purposes. Hakluyt confused Ingram's story through inept editing. But enough of Ingram's narrative has survived as he told it to show that his was a true account.

Accounts of America like Ingram's, which predate the catastrophic epidemics that swept away vast numbers of its inhabitants, are very important to modern readers. That is because the accounts describe a world that soon changed so much and so rapidly that later immigrants and their descendants could not perceive or accurately imagine what had existed just decades previously. Contact with Europeans introduced diseases so virulent that, once infected, local populations could suffer mortalities of 60 percent or more in a matter of weeks, or months at most.[3] Vast tracts of the continent were abandoned as shattered communities became scattered bands of refugees. People reduced in numbers were forced to merge with others, whether culturally alike or unlike them. Whole cultures dissipated or were reinvented by bands of survivors. Whole towns collapsed into the archaeological record. By the time the region was resettled, most of the area defined by modern Pennsylvania, Ohio, Indiana, Kentucky, and West Virginia was deserted and had become wilderness again for the first time in well over 10,000 years.[4] The hand of mankind that had used fire and farming to make much of the continent an anthropogenic landscape lost its grip. In the generation or two that passed before immigrants from Europe and elsewhere began resettlement, much of the land of North America had reverted to a primeval state that made it appear to most new settlers that the unwritten American Indian histories of 10 millennia had never occurred at all.

Ingram, and a few others, saw America when only the mild initial effects of exogenous diseases were being felt, before the great dying. They used an ancient trail network that had developed over the course of millennia, trails that were well known and still heavily traveled in 1568. They traveled widely, not only by trail but also by dugout canoes in regions where large straight-trunked trees grew. In the north, lighter birchbark canoes predominated, and still farther north people made and used skin kayaks. Ingram moved from one town to another, encountering communities of homes and public buildings of wood, bark, thatch, hide, plaster, earth, or sometimes excavated into the earth, depending on the opportunities and demands of climate and environment. There were hundreds of languages, which were descendant tongues of a small handful of ancestral languages that had been spoken by the first Americans well more than 14 millennia earlier.

The archaeological record of all of this was further complicated by the ways human beings universally behave. Marriage, growth, decline, collapse, technology, and death all led to episodes of expansion and contraction that had occurred sometimes very rapidly, sometimes very slowly over deep time. There were no fewer than 3.4 million people alive and well in America north of the Mexican deserts in the sixteenth century.[5]

None of this will surprise anthropologists, who have made it their task to understand how human beings behave over time and space. But it would have been a surprise to those who invaded the continent from the sixteenth century on. The newcomers had no good frame of reference for other cultures and no appreciation for the depth of America's ancient past. A modern popular writer who came up with the fatuous notion that native trails evolved recently from game trails had no clear grasp of these anthropological realities. Neither did the enthusiasts for the presumed contributions of largely mythical seaborne explorers before Columbus. Nor did the poorly educated gentlemen who interrogated David Ingram in 1582.

Much of what he told them was simply beyond their understanding at the time.

David Ingram's detailed contributions to African and American ethnology are in several cases the earliest known, and in some of those cases they would not be known at all were it not for Ingram. There are things we know better now about the sixteenth century because of Ingram's testimony. The native trail system of North America was ancient, elaborate, and heavily used. It was possible under aboriginal conditions to pass quickly across numerous tribal territories in eastern North America. Dugout canoes were often large and numerous in the portions of the Eastern Woodlands lying south of northern New England. Itinerant traders could make a good living in North America. Indians recovered and repurposed gold and silver found in Spanish shipwrecks. There was a productive pearl industry in the Caribbean. Apart from freshwater pearls, most artifacts called "pearls" by early sources were beads manufactured by Indians from marine shells. The word "penguin" was originally applied to great auks in the North Atlantic before being extended to similar species in the southern hemisphere. American Indians along the east coast used sheet mica to make scoops and containers for daily use. While the Timucuas of Florida were elaborately tattooed, the nations of the middle Atlantic seaboard preferred more temporary body decoration with paints of various colors.

Ingram tells us that the people of southern Texas valued mesquite seeds as a valuable trade item. Were it not for Ingram, we would not have a documentary source for the first appearance of Susquehannock towns in southern Pennsylvania. Ingram's testimony is the earliest clear evidence of Northern Iroquoian masked curing, a practice that would later become elaborated into the False Faces, a cultural feature for which the Northern Iroquoians are well known. Ingram provides evidence that the traditional enmity between Mohawks and Susquehannocks, as well as between the Mohawks and Abenakis, goes back to the middle of the sixteenth century.

Shakespeare, Ingram, and Caliban

Many people will be surprised to read that David Ingram had an early literary legacy that went beyond the scrambled report cobbled together by Richard Hakluyt. Contemporary authors often mined sixteenth-century travel journals for inspiration. Shakespeare in particular read such accounts, and there is evidence that Ingram's was among them.

A codicil to David Ingram's story derives from Hakluyt's editing of Ingram's relation. It is found only at the end of Hakluyt's version of "The Relation of David Ingram" in his *Principall Navigations*.[6] This is the entry that provides information on Curaçao in unusual detail. Hakluyt probably heard this from Ingram and Miles Phillips, possibly from both together in conversation. It reads like an odd postscript, but it appears to have captured the attention of William Shakespeare.

> Also, the said examinate saith that there is an island called Curaçao, and there are in it five or six thousand Indians at the least and all these are governed by one only negro who is but a slave to a Spaniard. And moreover the Spaniards will send but one of their slaves with 100 or 200 of the Indians when they go to gather gold in the rivers descending from the mountains, and when they shall be absent by the space of twenty or thirty days at the least every one of the Indians will nevertheless obey all the slave's commandments with as great reverence as if he were the natural king, although there be never a Christian near them by the space of one or two hundred miles, which argues the great obedience of these people and how easily they may be governed when they be once conquered.[7]

Scholars are uncertain about what Shakespeare was doing between 1585 and 1592, and when he began serious writing. Contemporary records show that several of his plays were on the London stage by 1592. Shakespeare liked to mine contemporary reports for ideas, and Hakluyt's *Principall Navigations* would have been grist for his mill. Robert Bromber has proposed that Hakluyt's version of Ingram's relation was at least part of the inspiration for Shakespeare's *The Tempest*.[8] The play was published in 1623.

Bromber is taken with Shakespeare's use of the name "Caliban" in *The Tempest*, which is apparently an anagram for "cannibal." He argues further that most of the marginal subject headings found in the Tanner manuscript and Hakluyt's 1589 published version correspond to topics in *The Tempest*, sometimes as direct paraphrasing. Bromber has argued that the last entry in the Tanner manuscript appears to set the stage for Shakespeare's play.

Scholarly consensus is that Shakespeare wrote *The Tempest* in 1610–1611, a dozen years before its publication. Ingram would have been approaching the age of 70 at that time, but it is unlikely that he lived that long. Elizabeth I lived to 69, and John Dee lived to 81, but most of the queen's men tended to die in their late 50s or early 60s. Ingram might have seen the turn of the seventeenth century if he was lucky, but it seems improbable that he did. However, Shakespeare would not have had to consult with Ingram or anyone else personally. He would have had access to Hakluyt's 1589 *Principall Navigations* as he began his career as a playwright.

Conclusions

Everybody has a personal history. Some are very long, some very brief. Some are generally regarded as fascinating, some are interesting to smaller audiences, most others are unable to attract much general interest at all. There are always individuals about whom we might want to know more but for whom the documentary evidence is too scant to invite attention. Others might leave records that are voluminous but too mundane to arouse interest. The latter can include many people perceived to have been notable in their day but of whom history takes little account.

There are also nearly anonymous people about whom we might wish to know much more, people who had extraordinary experiences, personal histories so amazing that many historians subsequently have had difficulty believing any of it. David Ingram was one such ordinary person, and the evidence he observed and reported was often unique. Ingram's legacy has been questioned often. He was later accused of lying on a grand scale, even though his contemporaries believed him. Some of them staked personal fortunes on the veracity of what Ingram told them in 1582. What Ingram testified to was evidence, but just what it was evidence of was debated at the time, and it has been debated off and on ever since.

As every accomplished liar knows, fraudulent fame can be made to work as effectively as legitimate fame so long as one does not get caught at it. Many liars do get caught. Others lie boldly and repeatedly, secure in the knowledge that repetition can garner wide belief of even the most absurd assertions. This works best for liars who are already trusted for other reasons. However, it is also the case that those looking to expose liars occasionally condemn the innocent.

To understand Ingram and his times, it has been necessary to explore the major personalities involved with him, the ideological biases of their times, and the slow emergence of scientific thinking from the fog of religious ideology that played out during the age of European exploration. Thus, this book has been about an ordinary man who had extraordinary experiences.

However, it also has been about evidence, how it has been used in the past, and how it should be used now.

Occasionally, Ingram has been abused by some authors for their own purposes. Authors promoting various demonstrably false propositions about history, religion, or archaeology often selectively mined Hakluyt's account for evidence to support their theses. For Ingram, this process began with George Peckham's ploys. But this kind of exploitation has continued to the present. For example, Ingram's mention of Norumbega, which he probably picked up from John Walker, has been cited often in support of various fantastic claims. None of these merit further mention here.[9]

David Ingram's story illustrates again that one can acquire a bad reputation easily, but reacquiring a good one takes much longer. It also demonstrates that as tested and validated knowledge grows, scholars must return to the reexamination of primary evidence that could not be adequately understood by less well-informed previous scholars. After more than four centuries, the time has at last come to take a new look at David Ingram's story.

Of all the scholars quoted here, the redoubtable David Quinn was apparently the only recent one who studied the manuscripts that were the basis of Hakluyt's 1589 publication. Quinn judged Ingram to have been a liar, but he allowed for the possibility that generations of historians citing each other rather than citing the primary evidence might have done both Ingram and their discipline a disservice. It turns out that Quinn was right, and there was much more to be learned from David Ingram.

Even Quinn did not delve deeply enough to understand what happened during and after Ingram's interrogation. However, he saw enough to suggest that someone else might succeed.[10] Quinn died in 2002, leaving the task for others to pick up. Until now, no one has taken up the challenge he offered in 1979.

David Ingram has been a name almost unknown to modern readers. Most contemporary scholars who do recognize his name still share the view that he was an outrageous liar. The evidence presented here shows that he was not that at all. Instead, it demonstrates that he was an ordinary Englishman, one who happened to be intelligent but probably also functionally illiterate. He showed himself to be a sympathetic ethnographic, botanic, and zoologic observer in the extraordinary world through which he journeyed. As he did so, he was also complicit in the creation of race-based slavery. Consequently, like all people, past and present, David Ingram was a person of contradictions. We all live with personal contradictions, and their specifics are generally defined by the times and places of our lives, along with our inherited prejudices. Ingram's context was Elizabethan England, where the contradictions were then very different from those that compli- cate the world today. But if the two situations are very different, the under- lying processes of science and reason remain the same. We can still learn many things from David Ingram.

Appendix

A New Transcript of David Ingram's Testimony

The entries in the three primary source manuscripts that recorded Ingram's 1582 testimony are here put in their proper chronological order. Spellings and punctuation have been modernized for clarity. Six entries that cannot be assigned appear at the end. This new transcription is intended to replace Richard Hakluyt's fatally flawed version of "The Relation of Dauid Ingram." Hakluyt mistakenly assumed that all of Ingram's testimony related only to his long walk through eastern North America, failing to understand that some of it relayed what Ingram had seen in Africa and the Caribbean. Ingram was probably not fully literate, but he told the truth as he remembered it 12 years after his return home. Transcripts of the three original manuscripts, color versions of maps, and supplementary tabular data are all available on the Companion Website.

1. The relation of David Ingram of Barking in the County of Essex, sailor being now about the age of forty years, of sundry things which he with others did see, in traveling [to Africa, the Caribbean Sea, and] by land from the most northerly part of the Bay of Mexico, (where he with many others were set on shore by Mr. Hawkins) through a great part of America until he came within 50 leagues or thereabouts of Cape Breton, which he reported to Sir Francis Walsingham, knight, her Majesty's principal secretary and to Sir George Peckham, knight, and diverse others of good judgement and credit in August & September Anno Domini 1582 (C1).[1]

The Agenda

2. Certain questions to be demanded of Davy Ingram, sailor, dwelling at Barking in the county of Essex—what he observed in his travel on the North side of the River of May, where he remained three months or thereabouts.[2]

    1. Imprimis: how long the said Ingram traveled on the north side of the River of May.
    2. Item: whether that country be fruitful, and what kind of fruits there be.
    3. Item: what kinds of beasts and cattle he saw there.
    4. Item: what kinds of people there be and how they be appareled.
    5. Item: what kinds of buildings and houses they have.
    6. Item: whether there is any quantity of gold, silver and pearl and of other jewels in that country.
    7. Item: whether he saw a beast far exceeding an ox in bigness (A1–7).[3]

Africa

Contrary to the introductory paragraph written by Hakluyt, the first 18 entries of the State Papers Colonial manuscript (Companion Website Appendix B) relate to Africa. That order is restored here in this new relation, except that entry B17 is moved up for clarity so that it now follows B4.

3. The People
    a. The people are of disposition courteously given if you use them courteously and do not abuse them either in their persons or goods (B1, C14.1).
    b. The killing and taking of their beasts, birds, fishes, or fruits cannot offend them, except it be their domestic cattle, for they do milk some of them. They keep beasts about their houses, cows, guinea hens, and such like. Also that there are wild horses [zebras] of goodly shape, but the people of the country have not the use of them (A3.2, B2, C14.2).
    c. If any of them do hold up both their hands at length together and kiss the backs of them on both sides, then you may undoubtedly trust them, for that is the greatest token of their friendship that may be.[4] Which if they break, they die for the same (B3, C15).

d. If any of them happens to come to you with a horsetail [zebra] in his hand then you may assure yourself that he is a messenger from the king, and to him you may safely commit yourself to go anywhere, or go to the king or anywhere else, or send by him any thing or message to the king, for those men are always either ensign bearers in the wars, or the king's messengers as aforesaid, who will never betray you (B4, C16).

e. There was given to the Captain Champaigne of Le Havre in France for one of those tails, a hundred pieces of silver. And a piece is eight ounces as he said he had heard (B17).

4. Silent Trade

a. If you will have any of the people come aboard your ship, hang out some white cloth or thing on a staff, for that is a sign of amity (B5, C17).

b. And if you will barter for wares with them, then leave the things that you will sell, on the ground, and go from it a pretty way off. Then they will come and take it, and set down such wares as they will for it in the place. If you think it is not sufficient, then leave their wares with signs that you do not like it, and then they will bring more until either they or you are satisfied or will give no more. Otherwise you may hang your wares on a long pike or pole's end and so put more or less on it until you have agreed on the bargain, and they will hang out their wares on a pole's end in like manner (B6, C18).

5. Customs and Clothing

a. Ballivo is a word of salutation, as among us good evening, or good morrow, god save you, or some such like (B7).

b. There is a kind of people, which when any of them is sick and like to die, they of the next of his kin, do cut his throat, and all his kin must drink up his blood, and so amongst them eat up his body. For they make a religion to have none of his blood lost. These be a courteous people, and not man eaters (B8).

c. The kings are always clothed or covered with some painted or colored garment, and by that you shall know him. Besides when he comes to speak with anybody, he is carried by or between men in a sumptuous chair of silver or crystal, garnished about with diverse sorts of precious stones (B9, C5).

d. The noble men or principal gentlemen and such as be in special favor with the king commonly wear feathers in the hair of their heads, for the most part of a bird as big as a goose of russet color, and this is the best mark that this examinate can give to know them by (B10, C7).

6. Tools
   a. They have crooked knives like a sickle, made of iron, with which they will carve most excellently, both in wood and bone (B11.1, C25).
   b. They make a kind of trumpet of elephant teeth, which they use in the wars (B11.2, C20).
   c. When they go to war they march in battle array, two and three in a rank (B11.3, C19).
   d. They have a kind of drum which they make of beast's skins and wicker (B12, C21.1).
   e. They do also make shields and targets of the thick skins of beasts, laid in salt and compassed with willow twigs, which after being dried are very strong and defensible (B13, C21.2).
   f. Their weapons are darts headed with iron. The blades are two fingers broad and half a foot long, which are fastened within a socket (B14, C22).
   g. They have also short bows strung with the bark of trees, being half an inch broad. The arrows are above a yard long, nocked, and headed the most part of them with silver and bone. The arrows are of small force within a stone's cast of them, and you may put them by [deflect them] with a staff or a stick (B15, C23).
   h. Their ensign in the wars is a horsetail, with a glass or piece of crystal in some of them, the hair being dyed with sundry colors, such as red, yellow, green (B16, C26).
   i. They have short broad swords of black iron, of the length very near a yard, which are edged thicker than the backs of any of our back swords, somewhat like the foils in our fencing schools (B18, C24).[5]
7. Crime and Punishment
   a. He says, that the people in those countries are allowed many wives, some five, some ten, and a king sometimes a hundred. And that adultery is very severely punished in the following manner: that is to say the woman taken in adultery must, with her own hands, cut the throat of the adulterer, and the next of his kindred likewise cut the throat of the adulteress. And being asked, in what manner they make their executions, he says that they are brought to execution by certain magistrates who deliver unto the woman the knife with which she cuts the throat of the adulterer. They lie both flat on their backs, and their hands and legs being held or tied, the executioner comes and kneels on their breasts, and with a crooked knife cuts both their throats, to which execution this reporter was an eye witness (B23, C78).

8. Their Kings
   a. If you will speak with the king at your first approaching near to him you must kneel down on both your knees and then arise again and come somewhat nearer him within your length. Then kneel down again as you did before. Then take of the earth or grass between both your hands, kissing the backside of each of them, and put the earth or grass on the crown of your head, and so come and kiss the king's feet. Those circumstances being performed you may then arise and stand up and talk with him (B24, C6).
   b. The kings in those countries are clothed with painted or colored garments and thereby you may know them. They wear great precious stones, long red stones, being four inches long and two inches broad, which this reporter thought to be a ruby. In the end of which is a hole, wherein they put a string, and hang it about the king's neck. If by any means whatsoever the stone is taken from him, by force or by slight, he who steals it shall be king in his place, for the time that he should so long have enjoyed the same, which is but the space of four or five years. And any king that hath this stone so stolen from him, is deprived of his kingdom or put to death (B25, C4).

9. Cannibals
   a. You shall know the men eaters by their teeth, for their teeth are long and sharp at the ends like dog teeth (B50, C27.2).

10. Their Industries
    a. The people do make their fires most in those countries of a kind of white turf or earth, which they dig out of their marshes or bogs, two or three feet [Tanner says a fathom] deep in the ground. It burns very clear, and it smells as sweet as musk. The earth is as wholesome, sweet, and comfortable to smell as any pomander.[6] The reporter [Ingram] made a ball for its delicate smell, and tied it to his hair, hanging down over his nose. The people make their fires of this earth even though they have great abundance of wood, because of its sweet and wholesome smell (B39, C42).
    b. They have great plenty of iron and there is also great plenty of mineral salt in the marsh grounds, which looks reddish, a thing necessary for the great fishing near the sea shore, which are there abundant and the fish very large and huge (B40, B51, C44).
    c. They melt metals down themselves, and (he thinks) through a plate of iron full of holes, casting the ore upon the plate and making fire over and about it, so the pure metal falls through the holes. He saw

them do it, but dared not approach near to see the manner of their
works (B41).

11. Palms and Gourds

    a. The which tree if you prick with your knife about two foot from
the root it will yield a wine in color like whey but in taste strong
and somewhat like bastard.[7] It is a most excellent drink, but it will
distemper by drunkenness both your head and body if you drink too
much of it, as our strong wines will do in these parts (B59.2, C48).

    b. They do use to draw the liquor of those trees into gourd bottles,
which they hang on the branches thereof. Whereof every traveler
knows which is stalest, and that is the best. Who having drunk thereof,
do again fill the bottle, and hang the next stalest in the place (B62).

    c. Also there is a red oil that comes out of the root of this tree, which is
most excellent against their poisoned arrows and weapons, for by it
they do recover themselves of their poisoned wounds (B61, C50).

    d. In their wars they do pitch their camp as near as they may unto
some woods of palm trees which yields them meat [food], drink, and
present remedy against poisoned arrows (C27.3).

12. Bananas

    a. There is also a tree called a plantain tree with a fruit growing on it
like a pudding, which is most excellent meat raw. And when it is ripe,
then it is yellow of color (A2, B63, C51).

13. Forest and Fields

    a. There is a great abundance of Brazil trees (B64.1).

    b. There is also great plenty of date trees (B64.2, C45.3).

    c. Also a great abundance of orange and lemon trees (B64.3).

    d. And there are many pepper trees (B64.4).

    e. And there is plenty of almond trees (B64.5).

    f. There is also abundance of bombasine or cotton trees and bushes,
which yield sufficient cotton to lade an infinite number of ships
(B64.6, C45.5).

    g. There are great plenty of worts, and of all sorts of flowers (B64.7).

14. Deer and Buffalos

    a. There is also great abundance of deer, both white, red, and of speckled
colors, the last kinds of them the examinate knew not (B70, C59).

    b. There is a great abundance of a kind of great beasts, in shape of body
not much different from an ox. They are as big as two of our oxen,
in length almost twenty feet, and which have ears like a bloodhound,

with long hair about their ears, breast and other parts of the body. Their horns are crooked like our rams' horns. Their eyes are very black, their hair very long and rough like a goat. The hides of these beasts are sold very dear. This beast keeps company only by couples, male and female. They always fight male to male and female to female when they meet. They kill those beasts thus: they have a forked iron, which being fastened on a pole, and made very sharp to cut, they come behind the beast and hough [hamstring] him (A7.1, B71, C58).

15. Elephants, Leopards, and Hippos
   a. He did also see in that country plenty of elephants, of whose teeth the people do make trumpets for their wars, and he saw ten of them very near together (B72, C66).
   b. There are also many ounces [leopards], which will also kill men, and follow them up the tree if they cannot defend them from coming up to them (B74, C66).

16. Birds
   a. There are in those countries an abundance of russet parrots as big as the common greater sort of green parrots, but very few green. To his remembrance he did not see two green parrots in his whole travel [in Africa] (B79, C68).
   b. There is a great plenty of guinea hens, which are tame birds and proper to the inhabitants, as big as geese, very black of color, having feathers like down (C70).

The Caribbean Sea

17. Margarita
   a. The people do dive and fish for pearl in three or four fathoms of water, which they have in oysters. They do cover, when they dive, their heads and upper parts of their bodies with leather to their waists, tied fast about their middles, whereby they take air under the water (B46).

18. Curaçao
   a. There is great plenty of wild goats, also great plenty of kine [cows] and cattle like ours, but they are all wild. There is great plenty of wild horses, also great plenty of sheep like ours (B68, C57.2).[8]

b. Also, the said examinate says that there is an island called Curaçao, and there are in it five or six thousand Indians at the least and all these are governed by one only negro who is but a slave to a Spaniard. And moreover the Spaniards will send but one of their slaves with 100 or 200 of the Indians when they go to gather gold in the rivers descending from the mountains, and when they shall be absent by the space of twenty or thirty days at the least every one of the Indians will nevertheless obey all the slave's commandments with as great reverence as if he were the natural king, although there be never a Christian near them by the space of one or two hundred miles, which argues the great obedience of these people and how easily they may be governed when they be once conquered (C99).

19. The People
   a. In the southern parts of those countries they all go naked, saving that the noblemen's privates are covered with the bark of a gourd, and the women's privates with the hair or leaf of an Adalmita palm tree. Further that the men go naked saving only the middle part of them covered with skins of beasts, and with leaves (A4.2, B20, C12.1).

20. Cassava
   a. Their bread is only made of the root of a cassado [cassava] tree, which they do dry and beat it as small as they can, and then temper it with water, and so bake it in cakes on a stone (B66, C56).

21. Pineapple
   a. The which tree carries a fruit like a pineapple with prickles, but somewhat less, which is the most delicate fruit to eat that may be, and you shall smell those trees a great way off through their strong hot and sweet savor (B58).

22. Wynter's Bark
   a. There is also a great abundance of those trees which carry a thick bark that bites like pepper, which young Mr. Wynter brought home from the Strait of Magellan (A7.4, B57, C45.6).

23. Manchineel
   a. There is a tree in those countries which bears a fruit like an apple, but is poison to eat, which being cut the apple being cut or broken there is a black liquor in the midst thereof that will come out very black like ink (A7.3, B65).

24. Lignum vitae
   a. And amongst the rest there is great abundance of Lignum Vitae, and sundry sweet woods which he knew not (B56, C45.4).

Birds

25. Flamingo
   a. There is a bird called a flamingo which is very red feathered, and is bigger than a goose, and billed like a shoveler, and which is very good meat (B81, C71).
26. Harpy Eagle
   a. There is also a very strange bird there as big as an eagle, very beautiful to behold. His feathers are more orient than a peacock's feathers, his eyes are as glistering as any hawk's eyes but as great as a man's eyes. His head and thigh as big as a man's head and thigh. It has a crest or tuft of feathers of sundry colors on the top of the head like a lapwing hanging backwards. His beak and talons in proportion like an eagle, but very huge and large (C73).

Mexico

27. The Tempest
   a. Touching Tempests and other strange monstrous things in those parts this examinate says that he has seen it lighten and thunder in summer season by the space of 24 hours together, the cause whereof he judges to be heat of that climate. He further says that there is a cloud sometime of the year seen in the air which commonly turns to great tempests (C74, C75).
28. Silk
   a. There is a great abundance of silkworms (B42).
29. The Landing
   a. About the beginning of October 1568, David Ingram, with the rest of his company, being 100 persons in all, were set on land by John Hawkins, about six leagues to the west of the river La Mina, or Rio de Minas, which stands about 140 leagues west by north from the Cape of Florida (C2.1).

North America

30. Autumn 1568

    a. He has traveled by land in those countries, from the most northerly parts of the Bay of Mexico through a great part of America, until he came within fifty leagues or thereabouts of Cape Breton, about 11 months in the whole, and about 7 months thereof in those countries which lie towards the north of the River of May. In which time (as the said Ingram thinks) he traveled by land 2000 miles at the least and never continued in any one place above 3 or 4 days, saving only at the city of Balma where he stayed 6 or 7 days (C2.2).

    b. When they want fire, they take briars and rub them very hard together between their fists, and so with hard and often rubbing they kindle and make a fire (C43).

    c. There are also curlews bigger than ours. (B82).

    d. They have also a wine which they make of a red berry called guyathos, that grows in a pod like a peasecod [pea pod], about 3 or 4 inches long which grows on short trees and bushes full of prickles, like a sloe or thorn tree. The fruit bites like a green raisin, but somewhat sharper. They pound this berry, and so make thereof wine, which they keep in vessels made of wood (B67, C52).

    e. There are in those parts, says he, very many kings, commonly within 100 or 120 miles one from another, who are at continual wars together. The first king that they came before dwelt in a country called Giricka, who caused them to be stripped naked, and wondering greatly at the whiteness of their skins, let them depart without further harm (C3).

    f. Also, they have a kind of grain the ear of which is as big as a man's wrist of his arm, the grain is like a flat piece. It makes very good white bread (C55).

    g. And that sometimes of the year there are great winds like whirlwinds (C76).

31. Winter 1568–1569

    a. Also, they passed over many great rivers in those countries in canoes or boats, some 4, some 8 some 10 miles over, whereof one was so large that they could scarce cross the same in 24 hours (C82).

    b. He did also see another strange beast bigger than a bear. It had neither head nor neck. His eyes and mouth were in his breast. This beast is very ugly to behold, and cowardly by nature. It bears a very fine skin like a rat, full of silver hairs (C67).

c. He has confessed that there are most goodly rivers, and in the heads of some of them there is great abundance of gold silver and pearl, and that he has seen at the heads of diverse springs and in small running brooks sundry pieces of cleaned gold, as big as a man's fist, and some as big as a egg, and as a man's thumb, and some less. He saw the earth having washed from it with the land floods, and waters which brought it out of the mines (A6.1, B38, C39).

d. All the men generally wear about their arms manilions [Sp. *manillas*], diverse hoops, bracelets, and sometimes of massy gold and silver, which are of good thickness, as big as a man's finger, and sometimes bigger on each of their arms. Which hoop are garnished with pearl, diverse of them as big as ones thumb. And likewise they wear the like on either of the small of their legs whereof commonly one of them is massy gold and two of them silver. Which hoops are garnished with pearl, diverse of them as big as ones thumb (A4.3, B26, C9).

e. That the women of the country go appareled with great plates of gold covering their whole bodies much like unto an armor, about the midst of their bodies they wear leaves, which have growing there one very long, much like hair. And likewise about their arms and the small of their legs they wear hoops and chains of gold and silver, garnished with chains of great pearl (A4.4, B27, C10.1).

f. And many of the women also do wear many bracelets & chains of great pearl, whereof many of them are as big as a man's thumb every way (B28, C10.2).

32. Palms

a. There are also trees called the palm, which carries hairs on the leaves thereof which reach to the ground whereof the Indians do make ropes and cords for their cotton beds and do use the same to many other purposes (B59.1, C47).

b. The branches of the top of the tree are most excellent meat raw after you have pared away the bark (B60, C49).

33. Buildings

a. Their buildings are weak and of small form. They build their houses round like dovecotes and have in like manner a louver on the tops of the houses.[9] They dwell together in towns and villages (A5.1, B32.1, C28.1).

34. Pearls

  a. They have among them in some of those countries a great abundance
     of pearl, and diverse strange stones of what sort or value he knew
     not. For in every cottage you shall find pearl, and in some houses
     a quart, in some a pottle [2 quarts], in some a peck, more and in
     some less, as it happens. He did see some as great as an acorn (A6.2,
     B29, C8.1).

  b. He said that he had in his own possession 27 pearls, every one as big
     as his thumb, he thinks. And Richard Browne, one of his companions
     found one of the great pearls in one of the canoes or boats, which
     pearl he gave to Monsieur Champaigne who took them aboard his
     ship and brought them to New Haven in France (B30, C8.2).

  c. The greatest wealth is, and most people do dwell, somewhat far
     up in the country about 30 or 40 leagues from the sea coast, as he
     found by his travel as far as he went. And in the higher countries
     their greatest wealth is both for metals and for good grass. And there
     are but few people dwelling near the sea coast, so far as he travelled,
     which was most [of it], but very little on the sea coast (B43).

  d. And the Country about the backside of the Cape of Florida is very
     barren and bare ground for fruits, and the people in that place very
     churlish and cruel (B48).

  e. The ground and country is most excellent, fertile, pleasant, and most
     delicate, especially towards the north of the River of May. The grass
     to the rest of the southwards of it is not so green as it is in those
     parts, for the rest is burned away with the heat of the sun. And as
     all the country is good and most delicate, compounded with great
     plains as fair in many places as you may see and more, and that is
     plain as a board, and then great woods, and after that plains again
     (B47, B52, C45.1).

  f. In other places great closes of pasture environed with most delicate
     trees instead of hedge, they being as it were set by the hands of men
     (B53, C46.1).

  g. Yet the best grass for the most part is in the high countries somewhat
     far from the seaside and great freshwater rivers. [This is] by reason
     that the low grounds there be so rank and unmanured that it makes
     the grass grow faster than it can be eaten, whereby the old grass
     lies withered there very thick and the new grass growing through
     it. Whereas in the upper countries the grass and ground is most

excellent and green, the ground not being overcharged with any old withered grass as before specified (B54, C46.2).

h. They have sundry canoes, which is their boats, which boats are also far up in the Country. In the most part of which boats you shall find a scoop of massy silver [mica sheets], wherewith they cast out their water (B31).

i. They have fine dishes made of wood, as thin as a paper leaf, most artificially carved (B34).

j. These people have also pots of earth very fine, like unto Venice clay (B35).

k. Also, there are larks bigger than ours (B83).

l. There are also birds of all sorts as we have in England, and many strange birds that he did not know (B80, C69).

m. They have also in many places vines which bear grapes as big as a man's thumb (C53).

n. They have in every house scoops, buckets and diverse other vessels of massy silver in which they carry diverse things, and with which they throw out water and dust and otherwise employ them to their necessary uses in their houses. All which this examinate did see commonly and usual in some of those countries, especially where he found the greater pearl (B33, C38).

o. The people commonly are of good favored features, and shape of body. The people are of growth tall and thick, above five feet high, somewhat thick like Turks, with their faces and skins of color very red or like an olive, and towards the north somewhat tawny. But many of them are painted with diverse colors. They are very swift of foot. The hair of their heads is shaved or cut in sundry spots and the rest of the hair of the head is traced (B19, C11).

35. Spring 1569

a. There is a mountain which lies to the northward of the sea coast about 30 leagues from the Bay of St. Mary's as he judges it, which is called Bauchoovan, and which seemed to be very rich of mines, both by the color thereof as by the plenty of silver among the inhabitants of those parts (B44).

b. There is also great plenty of herbs and of all kind of flowers as roses and gillyflowers like ours in England and many others which he knew not (C54).

36. Ingram's Itinerary
    a. This examinate did also see diverse towns and villages as: (C29).
    b. Gunda: a town a flight shot in length (C30).
    c. Ochala: a great town the mile long (C31).
    d. Balma: a rich city a mile and a half long (C32).
    e. [Norum] Bega: a country and the town of that name three quarters of a mile; there are good stores of ox hides (C33).
    f. Saganas: A town almost the mile in length (C34).
    g. Barmiah: A city a mile and a quarter long. Also, there is a river and town of that name but less than the first above named (C35).
    h. Guinda: A small town and the river both of that name and this is the most northerly part that this examinate was at (C36).
    i. There are besides these towns aforenamed many other great towns which this examinate passed being commonly distant 60 or 80 miles one from another which have diverse small villages within eight or ten miles from them (C37).

37. Balma
    a. Far into the land there are many people in towns and villages, and he saw one town a half (almost a) mile long, and the streets far broader than any street in London (A4.1, B32.2).
    b. And they have banquette houses that are made on the tops of them like the louver of a hall in England. Many of these banquette houses being built with pillars that uphold many things, framed square of crystal, and pillars of massy silver and some of them of gold beaten square. Many of the pillars are as big as a boy's leg of 15 years of age, and some lesser, and some as long as a man, and some twice as long, answerable to the height of the building (A5.2, B32.3, C28.2).
    c. In other places they did see great rocks of crystal at the heads of great rivers, being in quantities sufficient to load a great fleet of ships, as he imagined (B36, C40).
    d. The people are also something cruel towards the north of the River of May, as about the River of St. Mary's [Susquehanna River] or the northward of it, where [there] are some man eaters, but not many (B49).

38. Religion
    a. Touching their religion, he said that they do honor for their god a devil which they call Collochio, who speaks to them sometimes in

the likeness of a black dog and sometimes in the likeness of a black calf. And some do honor the sun the moon and the stars (B21, C77).

b. Then appeared their Collochio or devil in the likeness aforesaid and spoke unto them, and to that devil the parties brought to execution [they] do great reverence, and with many prayers to it do take their death (C79).

c. He said that such persons as are put to death in such sort have not any of their friends buried with them, but such as die naturally have [been] always buried quick, with them one of their dearest friends to keep them company and to provide necessaries and victuals for them who do willingly consent, being thereunto persuaded by their Collochio or devil, who they do worship (C80).

d. He said further that he & his two fellows, namely Richard Browne and Richard Twide went into a poor man's house and there they did see the said Collochio or devil with very great eyes like a black calf, upon which sight thereof Browne said "there is the devil," and thereupon blessed himself in the name of the father, the son, and the holy ghost. And Twide said very vehemently "I defy thee and all thy works," and presently the Collochio shrank away in a stealing manner forth of the doors and was seen no more unto them (C81).

39. Language

a. Gwando is a word of salutation, as among us good evening, or good morrow, god save you, or some such like (C92).

b. Garicona / A King (C93).

c. Garrucona /A Lord (C94).

d. Tona, Bread (C95).

e. Carmugnaz / The privities (C96).

f. Kerucca, the Sun (C97).

40. Summer 1589

a. And then great and huge woods of sundry kinds of trees [such] as cedar (C45.2).

b. Also, the said David Ingram traveling toward the north found the main[e] sea upon the north side of America and traveled in the sight thereof the space of 2 whole days (C98.1)

c. But in the north part they are clothed with beasts' skins the hairy side being next to their bodies in winter, after the manner of the country (C12.2).

d. There are in those parts plenty of wild beasts whose skins are most delicate and rare furs but what they were he knew not, dressed after the manner of the country (A7.2, B37, C41).

e. There are wolves (C62).

f. There are also bears, both black and white (B75, C61).

g. There are also an abundance of conies [rabbits] in every place, both white and gray, but black he saw none to his remembrance (B76, C64).

h. There is abundance of foxes with their skins of fairer silver hair, more grizzly than ours in England (B77, C63).

i. There is also great plenty of buffs, bears, horses, kine, wolves, foxes, deer, goats, sheep, hares, and conies (C57.1).

41. Autumn 1569

a. The people in those countries are professed enemies to the cannibals or man eaters. The cannibals do most inhabit between Norumbega and Barmiah (C27.1).

b. Where the people signified unto him that they had seen ships on that coast and did draw upon the ground the shape and figure of ships and of their sails and flags which thing especially proves the Northwest Passage and is agreeable to the experience of the Spanish Captain Vasquez De Coronado who found a ship of China or Cathay upon the Northwest of America (C98.2).

c. After long travel the aforesaid David Ingram with his two companions Browne and Twide came to the head of a river called Guinda, which is 60 leagues west from Cape Breton, where they understood by the people of that country of the arrival of a Christian. Whereupon they made their repair to the seaside and then found a French Captain named Monsieur Champaigne who took them into his ship and brought them unto Newhaven [Le Havre] and from thence they were transported into England, *anno domini* 1569 (C86).

d. This Monsieur Champaigne with diverse of his companions were brought into the village of Barmiah about 20 miles up into the country by the said examinate and his two companions, by whose means he had a trade with the people of diverse sorts of fine furs and of great red leaves of trees almost a yard long and about a foot broad. Whereof the Frenchman that brought home a great store with them, which he supposed to be good for dyeing, but the certainty thereof he knew not (B45, C87).

e. Also, the said Monsieur Champaigne had there for exchange of trifling wares a good quantity of rude and unwrought silver (C88).

f. And Richard Browne one of his Companions found one of the great pearls in one of the canoes or boats, which pearl he gave to Monsieur Champaigne, who took them aboard his ship and brought them to Newhaven [Le Havre] in France (C8.2).

g. This examinate did also see in those Countries a monstrous beast twice as big as a horse and in every proportion like unto a horse saving they be small towards the hinder legs like a greyhound. They are like unto a horse both in mane, hoof, hair, neighing, and of all colors like a horse, saving these beasts have two teeth or horns of a foot long growing straight out of or by their nostrils. They are most cruel and natural enemies to the horse, and will kill men if they cannot well defend themselves from them. He was put in great danger of his life, but he escaped by climbing up a tree, for so he saved himself (A3.1, B73, C65).

h. There is also a great plenty of another kind of great sheep which carry a kind of coarse wool red as blood, whose horns are very crooked and sharp. This sheep is very good meat, although the flesh is very red. They are exceedingly fat and by nature loath to rise when they are lain, which is always from five o'clock at night until five in the morning. All that time you may easily kill them. But after they are up on foot they are very wild and do not rest in one place. They live together in herds of 500, more or less as it happens, a thousand in some, a hundred in others, more or less. These red sheep are most about the Bay of St Mary's, or thereabouts, as this examinate guesses (A3.3, B69, C60).

i. There are to be seen many times about the Bay of St. Mary's fire dragons, which make the air very red as they fly, but they do neither move tempest nor other hurt to his knowledge (B22).

j. This examinate was embarked, when he came home, at the River called Banda [St. John], where he met a French ship of Newhaven [Le Havre] by chance. They came within sight of the Lizard within 20 days of sailing after they departed from the said coast [of Newfoundland] (B84.1,84.2).

k. There is also another kind of fowl in that country which haunts the rivers near unto the islands. They are of the shape and bigness of a goose, but their wings are covered with small callow feathers and

[they] cannot fly. You may drive them before you like sheep. They are exceedingly fat and have very delicate meat. They have white heads and therefore the countrymen call them penguins (which seems to be a Welsh name) and they have also in use diverse other Welsh words, a matter worthy of noting (C72).

l. He said further that diverse of the said Frenchmen which were in the said ship called the *Gargarine* are yet living in Honfluer, upon the Coast of France as he thinks, for he did speak with some of them within these 3 years [of 1582] (C89).

m. About a fortnight after their coming from Newhaven into England the said examinate and his two companions came to Mr. John Hawkins who had set them on shore upon the bay of Mexico and unto each of them he gave a reward (C90).

n. Richard Browne, his companion, was slain about five years past in the *Elizabeth* of Mr. Cockins of London, and Richard Twide, his other companion, died at Ratcliffe in John Sherewood's house there about three years past (C91).

o. Diverse other matters of great importance he has confessed (if they be true) which he says that upon his life, he offers to go to the place, to prove the same true (A7.5).

42. Unassigned Entries[10]

a. There are some monkeys which he saw the country people play with all (B78).

b. They are so brutish and beastly that they will not forbear the use of their wives in open presence (C13).[11]

c. Also, he said that in the same country the people have instruments of music made of a piece of a cane almost a foot long being open at both ends, which sitting down they smite upon their thighs and one of their hands making a pleasant kind of sound (C83).

d. And they do use another kind of instrument like a taber [drum] covered with a white skin somewhat like parchment (C84).

e. This examinate can very well describe their gestures, dancing, and songs (C85).[12]

f. There are in those countries most goodly and excellent trees and woods of sundry strange sorts that he knew not, as also like to our trees in Europe (B55).[13]

Notes

1. Ingram reported Browne's death and other details of the voyage of the *Elizabeth*, indicating that both of them were aboard in 1578. This is discussed in Chapter 10.
2. This was according to the "Old Style" Julian calendar.
3. This passage, like others quoted from manuscript sources, is modernized for clarity. It can be found in the second section (The Agenda) of the Appendix, "A New Transcription of David Ingram's Testimony."
4. This is the well-known Dunning-Kruger effect. Kruger, 1999; Darwin, 1871: (1)3.
5. See the introduction to an updated transcript of the State Papers Domestic manuscript titled *Examination of David Ingram*, Appendix A in the online Companion Website of this book.
6. Adams 1962: 132–134, 137.
7. What follows in this section is well-established factual history that can be confirmed by reference to a myriad of reliable sources.
8. Beginning in the 1540s, the king's representative came to be formalized as the role of the "Speaker" as presiding officer in the House of Commons. It was his unenviable job to convey news good and bad between the monarch and the lower chamber.
9. The literacy bar was set very low at the time. One needed only to be able to write one's name to be considered literate.
10. Barnhart 1995: 630.
11. Kelsey 2003: 18; Hazlewood 2004.
12. Cooper 2011.
13. Isaacson 2017. The example of Leonardo gave rise to Neil deGrasse Tyson's observation: "I know of no time in human history where ignorance was better than knowledge."
14. Quinn has found evidence that Gilbert was in Plymouth during a portion of the interrogation. Quinn 1967 I: 52, 64–66, 181–186.
15. Anonymous 1582d; Anonymous 1582c.
16. Anonymous 1582c.
17. Hakluyt 1965.
18. For example, Charles Bennett found sometimes egregious editorial errors in Hakluyt's publication of Laudonnière's narrative. Laudonnière 1975.

19. Purchas 1625.

20. The following chapters will show that Ingram and his two companions walked and canoed about 3,651 miles (5,876 km). It will also show that they could have done so averaging a modest 15 miles (24 km) a day for only eight or nine months.

21. A philosophical fad in the late twentieth century was based on the argument that there is no such thing as true history, only a multitude of representations of it. If that were true, there would be no basis for seeking historical accuracy. Consequently, there would also be no basis for expecting any valid system of justice based on factual evidence. This book takes the position that there is a sound basis for both science and justice. Bloom and Weisberg 2007.

22. All three documents must have been produced by different recorders having not just different handwriting but different spelling habits as well. The identities of the three recorders remain unknown.

23. The Calthorpe and Sloane manuscripts are both housed at the British Library. Both are available online. Anonymous 1582e; Anonymous 1582a. The Sloane manuscript is now held by the British Museum. It is mentioned here because David Quinn published a transcript of it in a 1967 publication that is often used by historians. There he collated the Sloane with Hakluyt's 1589 published version. He probably did this because he saw that the Tanner was virtually identical with Hakluyt's published version and possibly because he thought the Sloane might be the earlier of the two versions. The Sloane manuscript is derived from and is very similar to the Tanner, but they are not identical in detail. Inspection of the handwriting reveals that the Sloane and the Tanner were written by two different people. A careful reading of both manuscripts also shows that the Sloane is a flawed copy of the Tanner. In one place the Sloane copyist left out an entire paragraph. Thus, the evidence of mainly words or passages erroneously omitted by the copyist reveals that the Tanner is in fact the earlier version and that the Sloane was copied from it.

24. Dawson and Kennedy-Skipton 1966.

25. Refer to the updated transcription Companion Website Manuscript A. This manuscript is housed in the National Archives of the United Kingdom. Anonymous 1582b.

26. This manuscript is also housed in the National Archives of the United Kingdom. Anonymous 1582d. It incorporates a page previously filed with the State Papers Domestic manuscript. Anonymous 1582b.

27. The Calthorpe manuscript is a contemporary copy of the State Papers Colonial manuscript. Anonymous 1582e.

28. This manuscript is held by the Bodleian Library, Oxford University. Anonymous 1582c.

29. The Sloane manuscript is a contemporary copy of the Tanner manuscript. Anonymous 1582a.

30. The full, 107-word title is the first entry in the Appendix at 1.

CHAPTER 2

1. Luther 2009.
2. Durant 1957: 193.
3. Casas 1992.
4. Indigenous Americans were treated better than Africans under Spanish law, but not by much.
5. Hazlewood 2004: 91.
6. Hawkins 1589: 523.
7. Hazlewood 2004: 135–139.
8. Kelsey 2003: 41. Sugden provides a somewhat different accounting. Sugden 1990: 20.
9. This summary is taken from Kelsey's excellent biography of Hawkins. Kelsey 2003.
10. Antonio Luis and André Homem, the latter also sometimes known as Gaspar Caldeira.
11. Hortop 1591; Phillips 1589.
12. Kelsey 2003: 55–56. Sugden provides a somewhat different accounting. Sugden 1990: 23.
13. Kelsey 2003: 55–56.
14. Hortop 1591.
15. Hortop 1591; Kelsey 2003: 61–62.
16. Hortop 1591.

CHAPTER 3

1. Kelsey 2003: 64.
2. Newitt 2010: 205.
3. Recall that at this time January, February and much of March were considered late 1567, not early 1568 as is the case today.
4. Unwin 1960: 77–78. Unwin asserts the gourd of wine gift but does not provide a source. It is not mentioned in Kelsey (2003).
5. Akpan 2013. The two dominant ethnic groups of Sierra Leone are still the Temne and the Mende.
6. Fyfe 1962; Olson 1996: 552–553.
7. Appendix entry 3.
8. Richard Hakluyt would later claim in the title of his publication of Ingram's testimony that everything Ingram said in his testimony pertained to eastern North America. The full title of his version of Ingram's testimony is "The Relation of Dauid Ingram of Barking in the Countie of Essex Sayler of sundry things which he with others did see in traueiling by land from the most Northerly partes of the Baie of Mexico (where he with many others were set on shoare by Master Hawkins) through a great part of America vntill he came within fiftie leagues or thereabouts of Cape Britton." Hakluyt 1589a.

9. Appendix entry 4.

10. Sumner 1922; Schön 1884.

11. Appendix entry 5.

12. Appendix entry 6.

13. Today it is a long plastic horn that makes a loud monotone sound typically blown by South African fans at soccer matches.

14. At this point, Ingram's recorders abandoned the order of Ingram's narrative. It appears that questions began interrupting and redirecting his testimony, causing them to begin clustering his statements by topical categories that ignored geography. His words were taken down by all three recorders, but as should be expected, there were slight variations as the three men struggled to write fast enough to keep up with the testimony. For confirmation, compare the notes of any three people attending the same lecture.

15. Appendix entry 7.

16. Gibbs 1988: 213.

17. Kelsey 2003: 66–67. The twentieth-century Temne and Mende peoples like neighboring cultures still had highly developed systems for social, political, and legal controls. Secret societies, Poro for men and Sande for women, were vital institutions that worked together with political institutions to manage these controls. Polygyny was and still is common; senior men had more wives than lower-ranking men. Divorce has long been common, but by the twentieth century, adultery was punished mainly by monetary fines. More severe punishments like those described by Ingram were presumably later suppressed by colonial administrations.

18. Often incorrectly attributed to North America.

19. At this point in the manuscript the writer of State Papers Colonial appears to have grown tired of it all. There is a run of fourteen entries that from the evidence found in each of them must pertain to North America. After that the entries relating to Africa, the Caribbean, and North America are scattered singly or in sets of two to five. Fortunately, the scrambling is not as serious as in the case of the Tanner manuscript entries, so some semblance of geographic order is preserved here and there in the State Papers Colonial manuscript.

20. Appendix entry 9.

21. Brown 2020.

22. Appendix entry 10.

23. There are many sources describing African bloomery techniques, but Cline 1937 remains the classic work.

24. Appendix entry 11.

25. In the sixteenth century "bastard" was used to refer to second-rate Spanish sack wines.

26. This is asserted by Rayner Unwin but without a supporting citation. Unwin 1960: 77–78.

27. The likelihood that the Spanish introduced palm wine via their Caribbean colonies is suggested by one of the plates in the Drake Manuscript. There an

image of a palm includes a tap near the base with a ceramic bowl to catch the dripping sap. The caption states that the Indians made palm wine tasting like pear wine (Klinkenborg 1996: 257). There is nothing convincing to suggest that this was what Ingram observed but it remains possible.

28. The sabal (cabbage) palm and the saw palmetto are native to the northern Gulf Rim. Driver and Massey 1957: 267.

29. Poison arrows were in widespread use in South America. The cartographer Juan de la Cosa was killed by one near the native town of Turbaco in Colombia in 1509.

30. Wang et al. 2014.

31. Appendix entry 12.

32. Appendix entry 13.

33. These plant identifications are not controversial and sources are not required. They can be checked easily online.

34. Appendix entry 14.

35. "Hough" is a biblical reference (Joshua 11:9) used by Ingram to describe the disabling of a large animal by approaching it from behind and cutting its Achilles tendon with a Y-shaped spear point.

36. Appendix entry 15.

37. Hortop 1591.

38. Appendix entry 16.

39. Raffaele 1989: Plate 26.

40. Kelsey 2003: 64–67.

CHAPTER 4

1. Recall that this format accommodates both the current practice of starting the new year on January 1 and the "Old Style" practice of starting it on March 25.

2. Hawkins 1589: 553; Kelsey 2003: 71–74.

3. Appendix entry 17.

4. All quotes are Ingram's words unless otherwise identified.

5. Strack 2008; Southgate and Lucas 2008.

6. Herrera 1945 (2): 300–301. This translation is by the author.

7. Hortop 1591.

8. Barrett 1928: 156; Phillips 1589: 563.

9. Appendix entry 18. The State Papers Colonial manuscript is the better source on this because unlike the corresponding Tanner manuscript entry it does not conflate information pertaining to the Caribbean with information that could pertain to North America. This conflation was consistent with Hakluyt's mistaken belief that everything Ingram said had to do with North America.

10. Hakluyt might have got ten this part of the story outside the interrogation either from Ingram, his friend Miles Phillips, or the two of them together. Phillips had only recently escaped Spanish captivity at the time of Ingram's interrogation, returning to England in early 1582. Phillips and Ingram somehow

found each other and shared remembrances of their misbegotten voyage a dozen years earlier. Phillips was probably present at the interrogation. The Curaçao story might have come from either of them or it might even have been told in a back-and-forth conversation between them. After all, this is the mutually reinforcing way that people typically recount shared memories.

11. The entry appears to be one of the sources of inspiration for Shakespeare's *The Tempest*. Bromber 2001.

12. Sugden 1990: 61–77.

13. Hortop 1591.

14. Kelsey 2003: 81.

15. Hortop 1591.

16. Kelsey 2003: 83; Phillips 1589: 563.

17. Appendix entry 19.

18. This series of 199 paintings with annotations in French was probably produced in the 1590s. It has been called the *Drake Manuscript* because there are references to Francis Drake in two of the annotations labeled "Canoe of the South Sea" (f. 44) and the other one labeled "Indian of Loranbec" (f. 90). The first mentions Gilolo, an island in the Moluccas where Drake is said to have careened and cleaned the *Golden Hind* late in 1579. The second describes a man Drake encountered on the American east coast at around Lat. 36.5° in 1586. Klinkenborg 1996: 259, 264.

19. Appendix entry 20.

20. Appendix entry 21.

21. Klinkenborg 1996: folio 4,253.

22. Collingham 2007.

23. Appendix entry 22.

24. Appendix entry 23.

25. Nelson 2011: 165–166; Pitts et al. 1993.

26. Major 2010: 23.

27. Ponce de Leon's 1521 death after he was wounded in Florida is sometimes cited as evidence that manchineel was used by Florida Indians to poison their weapons. The source of these claims is uncertain. Fredrick Davis is cited, but he in turn cited an accurate translation of Herrera that did not mention manchineel or any other arrow poison. It is clear from Herrera that Ponce received a thigh wound made by an arrow shot by a Calusa warrior. Ponce de Leon died from the resulting infection after returning to Cuba. Ponce probably died from sepsis, and manchineel was not necessarily the cause of the infection. Jones et al. 2007: 29–35; Davis 2017: 51–53; Grunwald 2006: 25; Davis 1935; Herrera 1945 (4): 48.

28. Appendix entry 24.

29. Appendix entry 25.

30. Ingram's description of the harpy eagle certainly struck Rayner Unwin as ridiculous in 1960. This is merely evidence that Unwin did not consult a bird guide. Unwin 1960: 249–261.

31. Appendix entry 26.
32. Appendix entry 27.
33. Hogue 1993: 325.
34. Appendix entry 28.
35. Lewis 1937: 314.
36. Barrett 1928: 159–160.
37. Kelsey 2003: 88.
38. Hazlewood 2004: 261–262.
39. Phillips 1589: 566–567.
40. Appendix entry 29.
41. This total can be compiled from the relations of David Ingram and Miles Phillips.
42. Phillips 1589: 567.
43. Laughlin 1969; Mercado Ruvalcaba 2005: 260.
44. Phillips 1589: 567.
45. Phillips 1589.
46. Hortop 1591; Kelsey 2003: 112; Phillips 1589.
47. Sugden 1990: 36–37.
48. Phillips 1589: 568.

CHAPTER 5

1. Appendix entry 30. The complete title was originally a run-on sentence of 107 words. Six words have been added in brackets for clarification in the Appendix. Hakluyt 1589a.
2. Two methods were used to measure the distances of legs of the journey: MapInfo v. and Google Maps. The two techniques varied slightly. The larger of the two measures was selected in each case as a means to avoid artificially minimizing the length of the long walk.
3. For example, David Quinn's opinion was that "Ingram could less incredibly have walked to some part of the coast north of the Spanish posts. . . . An accidental meeting with a French ship on this coast is credible the distance less unlikely. More plausibly still he could have been picked up by a French privateer on the Gulf of Mexico . . . conceivable [sic] ending up with a call near Cape Breton before sailing for Europe." Quinn 1979b.
4. The following chapters will show that Ingram and his two companions could have completed their long walk averaging a modest 15 miles a day for only eight or nine months. Holly Harrison was interviewed twice along the way by Harry Smith of NBC News.
5. Richard Nathan, who replicated the long walk in 1999–2000, was guided by these leads and sensibly followed a route that kept to the coastal plain of the Atlantic and Gulf Coasts. Nathan might have read Eric Kelly's 1949 historical novel about a fictionalized David Ingram which includes a map showing the same coastal plain route. Kelly 1949.
6. Hudson et al. 1984: 66.

7. The kilometers sum is slightly different in Table 5.1 due to roundings in the conversions from miles.

8. Phillips 1589.

9. DeGolyer 1947.

10. Quinn 1967 (2): 311.

11. Covey 1961: 66–67; Driver and Massey 1957: 267–268.

12. Such creative linguistic juggling continued to be a popular parlor game throughout the twentieth century. Hakluyt 1589a: 560; Peckham 1583: 459.

13. Phillips 1589: 570.

14. Newcomb Jr. 1961: 42.

15. Reséndez 2007.

16. Hallenbeck 1940; Newcomb Jr. 1961: 67; Newcomb Jr. 1983; Reséndez 2007.

17. David Ingram and his partners probably encountered no fewer than 25 mutually unintelligible Indian languages between their landing place near Tampico, Mexico, and their place of rescue in New Brunswick. The total could conceivably have been twice that many, but the evidence is too scanty to be certain.

18. Wurtzburg and Campbell 1995.

19. Wurtzburg and Campbell 1995: 155.

20. Covey 1961: 66–67.

21. Smith 2012: 114–119.

22. Whalen 2013.

23. Reséndez 2007: 161–162.

24. Stephens and Holmes 1989: 20.

25. Newcomb Jr. 1961: 62; Bargatzky 1980; Chipman 1987.

26. The Archaeological Conservancy recently acquired the Shackleford Creek site about 70 miles (113 km) northwest of Nacogdoches. This Caddoan village was thriving at the time of Cabeza de Vaca's trading trips.

27. Rogers and Sabo 2004; Tooker 1971.

28. Newcomb Jr. 1961: 292, 321.

29. Myer 1923.

30. Henige 1998; Snow 1995a; Snow and Lanphear 1988; Ubelaker 1988.

31. Elliott Jr. 1997; Swanton 1928.

32. George Chaplin recently took the lead in compiling an electronic map of these and other Eastern Woodland trails. Milanich 1993: 11–12; Hudson 1997; Sanger et al. 2019.

33. At least one historian imagined that they hiked to the Great Lakes before turning eastward. Burrage 1914.

34. Kniffen et al. 1987: 48, 208; Myer 1923; Goins and Caldwell 1986: 17.

35. Foster 1996: 109; Wurtzburg and Campbell 1995.

36. Swanton 1928b: 748.

37. Swanton 1928b.

38. Henige 1998; Snow 1995a; Snow and Lanphear 1988; Ubelaker 1988.

CHAPTER 6

1. Appendix entry 31.
2. Snow 1972b: 211; Quinn 1955 (1): 433.
3. Driver and Massey 1957: 291; Snow 1972b; Snow 1975; Wood 2018: 210; Wroth 1970: 139.
4. Swanton 1928b: 748.
5. Worth 2020.
6. Swanton 1928b: 748.
7. Appendix entry 31b.
8. Swanton 1928b: 748.
9. Milanich 2004: 225.
10. Milanich 1996: 47–79.
11. Hulton 1979: 195.
12. Hulton 1977 (1): Plate 106.
13. McKnight 2007: 73.
14. Lewis and Loomie 1953: 13.
15. The American Indian preference for copper over gold might not have been news to any European by this time because Columbus had made the same observation on his second voyage to the Caribbean over 70 years earlier. Laudonnière 1964: 38; Laudonnière 1975: 116; Major 2010: 55.
16. Laudonnière 1975: 9.
17. Laudonnière 1964: 15, 39b, 40.
18. Jerald Milanich argues in a 2016 Hakluyt Society blog that le Moyne was unlikely to have been able to salvage much of his Florida artwork when he returned home and that deBry probably exercised a considerable amount of his own invention for his illustrations in Harriot's 1590 publication. Harriot 1972.
19. Quinn 1955 (1): 462.
20. Laudonnière 1975.
21. Copper plates are confirmed archaeologically. Milanich et al. 1997.
22. Laudonnière 1975: 110; Milanich 1996: 59–60.
23. Hakluyt already had French and English sources in his possession in the 1580s. He could have embellished the Tanner manuscript from Laudonnière or other sources prior to publishing it in 1589. However, in this case the Tanner manuscript has the least amount of content on the subject, all of which is clearly derived from the other two manuscripts.
24. Appendix entry 32; Austin 2004: 585–586.
25. Appendix entry 33.
26. Hudson et al. 1984: 66.
27. Hudson et al. 1984: 66; Smith 1968: 79; Milanich and Hudson 1993: 42.
28. Reséndez 2007: 107–108; Cortés 1962.
29. Milanich and Hudson 1993: 218.
30. Researchers previously hypothesized that de Soto had spent the winter in the province of Apalachee, the town being unidentified. More recent research has

revealed that the town was at the Governor Martin site in Tallahassee. De Soto called the town Iniahica, and that is how it is identified here. Ewen and Hann 1998; Milanich 1989: 86; Hudson et al. 1984: 68.

31. Many of de Soto's horses were killed during the *entrada*, and it is remotely possible that an American Indian found and kept a few exotic horsetails, but it appears that no other source corroborates the possible use of horsetail insignias in eastern North America. This supports the likelihood that Ingram's descriptions of horsetails related only to his experiences in Africa, as described in Chapter 3. Driver and Massey 1957: 284–285.

32. Milanich and Hudson 1993: 180,231; Varner 1962: 253.

33. Appendix entry 34. Varner and Varner 1962: 313–314.

34. A transcript of de Soto's experience in the original Spanish reveals that there is no confusion on this point in the English translation. Varner and Varner 1962: 489; Vega 1956: 341.

35. Smith 1968: 124; Varner and Varner 1962: 337.

36. Snow 1995: 103.

37. The whelks, which spiral in the opposite direction of conchs, reach a size of 16 inches (40 cm) in length. A whelk of that size has a solid conical inner column about half that long. The solid column tapers to a point having a base about an inch (2.5 cm) in diameter. This means that the lower 3-inch (8-cm) segment of its length is comparable to the size of a man's thumb. Milanich and colleagues illustrate some examples from smaller whelks that were ground into ear pins that were up to 5.5 inches (14 cm) long. These were each headed like modern golf tees at one end so they could be worn dangling from holed earlobes. Ingram's large pearls could not have been true pearls at all. Because of hoarding and burial with the dead, the supply of marine shell diminished northward, even though the demand there was strong. Archaeological examples from interior New York are known, but they are rare. The rarity of Gulf Coast marine shell this far north contributed to the popularity of more readily available northern shell species, particularly quahog (*Mercenaria*) shell. Once Europeans introduced metal tools that could be used to make small tubular beads, the production of such "wampum" exploded across the northern region in the seventeenth century. Strings and belts of wampum, some of the latter being very large, were made from small purple and white wampum beads and used in elaborate political and religious ceremonies across the Northeast. However, this was long after Ingram passed through. The point is that marine shell was long perceived as no less powerful here than elsewhere in the Eastern Woodlands. Milanich et al. 1997.

38. Emerson et al. 2016; Whalen 2013.

39. Quinn 1967 (2): 311.

40. Adair 1775: 79.

41. Adair 1775: 17–18, 447, 456; Tooker 1971.

42. Jones 2020.

43. Swanton 1928c: 452–453; 1928a: 723; Adair 1775: 456.

44. Swanton 1928b: 747.

45. DeMallie 2004: 287; Swanton 1928: 748.
46. Smith 1968: 72; Hudson et al. 1984: 66.
47. Beck et al. 2018: 579.
48. Swanton 1928a: 723; Davis Jr. et al. 1998; Swanton 1953: 66, 90–92.
49. Wroth 1970: 136.
50. Quinn 1955 (1): 330; Rights 1931: 404.
51. So named by English colonists after the settlement of Jamestown. Hundreds were tracts that were each intended to support a hundred homesteads.
52. Boyce 1978; Rudes 2011.
53. Binford 1967: 138.
54. Feest 1978b: 272.
55. "Out of this bay he signified unto me that this king had so great quantity of pearl [shell beads], and does so ordinarily take the same as that not only his own skins that he wears and the better sort of his gentlemen and followers are full set with the said pearl, but also his beds and houses are garnished with them, and that he has such quantities of them that it is a wonder to see." Quinn 1955 (1): 260, 415.
56. Milner 2004: 65.
57. Quinn 1955 (1): 440–442.
58. Quinn 1955 (1): 417.
59. Harriot 1972: Fig. 7; Quinn 1955 (1): 438–439.
60. Quinn 1955 (1): 268–270.
61. Bourque and Whitehead 1994: 132; Grumet 1995: 297; McKnight 2007.

CHAPTER 7

1. Appendix entry 35.
2. Meaning uncertain.
3. Lewis and Loomie 1953: 12–18.
4. Lewis and Loomie 1953: 26–64.
5. Quinn 1971: 172.
6. Personal communications: Joanne Brown, Melinda Zeder, Heather Lapham, Lorena Walsh, and Henry Miller.
7. Appendix entry 35.
8. Appendix entry 37.
9. Quinn 1979b.
10. Wallace 1952.
11. Appendix entry 36.
12. Appendix entry 37.
13. The story of fish fertilizer in New England is a popular Thanksgiving tale, but if it was used at all in the sixteenth century it was probably restricted to a few locales. Ceci 1975.
14. Raber 2019; Mooney 1910: 54, 118, 350; Snow 1994: 40–46; Snow 1997.

15. Kent 1984: 117.
16. In this case even high-precision radiocarbon dating does not help resolve the issue, because six years would be well within the range of standard error. Kent 1984: 18; Snow 2019.
17. Snow 1997.
18. Snow 1997.
19. Hakluyt, 1589a: 558.
20. Krusche 1986; Snow 1995b: 100, 124–126.
21. "He wrote an account of his trip and liberally embellished it from his imagination, describing the mythical city of Norumbega containing houses with pillars of crystal and silver and abounding in fur pelts." Verner 1950: 5–6.
22. Snow 1994: 86.
23. Fenton and Tooker 1978: 478; Snow 1994: 86.
24. Feest 1978a: 241; Feest 1978b: 256; Feest 1978c.
25. Pendergast 1991; Smith 1910: 54; Simms 2016.
26. English modernized except for "Sasquesahanocks." Smith 1910: 118.
27. English modernized. "Six-hundred" men implies a town population of around 2,400 inhabitants. Smith 1910: 350.
28. Smith's lithographer copied this from de Bry's plate 3, with edits based on Smith's narrative. de Bry 1591.
29. This magnificent tribute to nature is still delivered in a variety of languages by Northern Iroquoian people. Snow 1994: 24. Appendix entry 38.
30. For example, Mohawk for "devil" or "demon" is *atku*, while "witch" is *rata?dv:nears* or *wata?vineras*, depending upon gender. Mohawk for (he is a) "doctor" is *ratétsv?ts*. Michelson 1973: 34, 39, 109, 145; Mithun 1981.
31. Francis Scardera (personal communication) has suggested that Ingram could have picked up *malocchio* "evil eye" from an Italian-speaking shipmate. However, the necessary shift of the first phoneme from *m* to *c* seems unlikely to linguists.
32. Smith 1910: 50–51.
33. English modernized. Smith 1910: 54.
34. Champlain 1907: 324–326; Sagard 1968: 115–118.
35. Fenton 1987.
36. Marianne Mithun and Ives Goddard, personal communications. Appendix entry 39.
37. Ives Goddard, personal communication. Speck 1927.
38. Words that begin with "g" (often interchangeable with "k") are common in those languages. So too are words beginning with "t." Words having initial bilabials, "b" or "p," are never encountered in Northern Iroquoian. The "l" sound is also absent, although the reflexive "r" is common.
39. Mithun 1981.
40. Michelson 1973: 95; Woodbury 2003: 329.
41. Appendix entry 40.
42. Bakker 1990.

43. Wallace 1952: 433.
44. Snyder 1973: 41.
45. de Conte and Dupont 2009.
46. To the Manhattan people this was an occasion that called for an exchange of gifts as a means to establish mutual goodwill.
47. D'Abate 1994.
48. Griswold 1930; Russell 1980: 200.
49. Wroth 1970: 139.
50. Sturtevant 1975.
51. Salwen 1978: 165.
52. Bradford 1908; Heath 1963; Speiss 1987.
53. Heath 1963: 27.
54. Heath 1963: 23, 64.

CHAPTER 8

1. Appendix entry 40.
2. *Betula papyrifera* is the American white (canoe) birch, not the smaller gray birch (*Betula populifolia*).
3. Russell 1980: 202.
4. Grant 1907: 44–77; Purchas 1625 (4): 1873–1875; Smith 1910.
5. Champlain 1907: 44–77; Purchas 1625; Smith 1910: 192; Snow 1980: 37–38.
6. English modernized. Smith 1910: 192.
7. Village populations are assumed to have been 25 percent adult men, allowing the derivations of whole communities to be calculated by simply multiplying adult male counts by four. This is amended from an earlier standard of 30 percent I used in 1980 (Snow 1980: 37).
8. Snow 1980: 45.
9. Wroth 1970: 140–141.
10. Axtell 1994.
11. Quinn 1998: 50; Winship 1905: 99–151.
12. Winship 1905: 124.
13. Snow 1976a; Snow 1976b.
14. Hugh Honour combined unrelated fragments from various parts of Hakluyt's published version to make Ingram appear foolish. "An English sailor David Ingram boasted of finding near the Penobscot estuary the city of Norumbega with streets larger than any of those in London, and inhabitants who wore hoops of gold and silver garnished with pearles divers of them as big as one's thumb." Honour 1975.
15. A 1541 translated account of this portion of the voyage was published by Ganong and Layng 1964: 129–130.
16. Outcrops of the metamorphic Ellsworth Schist formation are found between Penobscot Bay and Mount Desert Island, near intrusions of Devonian granite.

The schist sparkles with metal sulfides, particularly fool's gold and mica. It is easy to see how early explorers jumped to the conclusion that they had found valuable ore in these rocks. Outcrops are visible from boats along the rocky coast, and samples were easy to acquire. Good exposures are particularly accessible on the north end of Mount Desert Island. Caldwell 1998: 74.

17. Ganong and Layng 1964: 94.
18. Hornsby and Judd 2015: Part 1, Plate 5.
19. Note that like many early maps this one has labels and illustrations that do not assume any particular map orientation.
20. This is a copy of *Terre de las Franciscane* by Jean Alfonse, 1545, showing the Penobscot River as the *Riviere de Norombergue*. Published with his *Cosmographie* in 1904. Alfonce 1904: 507. A derivative sketch was published by Ganong and Layng 1964: 130. This and other Alfonse original sketch maps are in the Bibliotheque Nationale, Paris.
21. Ganong and Layng 1964; Snow 1994: 52–76.
22. D'Abate 1994: 87; Eckstorm 1941: 15, 250.

CHAPTER 9

1. Goddard 1996: 19; Sanger et al. 2003; Bourque and Whitehead 1994.
2. Appendix entry 36.
3. Appendix entry 41.
4. Turgeon 1986; Wroth 1970.
5. This name of the St. John River is given as "Banda" in the State Papers Colonial manuscript (B84).
6. Morison spoke for the consensus in 1971 writing that Ingram was rescued at the mouth of the St. John but without providing any evidence. Morison 1971: 467.
7. The crucial choice at the end of the trail was merely the last of many that have caused later historians to doubt that any of the long walk happened at all. Percy Adams included Ingram in his 1962 rogue's gallery of travel liars. But it was Adams who was making things up. There is no evidence to support his pathless forests, savage Indians, or uphill rivers at least as far as the end of the trail at Saganas. Like so many others, Adams misrepresents Ingram in many errors great and small but that is to be expected given Hakluyt's editing. What almost certainly happened next explains how Ingram and his companions completed their journey as autumn arrived in the boreal forest.
8. Maine was previously a province of Massachusetts. It was granted statehood in 1820 as part of the Missouri Compromise.
9. Eckstorm 1945.
10. Pawling 2007; Thoreau 1966: 305–306.
11. Erickson 1978: 124; Thoreau 1966: 305–306.
12. Speck 1940: 56.

13. Appendix entry 41.

14. Thoreau 1966: 177.

15. Samuel Morison agreed that Ingram "hailed a French ship at the mouth of the St. John River New Brunswick and returned to Europe." However, Morison simply asserted this and did not discuss his reasoning. He then went on to claim on the basis of no evidence that "David made a living telling in sundry taverns the tale of his incredible journey—a profitable sort of pub-crawling." All of this was to set up passages ridiculing Ingram's testimony Morison (1971: 467, 489). According to Ogburn, William Sturtevant echoed this by saying that Ingram had "been cadging food and drink with his story for years the wonders growing with every telling." Ogburn 1979.

16. The following Ingram quotes can all be found in Appendix entry 41.

17. However, it is also foremost among the things that Morison and several other historians have ridiculed. It only appears ridiculous if one begins with the assumption that Ingram is trying to describe a moose, a mistake in which so many have followed Morison. The fragments Morison patched together are in fact Ingram's separate descriptions of a walrus, Newfoundland sheep, and an African buffalo, accompanied by a baseless assertion Morison found in two manuscripts that the animal chased Ingram up a tree. Morison 1971: 467–468, 489; Sylvester 1909.

18. Ganong and Layng 1964: 171.

19. Hayes 1589: 689.

20. Alternatively, it is possible to hypothesize that Ingram might have seen muskoxen (*Ovibos moschatus*) and mistook them for large sheep. However, muskoxen live in the high Arctic far beyond any English exploration up to this point in time.

21. This is a weather phenomenon in which luminous plasma is created by a corona discharge—in this case, from a ship's mast.

22. The distance from St. John's, New foundland, to the Lizard Point is 3,223 miles (5,186 km). That converts to 2,800 nautical miles. The *Gargarine* thus averaged 140 nautical miles per day for an average speed of nearly six knots. Fair winds and the Gulf Stream made this possible.

23. Hawkins published a report of the voyage in 1569, which Hakluyt 20 years later reprinted with only minor edits in his *Principall Navigations*. Hawkins 1569.

CHAPTER 10

1. Kelsey 2003: 117–138.

2. Kelsey (2003) provides an excellent source for these and other details of the life of Hawkins.

3. Hawkins 1589: 556.

4. Crouch 1692: 7.

5. Sugden 1990: 45–53.

6. Hakluyt 1589b.

7. The expression "beyond the pale" is still used in modern English.

8. Sugden 1990: 80–88.

9. Best et al. 1938.

10. Banfield 1974: 307, 312; Kintisch 2016; Star et al. 2018.

11. Best et al. 1938: 97.

12. Best et al. 1938: 58.

13. Best et al. 1938: 62.

14. The *Aid* made landfall in Wales on September 23. Kalicho died and was buried on November 8. Amaq attended the funeral stoically, then she too died suddenly of measles and was buried four days later. The baby Nutaaq was taken to London in a nurse's care but the child soon also died probably of measles. Best et al. 1938: 235.

15. Sturtevant 1976: 440–441.

16. Vaughn 2006: 3–10.

17. Lok 1578.

18. Best et al. 1938: 220–222.

19. Taylor 1930: 149; Cooke 1854; Cliffe 1854; Drake 1854.

20. Cliffe 1854: 279.

21. Drake 1628; Drake 1854: 72.

22. Taylor 1930: 140, 149.

23. Cliffe 1854: 277.

24. Cliffe 1854: 282.

25. Gallay 2019: 63–65.

26. Quinn 1967 (1): 3–49; Gallay 2019.

CHAPTER 11

1. Appendix entry 22.

2. The *Golden Hind* lived on as a floating museum piece until 1650, by which time its deterioration would lead to its demolition.

3. Hakluyt 1589a; Parry 2011.

4. Hakluyt 1582.

5. Dunham Jr. 1938: 322; Hakluyt 1877; Marsh 1962; Quinn 1979a.

6. Hakluyt 1877: 128, 61. English modernized.

7. At this time there was a colony of English merchants at Rouen, France. Etienne Bellenger sailed from there to the Gulf of Maine in early 1583, but there is nothing to suggest that Ingram was with him (Marsh 1962; Quinn 1962).

8. Cooper 2011.

9. Hakluyt 1589a.

10. Simon Fernandes might have made his own brief trip to the Maine coast in 1579 for Francis Walsingham. If he did, it was a voyage of prodigious seamanship on the little frigate *Squirrel*. However, the evidence for this is scanty—not

enough to justify the belief of some historians that he penetrated up the Penobscot all the way to the site of modern Bangor (Morris 1976: Plate 2; Quinn 1967 [1]: 239–240, 282, 309).

11. Quinn 1967 (1): 52. Appendix entry 2.

12. Quinn 1967 (2): 309–310.

13. Quinn 1967 (1): 71–72, 199.

14. Quinn 1967 (2): 245–278.

15. Quinn 1967 (1): 52, 64–66, 81–186.

16. At the time, the English still used the Julian calendar, and the beginning of the year was set to March 25. In England it was not changed to January 1 until 1752. To avoid confusion, historians often cite dates between these dates with both years, as in the case of February 1, 1591/1592. February here is treated as a month in early 1582 (Phillips 1589: 574, 76–580).

17. Nothing is known of the fates of those men (Phillips 1589: 568; Quinn 1967 [1]: 66; Arianrhod 2019).

18. Quinn 1967 (1): 71–72, 99; (2): 239–242.

19. Peckham 1583.

20. For example, two centuries later colonial English politicians would fabricate a vast Iroquois empire in eastern North America so they could use their allies, the nations of the Iroquois Confederacy, as proxies in claiming it (Colden 1958; Jennings 1984).

21. Williams 1979: 31–36.

22. Appendix entry 30.

23. Quinn 1967 (2): 459; Williams 1979: 43. Appendix entry 39.

24. Montevecchi 1994.

25. Modern lexicographers attribute the origin of "penguin" to Drake's report of his circumnavigation, Ingram's 1582 interrogation, and the events surrounding them (Williams 1949: 282–283; Drake 1628; Drake 1854; Peckham 1583; Barnhart 1995: 552).

26. Appendix entry 39.

27. The real and presumed American exploits of both Welsh and Norse explorers led to sea-voyage reenactments in the twentieth century. Fake claims of archaeological evidence, more pseudo-linguistics, and other popular enthusiasms were also deployed. However, nothing substantive apart from the Norse outpost discovered in northernmost Newfoundland has turned up.

28. Peckham 1583: 459–460, English modernized. Muñoz Camargo 1981: 257 recto.

29. Cortés 1967: 42.

30. Cortés 1962: 70.

31. Peckham, unlike Walter Ralegh, also did not mind preferring conquest over accommodation. Peckham distinguished between "savages" and "cannibals," the former being redeemable but the latter not deserving of consideration. This plus the Elizabethan fascination with cannibalism explains why Ingram had been questioned so closely about evidence for it. They believed that

American colonization could be built on recruitment of the indigenous savages and the extermination of indigenous cannibals (Gallay 2019: 72).

32. Clement is described as a "seamaster," but he was not the master of any of the five ships that made up the fleet Gilbert would take to Newfoundland the following June. He might have been the Joseph Clements who made a voyage to Constantinople in 1575.

33. Peckham 1583: 452; Quinn 1967 (2): 313.

34. Gallay 2019: 56.

35. Quinn 1967 (1): 83–90; Gallay 2019: 63–65.

36. Peckham 1583: 452.

37. Gallay 2019: 26.

38. The spelling of "Ralegh" is what he used in later life and which is now current among historians (Gallay 2019: 1–8).

39. Arianrhod 2019: 8.

40. Gallay 2019: 75.

41. Oberg 2020.

42. John Hart had previously worked on phonetically rendering English dialects as well as Irish and Welsh, but it is not known whether Harriot was aware of Hart's work (Arianrhod 2019: 58–59; Harriot 1972).

43. Arianrhod 2019: 70.

44. Gallay 2019: 134–142.

45. No drawings or records concerning the original Elizabeth survive.

46. Cavendish made his own reputation later in 1586–1588 duplicating Francis Drake's circumnavigation of the world. For that long journey Cavendish would sail from Plymouth in a brand-new flagship and two other ships. It is very unlikely that Ingram went with him.

47. A replica of one of the seven ships, the Elizabeth, can be visited at Roanoke Island Festival Park. Arianrhod 2019: 71–78.

48. Quinn 1955 (1): 260, 333–334.

49. White's surviving watercolors have been published in a definitive two-volume set. William Sturtevant provided separately a critical description of the ethnographic details they illustrate. Hulton and Beers 1964; Sturtevant 1965.

50. Sturtevant 1976: 443.

51. There is some evidence that White had been on the previous 1584 voyage as well, but that is uncertain.

52. Hulton and Beers 1979: 199.

53. Hulton and Beers 1979: 197.

54. There had been an eclipse visible in North America on April 29, the only one visible there between 1584 and 1587, but it tracked so far north that it probably would have gone unnoticed on Roanoke Island. Harriot 1972: 2, 9 NASA 2019.

55. Klinkenborg 1996: f 90, 64–265; Sturtevant 1976: 443.

56. Gallay 2019: 33.

57. Quinn 1955 (1): 293, 333–334.
58. Arianrhod 2019: 90–92; Sugden 1990: 198.
59. de Bry 1591; Harriot 1972; Gallay 2019: 171.
60. Kelsey 2003: 173–182.
61. Sugden 1990: 203–217.
62. Remember that the English were still using the "Old Style" Julian calendar.
63. Sugden 1990: 28; Laughton 1895: 324–342.
64. Charles Howard was Baron Howard of Effingham who led the English fleet against the Spanish Armada as Lord High Admiral of England Lord Howard of Effingham. He later became the 1st Earl of Nottingham. He is referred to in this book as "Howard."
65. Sugden 1990: 208.
66. The modern Gregorian calendar was introduced in 1582, but Protestant countries continued to use the old Julian calendar. Consequently, the dates recorded by English and Spanish sources differ by 11 days. England would not adopt the Gregorian calendar until 1752.
67. Lawler 2018.
68. White 1906: 294.
69. Malakoff 2020.
70. Gallay 2019: 219.
71. Arianrhod 2019: 116.
72. Harriot 1972.
73. Arianrhod 2019.
74. Hulton and Beers 1979: 213n.
75. Andrews et al. 1979: 198; Hulton and Beers 1979: 198, 01; Sturtevant 1976: 418, 43; Quinn 1955 (1): 390–464.

CHAPTER 12

1. Hakluyt 1589a.
2. "*Mestizo*" identifies a person of mixed European and indigenous American ancestry. Mexicans typically regard themselves as *mestizos*, a self-identification that intends no negative connotations.
3. Snow and Lanphear 1988; Snow 1995a.
4. Trigger 1978.
5. Snow 2001.
6. Hakluyt 1589a: 562.
7. Appendix entry 18.
8. Bromber 2001.
9. Feder 2017; Fritze 1993: 183–188.
10. Quinn 1979b.

Appendix

1. For reasons unknown, Hakluyt decided to shorten this by leaving out every-thing following the words "Cape Breton" in the final published version. Hakluyt's words represent everything Ingram said in his testimony as refer-ring to what he saw and experienced in his nearly year-long walk in North America. It was a false characterization. None of the information from Africa or the Caribbean that Ingram mentioned in his testimony should have been part of what followed this introduction. The information in brackets corrects Hakluyt's erroneous characterization. The parenthetical insertion is original in the Tanner manuscript.

2. Other evidence shows that three months was incorrect. Either this was Ingram's estimate of the time he spent in Africa, or the recorder mistook a 7 for a 3.

3. The parenthetical A1-7 indicates that the source for this section of text can be found as the first seven entries in the manuscript transcript reproduced in Appendix A (Anonymous, 1582 #4854) on the Companion Website. All entries in the new transcript are linked to this and transcripts of the other two primary source manuscripts, Appendices B and C .

4. It is possible that Ingram witnessed the kissing of hands both in Africa and in the American Southeast, for de Soto reported something similar there earlier in the century. Because of Hakluyt's muddling, we cannot be entirely sure.

5. The order of the first 18 entries in the State Papers Colonial (B) manuscript (*Reports of the country Sir Humphrey Gilbert goes to discover*) is retained to this point. From this point on, scrambling by the recorders and editor(s) compel extensive rearranging to put topics in their correct chronological order.

6. This is an aromatic ball, from the French *pomb d'ambre*. The identity of this substance is uncertain.

7. In the sixteenth century, "bastard" was used to refer to second-rate Spanish sack wines.

8. The State Papers Colonial manuscript is the better source on this because, unlike the corresponding Tanner entry, it does not conflate information pertaining to the Caribbean with information that could pertain to North America. This conflation was consistent with Hakluyt's mistaken belief that everything Ingram said had to do with North America.

9. The false reference to louvers in this entry resulted from the confusion of the recorder of the State Papers Domestic manuscript (A5.1).

10. Only two brief entries in the State Papers Colonial manuscript and four in the Tanner manuscript cannot be assigned to specific regions through which Ingram traveled: Africa, the Caribbean, North America, or to places on the return voyage. In these cases, his testimony could have referred to almost any-where. For example, monkeys are found in both Africa and South America. Although the South American species have prehensile tails and the African species do not, Ingram does not say anything about this detail.

11. Ingram also made a negative remark about the treatment of women by men, but this too could apply to anywhere or to nowhere.
12. Hakluyt clustered three entries regarding music and dancing. These too could pertain to any of the three main regions Ingram mentioned in his testimony.
13. Ingram mentioned several trees, which can be identified well enough to identify and assign in several preceding chapters. However, this single entry in the State Papers Colonial manuscript remains so vague that it cannot be assigned.

Sources

Adair, James

    1775   *History of the American Indians*. Edward and Charles Dilly, London.

Adams, Percy C.

    1962   *Travelers and Travel Liars 1660–1800*. University of California Press, Berkeley.

Akpan, Otoabasi

    2013   *Introduction to the Modern Gulf of Guinea: People, History, Political Economy and Strategic Future*. Adonis and Abbey, London.

Alfonce, Jean

    1904   *La Cosmographie avec L'Espère et Régime du Soleil et du Nord*. Ernest Leroux, Paris.

Andrews, K. R., N. P. Canny, and P. E. H. Hair

    1979   *The Westward Enterprise*. Wayne State University Press, Detroit.

Anonymous

    1582a David Ingram's Record of a Voyage to Mexico and Nova Scotia. Vol. MSS Sloane. British Library.

    1582b Examination of David Ingram. In *State Papers Domestic, SP12/575*. National Archives of the United Kingdom, Quinn 1967: 281–283.

    1582c Relation of David Ingram, Tanner MS. Oxford University.

    1582d Reports of the country Sir Humphrey Gilbert goes to discover. In *State Papers Colonial*. British Library, Quinn 1967: 296–310.

    1582e Sondrie Reportes of the contrie which Sir Humfrie Gilberte goeth to discover. In *Papers of Robert Beale*, MS 48151. British Library.

Arianrhod, Robyn

    2019   *Thomas Harriot: A Life in Science*. Oxford University Press, New York.

Austin, Daniel F.

    2004   *Florida Ethnobotany*. CRC Press, Boca Raton.

Axtell, James

    1994   The Exploration of Norumbega: Native Perspectives. In *American Beginnings: Exploration, Culture, and Cartography in the Land of Norumbega*, edited by E. W. Baker, E. A. Churchill, R. D'Abate, K. L. Jones, V. A. Konrad, and H. Prins, pp. 149–165. University of Nebraska Press, Lincoln.

Bakker, P.

    1990   A Basque Etymology for the Word "Iroquois." *Man in the Northeast* 40: 89–93.

Banfield, A. W. F.

    1974   *The Mammals of Canada*. University of Toronto Press, Toronto.

Bargatzky, Thomas

   1980   Aspects of Aboriginal Trade and Communication between Northeast
          Mexico and Southwest Texas in the 16th Century. *Anthropos* 75 (3/4):
          447–464.

Barnhart, Robert K. (editor)

   1995   *The Barnhart Concise Dictionary of Etymology.* HarperCollins, New York.

Barrett, Robert

   1928   Robert Barrett, deposition, Jalapa, October 8, 1568. In *Spanish Documents
          Concerning English Voyages to the Caribbean, 1527–1568,* edited by I. A.
          Wright, pp. 153–160. Hakluyt Society, London.

Beazley, Charles Raymond

   1903   The Third Hawkins Voyage: First Narrative by a Survivor. In *Voyages
          and Travels Mainly During the 16th and 17th Centuries,* edited by Thomas
          Seccombe. Archibald Constable and Co.

Beck, Robin A., David G. Moore, Christopher B. Rodning, Timothy J. Horley, and
   Sarah C. Sherwood

   2018   A Road to Zacatecas: Fort San Juan and the Defenses of Spanish La
          Florida. *American Antiquity* 83 (4): 577–597.

Best, George, Vilhjalmur Stefansson, Wilberforce Eames, and Eloise McCaskill

   1938   *The Three Voyages of Martin Frobisher.* Argonaut Press, London.

Binford, Lewis R.

   1967   An Ethnohistory of the Nottoway, Meherrin and Weanock Indians of
          Southeastern Virginia. *Ethnohistory* 14 (3–4): 103–218.

Bloom, Paul and Deena Skolnick Weisberg

   2007   Childhood Origins of Adult Resistance to Science. *Science* 316: 996–997.

Bourque, Bruce J. and Ruth H. Whitehead

   1994   Trade and Alliances in the Contact Period. In *American Beginnings:
          Exploration, Culture, and Cartography in the Land of Norumbega,* edited by
          E. W. Baker, E. A. Churchill, R. D'Abate, K. L. Jones, V. A. Konrad, and H.
          Prins, pp. 131–147. University of Nebraska Press, Lincoln.

Boyce, Douglas W.

   1978   Iroquoian Tribes of the Virginia–North Carolina Coastal Plain. In
          Northeast, edited by B. G. Trigger, pp. 282–289. Handbook of North
          American Indians. Vol. 15, W. C. Sturtevant, general editor. Smithsonian
          Institution, Washington.

Bradford, William

   1908   *Bradford's History of Plymouth Plantation: 1606–1646.* Barnes and Noble,
          New York.

Bradley, James W.

   1987   *Evolution of the Onondaga Iroquois: Accommodating Change, 1500–1655.*
          Syracuse University Press, Syracuse.

Bromber, Robert

   2001   The Liar and the Bard: David Ingram, William Shakespeare and The
          Tempest. *Sociedad Española de Estudios Renacentistas Ingleses* 12: 123–133.

Brown, Marley
  2020   The First Enslaved Africans in Mexico. *Archaeology* 74 (1): 28.
Burrage, Henry S.
  1914   *The Beginnigs of Colonial Maine: 1602–1658.* State of Maine, Augusta.
Caldwell, D. W.
  1998   *Roadside Geology of Maine.* Mountain Press, Missoula.
Casas, Bartolomé de las
  1992   *A Short Account of the Destruction of the Indies.* Translated by N. Griffin.
          Penguin Books, New York.
Ceci, Lynn
  1975   Fish Fertilizer: A Native North American Practice? *Science* 188: 26–30.
Champlain, Samuel de
  1907   *Voyages of Samuel de Champlain 1604–1618.* Original Narratives of Early
          American History. Charles Scribner's Sons, New York.
Chipman, Donald E.
  1987   In Search of Cabeza de Vaca's Route across Texas: An Historiographical
          Survey. *Southwestern Historical Quarterly* 91 (2): 127–148.
Cliffe, Edward
  1854   The Voyage of M. John Winter into the South sea by the Streight of
          Magellan, in consort with M. Francis Drake, begun in the yeere 1577. In
          The World Encompassed by Sir Francis Drake, edited by W. S. W. Vaux, pp.
          269–284. Hakluyt Society, London.
Cline, W. W.
  1937   *Mining and Metallurgy in Negro Africa.* George Banta, Menasha.
Colden, Cadwallader
  1958   *The History of the Five Indian Nations Depending on the Province of New-York
          in America.* Cornell University Press, Ithaca.
Collingham, I.
  2007   *Curry: A Tale of Cooks and Conquerors.* Oxford University Press, Oxford.
Cooke, John
  1854   Narrative of John Cooke, Entituled "For Francis Drake." In *The World
          Encompassed by Sir Francis Drake*, edited by W. S. W. Vaux, pp. 187–218.
          Hakluyt Society, London.
Cooper, John
  2011   *The Queen's Agent: Sir Francis Walsingham and the Rise of Espionage in
          Elizabethan England.* Pegasus Books, New York.
Cortés, Hernando
  1962   *5 Letters of Cortés to the Emperor.* Translated by J. B. Morris. W. W. Norton,
          New York.
  1967   *Cartas de Relación.* Editorial Porrúa, Mexico City.
Covey, Cyclone
  1961   *Cabeza de Vaca's Adventures in the Unknown Interior of America.* University of
          New Mexico Press, Albuquerque.

Crouch, Nathaniel

    1692   *The English Hero, or Sir Francis Drake Revived.* Wogan, Bean, and Pike, Dublin.

D'Abate, Richard

    1994   On the Meaning of a Name: "Norumbega" and the Representation of North America. In *American Beginnings: Exploration, Culture, and Cartography in the Land of Norumbega*, edited by E. W. Baker, E. A. Churchill, R. D'Abate, K. L. Jones, V. A. Konrad, and H. Prins, pp. 61–88. University of Nebraska Press, Lincoln.

Darwin, Charles

    1871   *The Descent of Man, and Selection in Relation to Sex.* J. Murray, London.

Davis, Jack E.

    2017   *The Gulf: The Making of an American Sea.* Liveright, New York.

Davis Jr., R. P. Stephen, Patrick Livingood, H. Trawick Ward, and Vincas Steponaitis

    1998   *Excavating Occaneechi Town.* University of North Carolina Press, Chapel Hill.

Davis, T. Frederick

    1935   History of Juan Ponce de Leon's Voyages to Florida. *Florida Historical Society Quarterly* 14 (1).

Dawson, Giles E. and Laetitia Kennedy-Skipton

    1966   *Elizabethan Handwriting 1500–1650: A Manual.* W. W. Norton, New York.

de Bry, Theodor

    1591   *America: Brevis narratio eorum quae in Florida Americae provi[n]cia Gallis acciderunt, secunda in illam navigatione, duce Renato de Laudo[n]iere classis praefecto, Anno 1564, Volume 2.* Wechel, Frankfurt.

de Conte, Paul and Ronald Dupont Jr.

    2009   *Hiking New Jersey: A Guide to 50 of the Garden State's Greatest Hiking Trails.* Globe Pequot Press, Guilford.

DeCosta, B. F.

    1883a   Ingram's Journey through North America 1567–69. *Magazine of American History* 9 (1): 168–176.

    1883b   The Relation of David Ingram. *Magazine of American History* 9 (1): 200–208.

DeGolyer, Everette

    1947   Across Aboriginal America. The Journey of Three Englishmen across Texas. *Southwest Review* 26 (2): 167–187.

DeMallie, Raymond J.

    2004   Tutelo and Neighboring Groups. In *Southeast*, edited by R. Fogelson, pp. 286–300. Handbook of North American Indians. Vol. 14, W. C. Sturtevant, general editor. Smithsonian Institution, Washington.

Drake, Francis

    1628   *The World Encompassed.* Nicholas Bourne, London.

    1854   The Voyage about the World. In *The World Encompassed by Sir Francis Drake*, edited by W. S. W. Vaux, pp. 11–162. Hakluyt Society, London.

Driver, Harold E. and William C. Massey

1957   Comparative Studies of North American Indians. *Transactions of the American Philosophical Society*, New Series 47 (2). American Philosophical Society, Philadelphia.

Durant, Will

1957   *The Reformation. The Story of Civilization*. Simon and Schuster, New York.

Eckstorm, Fannie Hardy

1941   *Indian Place-Names of the Penobscot Valley and the Maine Coast*. University Press, Orono.

1945   *Old John Neptune and Other Maine Indian Shamans*. Southworth-Anthoensen Press, Portland.

Elliott Jr., Jack D.

1997   Of Roads and Reifications: The Interpretation of Historical Roads and the Soto Entrada. In *The Hernando De Soto Expedition: History, Historiography, and "Discovery" in the Southeast*, edited by P. Galloway, pp. 246–258. University of Nebraska Press, Lincoln.

Emerson, Thomas E., Kristin M. Hedman, Eve A. Hargrave, Dawn E. Cobb, and Andrew R. Thompson

2016   Paradigms Lost: Configuring Cahokia's Mound 72 Beaded Burial. *American Antiquity* 81 (3): 405–425.

Erickson, Vincent O.

1978   Maliseet-Passamaquoddy. In *Northeast*, edited by B. G. Trigger, pp. 123–136. Handbook of North American Indians. Vol. 15, W. C. Sturtevant, general editor. Smithsonian Institution, Washington.

Ewen, Charles R. and John H. Hann

1998   *Hernando De Soto among the Apalachee: The Archaeology of the First Winter Encampment*. University Press of Florida, Gainesville.

Feder, Kenneth L.

2017   *Frauds, Myths, and Mysteries: Science and Pseudoscience in Archaeology*. Oxford University Press, New York.

Feest, Christian F.

1978a   Nanticoke and Neighboring Tribes. In *Northeast*, edited by B. G. Trigger, pp. 240–252. Handbook of North American Indians. Vol. 15, W. C. Sturtevant, general editor. 20 vols. Smithsonian Institution Press, Washington.

1978b   North Carolina Algonquians. In *Northeast*, edited by B. G. Trigger, pp. 271–281. Handbook of North American Indians. Vol. 15, W. C. Sturtevant, general editor. 20 vols. Smithsonian Institution Press, Washington.

1978c   Virginia Algonquians. In *Northeast*, edited by B. G. Trigger, pp. 253–270. Handbook of North American Indians. Vol. 15, W. C. Sturtevant, general editor. 20 vols. Smithsonian Institution Press, Washington.

Fenton, William N.

1987   *The False Faces of the Iroquois*. University of Oklahoma Press, Norman.

Fenton, William N. and Elisabeth Tooker

    1978   Mohawk. In *Northeast,* edited by B. G. Trigger, pp. 466–480. Handbook of North American Indians, Vol. 15, W. C. Sturtevant, general editor. 20 vols. Smithsonian Institution Press, Washington.

Foster, Michael K.

    1996   Language and the Culture History of North America. In *Languages,* edited by I. Goddard, pp. 64–110. Handbook of North American Indians, Vol. 17, W. C. Sturtevant, general editor. 20 vols. Smithsonian Institution, Washington.

Fritze, Ronald H.

    1993   *Legend and Lore of the Americas before 1492.* ABC-CLIO, Santa Barbara.

Fyfe, Christopher

    1962   *A History of Sierra Leone.* Oxford University Press, Oxford.

Gallay, Alan

    2019   *Walter Ralegh.* Basic Books, New York.

Ganong, William Francis and Theodore E. Layng

    1964   *Crucial Maps in the Early Cartography and Place-Nomenclature of the Atlantic Coast of Canada.* University of Toronto Press, Toronto.

Gibbs, James L.

    1988   *Peoples of Africa.* Waveland, Prospect Heights.

Goddard, Ives (editor)

    1996   *Languages.* Handbook of North American Indians, Vol. 17, W. C. Sturtevant, general editor. Smithsonian Institution, Washington.

Goins, Charles Robert and John Michael Caldwell

    1986   *Historical Atlas of Louisiana.* University of Oklahoma Press, Norman.

Grant, W. L. (editor)

    1907   *Voyages of Samuel de Champlain.* Scribner's Sons, New York.

Griswold, Hayden L.

    1930   Map of the State of Connecticut Showing Indian Trails, Villages, and Sachemdoms. Connecticut Society of the Colonial Dames of America, Wethersfield.

Grumet, Robert Steven

    1995   *Historic Contact: Indian People and Colonists in Today's Northeastern United States in the Sixteenth through Eighteenth Centuries.* University of Oklahoma Press, Norman.

Grunwald, Michael

    2006   *The Swamp.* Simon and Schuster, New York.

Hakluyt, Richard

    1582   *Divers Voyages touching the Discoverie of America, and the ilands adjacent unto the same.* T. Dawson for T. Woodcocke, London.

    1584   *A Discourse Concerning Western Planting.* John Wilson and Son, Cambridge.

    1589a The Relation of David Ingram of Barking. In *The Principall Navigations, Voiages and Discoveries of the English Nation,* edited by R. Hakluyt, pp. 557–562. George Bishop and Ralph Newberie, London.

1589b   The voyage of John Oxnam of Plymmouth. In *The Principall Navigations, Voiages and Discoveries of the English Nation*, edited by R. Hakluyt, pp. 595–596. George Bishop and Ralph Newberie, London.

1877   *Discourse on Western Planting, Written in the Year 1584*. Documentary History of the State of Maine, Vol. 2. Maine Historical Society, Portland.

Hallenbeck, Cleve

1940   *Alvar Nuñez Cabeza de Vaca: The Journey and Route of the First European to Cross the Continent of North America 1534–1536*. Arthur H. Clark Co., Glendale.

Harriot, Thomas

1972   *A Briefe and True Report of the New Found Land of Virginia*. Dover, New York.

Hawkins, John

1569   *A true declaration of the troublesome voyadge of M. John Hawkins to the parties of Guynea and the West Indies: in the years of our Lord 1567 and 1568*. Thomas Purfoote for Lucas Harrison, London.

1589   The 3rd vnfortunate voyage made with the Iesus, the Minion, and foure other shippes. In *The Principall Navigations, Voiages and Discoveries of the English Nation*, edited by R. Hakluyt, pp 553–557. George Bishop and Ralph Newberie, London.

Hayes, Edward

1589   A briefe relation of the Newfoundland and commodieties thereof. In *The Principall Navigations, Voiages and Discoveries of the English Nation*, edited by R. Hakluyt, pp. 688–691. George Bishop and Ralph Newberie, London.

Hazlewood, Nick

2004   *The Queen's Slave Trader*. HarperCollins, New York.

Heath, Dwight B.

1963   *A Journal of the Pilgrims at Plymouth: Mourt's Relation*. Corinth Books, New York.

Henige, David P.

1998   *Numbers from Nowhere: The American Indian Contact Population Debate*. University of Oklahoma Press, Norman.

Herrera, Antonio de

1945   *Historia General de los Hechos de los Castellanos, en las Islas, y Tierra-Firme de el Mar Océano*. 10 vols. Editorial Guarania, Buenos Aires.

Hogue, Charles Leonard

1993   *Latin American Insects and Entomology*. University of California Press, Berkeley.

Honour, Hugh

1975   *The New Golden Land: European Images of America from the Discoveries to the Present Time*. Pantheon Books, New York.

Hornsby, Stephen J. and Richard W. Judd (editors)

2015   *Historical Atlas of Maine*. University of Maine Press, Orono.

Hortop, Job

1591   *The rare trauailes of Iob Hortop*. William Wright, London.

Hudson, Charles
  1976   *The Southeastern Indians.* University of Tennessee Press, Knoxville.
  1997   *Knights of Spain, Warriors of the Sun: Hernando de Soto and the South's Ancient Chiefdoms.* University of Georgia Press, Athens.
Hudson, Charles, Marvin T. Smith, and Chester B. DePratter
  1984   The Hernando de Soto Expedition from Apalachee to Chiaha. *Southeastern Archaeology* 3 (1): 65–77.
Hulton, Paul (editor)
  1977   *The Work of Jacques Le Moyne de Morgues.* 2 vols. British Museum Publications, London.
  1979   Images of the New World: Jacques Le Moyne de Morgues and John White. In *The Westward Enterprise*, edited by K. R. Andrews, N. P. Canny, and P. E. H. Hair, pp. 195–214. Wayne State University Press, Detroit.
Hulton, Paul and David Beers
  1964   *The American Drawings of John White, 1577–1590, with Drawings of European and Oriental Subjects.* 2 vols. University of North Carolina Press, Chapel Hill.
Isaacson, Walter
  2017   *Leonardo da Vinci.* Simon and Schuster, New York.
Jennings, Francis
  1984   *The Ambiguous Iroquois Empire: The Covenant Chain Confederation of Indian Tribes with English Colonies from Its Beginning to the Lancaster Treaty of 1744.* W. W. Norton, New York.
Jones, David E.
  2007   *Poison Arrows: North American Indian Hunting and Warfare.* University of Texas Press, Austin.
Jones, E., M. Krause, C. Watson, and G. O'Saile
  2020   Economic and Social Interactions in the Piedmont Village Tradition— Mississippian Boundarylands of Southeastern North America, AD 1200– 1600. *American Antiquity* 85 (1): 72–92.
Kelly, Eric P.
  1949   *The Amazing Journey of David Ingram.* Lippincott, New York.
Kelsey, Harry
  2003   *Sir John Hawkins.* Yale University Press, New Haven.
Kent, Barry C.
  1984   *Susquehanna's Indians.* Pennsylvania Historical and Museum Commission, Harrisburg.
Kintisch, Eli
  2016   The Lost Norse. *Science* 354 (6313): 696–701.
Klinkenborg, Verlyn (editor)
  1996   *The Drake Manuscript.* André Deutsch Limited, London.
Kniffen, Fred B., Hiram F. Gregory, and George A. Stokes
  1987   *The Historic Indian Tribes of Louisiana.* Louisiana State University Press, Baton Rouge.

Kruger, Justin and David Dunning
  1999   Unskilled and Unaware of It: How Difficulties in Recognizing One's Own
          Incompetence Lead to Inflated Self-Assessments. *Journal of Personality and
          Social Psychology* 77 (6): 1121–1134.

Krusche, Rolf
  1986   The Origin of the Mask Concept in the Eastern Woodlands of North
          America. *Man in the Northeast* 31: 1–47.

Laudonnière, René Goulaine de
  1964   *A Notable History Containing Four Voyages Made by Certain French
          Captains unto Florida*. Henry Stevens, Son & Stiles, Larchmont.
  1975   Three Voyages. In *Three Voyages*, edited by C. E. Bennett and J. T. Milanich.
          University Press of Florida, Gainesville.

Laughlin, Robert M.
  1969   The Huastec. In *Ethnology: Part One*, edited by E. Z. Vogt, pp. 298–311.
          Handbook of Middle American Indians. Vol. 7, R. Wauchope, general
          editor. 16 vols. University of Texas Press, Austin.

Laughton, John Knox
  1895   *State Papers Relating to the Defeat of the Spanish Armada* 2. Naval Records
          Society, London.

Lawler, Andrew
  2018   *The Secret Token: Myth, Obsession and the Search for the Lost Colony of
          Roanoke*. Doubleday, New York.

Lewis, C. M. and A. J. Loomie
  1953   *The Spanish Jesuit Mission in Virginia, 1570–1572*. University of North
          Carolina Press, Chapel Hill.

Lewis, Michael
  1937   Fresh Light on San Juan de Ulua. *Mariner's Mirror* 23 (3): 295–315.

Lok, Michael
  1578   Accounts, with subsidiary documents, of Michael Lok, treasurer of the
          first, second and third voyages of Martin Frobisher to Cathay by the
          North-West passage. In *Exchequer: King's Remembrancer: Miscellaneous
          Books, Series I*. Records of accounts pertaining to the Martin Frobisher
          expeditions. ed. Vol. E 164/35. The National Archive, London.

Luther, Martin
  2009   *D. Martin Luthers Werke: kritische Gesammtausgabe*. Werke 15, Predigten und
          Schriften 1524. Heidelberger Akademie der Wissenschaften, Heidelberg,

Major, R. H. (editor)
  2010   *Select Letters of Christopher Columbus, with Other Original Documents, Relating
          to His Four Voyages to the New World*. Vol. 63. Hakluyt Society, London.

Malakoff, David
  2020   New Evidence of the Lost Colony. *American Archaeology* 24 (4): 11.

Marsh, T. N.
  1962   An Unpublished Hakluyt Manuscript? *New England Quarterly* 35: 247–252.

McKnight, Matthew D.
  2007 The Copper Cache in Early and Middle Woodland North America. Doctoral dissertation, Anthropology, Pennsylvania State University.
Mercado Ruvalcaba, Jesús (editor)
  2005 *The Huastec Maya*. University of Arizona Press, Tucson.
Michelson, Gunther
  1973 *A Thousand Words of Mohawk*. National Museum of Man, Ethnology Division, Mercury Series 5. National Museum of Man, Ottawa.
Milanich, Jerald T.
  1996 *The Timucua*. Blackwell, Cambridge.
  2004 Timucua. In *Southeast*, edited by R. Fogelson, pp. 219–228. Vol. 14. W. C. Sturtevant, general editor. Smithsonian Institution, Washington.
Milanich, Jerald T., Ann S. Cordell, Vernon J. Knight, Jr., Timothy A. Kohler, and Brenda J. Sigler-Lavelle
  1997 *McKeithen Weeden Island: The Culture of Northern Florida, A.D. 200–900*. University of Florida Press, Gainesville.
Milanich, Jerald T. and Charles Hudson
  1993 *Hernando de Soto and the Indians of Florida*. University Press of Florida, Gainesville.
Milanich, Jerald T. and Susan Milbrath (editors)
  1989 *First Encounters: Spanish Explorations in the Caribbean and the United States, 1492–1570*. University of Florida Press, Gainesville.
Milner, George R.
  2004 *The Moundbuilders: Ancient Peoples of Eastern North America*. Thames and Hudson, New York.
Mithun, Marianne
  1981 Stalking the Susquehannocks. *International Journal of American Linguistics* 47 (1): 1–26.
Montevecchi, Bill
  1994 The Great Auk Cemetery. *Natural History* (August): 6–8.
Mooney, James
  1910 Population. In *Handbook of American Indians North of Mexico*, edited by F. W. Hodge, pp. 286–287. Bureau of American Ethnology Bulletin. Vol. 30. Smithsonian Institution, Washington.
Morison, Samuel Eliot
  1971 *The European Discovery of America: The Northern Voyages A.D. 500–1600*. Oxford University Press, New York.
Morris, Gerald E. (editor)
  1976 *The Maine Bicentennial Atlas: An Historical Survey*. Maine Historical Society, Portland.
Muñoz Camargo, Diego
  1981 *Descripción de la Ciudad y Provincia de Tlaxcala*. Universidad Nacional Autónoma de México, Mexico, D.F.

Myer, William E.

    1923   The Trail System of the Southeastern United States. Forty-Second Annual
           Report, Plate 15. Bureau of American Ethnology, Washington.

NASA

    2019   Catalog of Solar Eclipses: 1501 to 1600. NASA, Washington.

Nelson, Gil

    2011   *The Trees of Florida: A Reference and Field Guide*. Pineapple Press, Sarasota.

Newcomb Jr., W. W.

    1961   *The Indians of Texas*. University of Texas Press, Austin.

    1983   Karankawa. In *Southwest*, edited by A. Ortiz, pp. 359–367. Handbook
           of North American Indians. Vol. 10, W. C. Sturtevant, general editor.
           Smithsonian Institution, Washington.

Newitt, Malyn

    2010   *The Portuguese in West Africa, 1415–1670*. Cambridge University Press,
           New York.

Oberg, Michael Leroy

    2020   Tribes and Towns: What Historians Still Get Wrong about the Roanoke
           Ventures. *Ethnohistory* 67 (4): 549–602.

Ogburn, Charlton

    1979   The Longest Walk: David Ingram's Amazing Journey. *American Heritage*
           30 (3).

Olson, Donald James S.

    1996   *The Peoples of Africa: An Ethnohistorical Dictionary*. Greenwood, Westport.

Parry, Glyn

    2011   *The Arch-Conjuror of England, John Dee*. Yale University Press, New Haven.

Pawling, Micah A.

    2007   *Wabanaki Homeland and the New State of Maine*. Native Americans of
           the Northeast: Culture, History, and the Contemporary. University of
           Massachusetts Press, Amherst.

Peckham, George

    1583   A true report of the late discoveries. In *The Voyages and Colonising
           Enterprises of Sir Humphrey Gilbert*, edited by D. B. Quinn, pp. 435–480.
           Vol. 2. 2 vols. Hakluyt Society, Reprinted by Kraus Reprint, Wilmington.

Pendergast, James F.

    1991   *The Massawomeck: Raiders and Traders into the Chesapeake Bay in the
           Seventeenth Century*. Transactions of the American Philosophical Society
           81 (2). American Philosophical Society, Philadelphia.

Phillips, Miles

    1589   A discourse written by one Miles Phillips Englishman. In *The Principall
           Navigations, Voiages and Discoveries of the English Nation*, pp. 562–580. Edited
           by R. Hakluyt. George Bishop and Ralph Newberie, London.

Pitts, John F., Nigel Barker, D. Clive Gibbons, and Jeffrey L. Jay

    1993   Manchineel keratoconjunctivitis. *British Journal of Ophthalmology* 77:
           284–288.

Purchas, Samuel
  1625   *Hakluytus Posthumus or Purchas his Pilgrimes*. 4 vols. Henrie Fetherstone, London.
Quinn, David Beers (editor)
  1955   *The Roanoke Voyages, 1584–1590*. Vols. 1 & 2. Hakluyt Society, London.
  1962   The Voyage of Etienne Bellenger to the Maritimes in 1583: A New Document. *Canadian Historical Review* 43 (4): 328–343.
  1967   *The Voyages and Colonising Enterprises of Sir Humphrey Gilbert*. Vols. 1 & 2 bound together. Kraus Reprint Limited, Wilmington.
  1971   *North American Discovery circa 1000–1612*. University of South Carolina Press, Columbia.
  1979a Bellenger, Étienne. In *Dictionary of Canadian Biography*. Vol. 1. University of Toronto/Université Laval, Toronto/Quebec.
  1979b Ingram, David. In *Dictionary of Canadian Biography*. Vol. 1. University of Toronto/Université Laval, Toronto/Quebec.
  1998   The Early Cartography of Maine in the Setting of Early European Exploration of New England and the Maritimes. In *European Approaches to North America, 1450–1640*, edited by D. B. Quinn, pp. 41–67. Ashgate Publishing, Brookfield.
Raber, Paul A. (editor)
  2019   *The Susquehannocks: New Perspectives on Settlement and Cultural Identity*. Pennsylvania State University Press, State College.
Raffaele, Herbert A.
  1989   *A Guide to the Birds of Puerto Rico and the Virgin Islands*. Princeton University Press, Princeton.
Reséndez, Andrés
  2002   *A Land So Strange: The Epic Journey of Cabeza de Vaca*. Basic Books, New York.
Rights, Douglas L.
  1931   The Trading Path to the Indians. *North Carolina Historical Review* 8 (4): 8–24.
Rogers, J. Daniel and George Sabo III
  2004   Caddo. In *Southeast*, edited by R. Fogelson, pp. 616–631. Handbook of North American Indians. Vol. 14, W. C. Sturtevant, general editor. Smithsonian Institution, Washington.
Rudes, Blair A.
  2011   The First Description of an Iroquoian People: Spaniards among the Tuscaroras before 1522. In *Tuscarora Archives*, edited by C. C. I. Center, Coastal Carolina Indian Center, Emerald Isle.
Russell, Howard S.
  1980   *Indian New England before the Mayflower*. University Press of New England, Hanover.
Sagard, Gabriel
  1968   *Sagard's Long Journey to the Country of the Hurons*. Greenwood Press, New York.

Salwen, Bert
  1978   Indians of Southern New England and Long Island: Early Period. In *Northeast*, edited by B. G. Trigger, pp. 160–176. Handbook of North American Indians. Vol. 15, W. C. Sturtevant, general editor. Smithsonian Institution, Washington.

Sanger, David
  2003   Who Lived in Pre-European Maine? A Cosmology Approach to Social Patterning on the Landscape. *Northeast Anthropology* 66: 29–39.

Sanger, Matthew C., Brian D. Padgett, Clark Spencer Larsen, Mark Hill, Gregory D. Lattanzi, Carol E. Colaninno, Brendan J. Culleton, Douglas J. Kennett, Matthew F. Napolitano, Sébastien Lacombe, Robert J. Speakman, and David Hurst Thomas
  2019   Great Lakes Copper and Shared Mortuary Practices on the Atlantic Coast: Implications for Long-Distance Exchange during the Late Archaic. *American Antiquity* 84 (4): 591–609.

Schön, J. F.
  1884   *Vocabulary of the Mende Language*. Society for Promoting Christian Knowledge, London.

Simms, William G.
  2016   *The Life of Captain John Smith*. University of South Carolina Press, Columbia.

Smith, Buckingham (editor)
  1968   *Narratives of de Soto in the Conquest of Florida*. Palmetto Books, Gainesville.

Smith, John
  1910   *Travels and Works of John Smith*. Burt Franklin, New York.

Smith, Michael E.
  2012   *The Aztecs*. 3rd ed. The Peoples of America. Blackwell, Cambridge.

Snow, Dean R.
  1972a   Classic Teotihuacan Influences in North-Central Tlaxcala. In *Teotihuacan, XI Mesa Redonda*, edited by A. R. L. Sociedad Mexicana de Antropologia, Mexico City.
  1972b   Rising Sea Level and Prehistoric Cultural Ecology in Northern New England. *American Antiquity* 37 (2): 211–221.
  1975   The Passadumkeag Sequence. *Arctic Anthropology* 12 (2): 46–59.
  1976a   Abenaki Fur Trade in the Sixteenth Century. *Western Canadian Journal of Anthropology* 6 (1): 3–11.
  1976b   The Ethnohistoric Baseline of the Eastern Abenaki. *Ethnohistory* 23 (3): 291–306.
  1978   Eastern Abenaki. In *Northeast*, edited by B. G. Trigger, pp. 137–147. Handbook of North American Indians. Vol. 15, W. C. Sturtevant, general editor. Smithsonian Institution, Washington.
  1980   *The Archaeology of New England*. New World Archaeological Record. Academic Press, New York.
  1994   *The Iroquois*. The Peoples of America. Blackwell, Cambridge.
  1995a   Microchronology and Demographic Evidence Relating to the Size of Pre-Columbian North American Indian Populations. *Science* 268 (5217): 1601–1604.

1995b *Mohawk Valley Archaeology: The Sites*. Occasional Papers in Anthropology 23. Matson Museum of Anthropology, University Park.

1997 The Architecture of Iroquois Longhouses. *Northeast Anthropology* 53: 61–84.

2001 Setting Demographic Limits, the North American Case. In *Computing Archaeology for Understanding the Past*, edited by Z. Stancic and T. Veljanovski, pp. 259–261. BAR International Series. Vol. 931. British Archaeological Reports, Oxford.

2019 Introduction: Susquehannock Archaeology. In *The Susquehannocks: New Perspectives on Settlement and Cultural Identity*, edited by P. A. Raber, pp. 1–15. Pennsylvania State University Press, University Park.

Snow, Dean R. and Kim M. Lanphear

1988 European Contact and Indian Depopulation in the Northeast: The Timing of the First Epidemics. *Ethnohistory* 35 (1): 15–33.

Snyder, John P.

1973 *The Mapping of New Jersey*. Rutgers University Press, New Brunswick.

Southgate, Paul C. and John S. Lucas (editors)

2008 *The Pearl Oyster*. Elsevier, Oxford.

Speck, Frank G.

1927 *The Nanticoke and Conoy Indians* n. s. 1. Historical Society of Delaware, Wilmington.

1940 *Penobscot Man*. University of Pennsylvania Press, Philadelphia.

Speiss, Arthur E. and B. D. Speiss

1987 New England Pandemic of 1616-1622: Cause and Archaeological Implication. *Man in the Northeast* Vol. 34.

Star, Bastiaan, James H. Barrett, Agata T. Gondek, and Sanne Boessenkool

2018 Ancient DNA Reveals the Chronology of Walrus Ivory Trade from Norse Greenland. In *Proceedings of the Royal Society B: Biological Sciences*. Vol. 285.

Stephens, A. Ray and William M. Holmes

1989 *Historical Atlas of Texas*. University of Oklahoma Press, Norman.

Strack, Elizabeth

2008 Introduction. In *The Pearl Oyster*, edited by P. C. Southgate and J. S. Lucas, pp. 1–35. Elsevier, Oxford.

Sturtevant, William C.

1965 Ethnographic Details in the American Drawings of John White. *Ethnohistory* 12 (1): 54–63.

1975 Two 1761 Wigwams at Niantic, Connecticut. *American Antiquity* 40 (4): 437–444.

1976 Visual Images of Native America. In *First Images of America*, edited by F. Chiappelli, pp. 417–454. Vol. 1. 2 vols. University of California Press, Berkeley.

Sugden, John

1990 *Sir Francis Drake.* Henry Holt, New York.

Sumner, A. T.

1922 *A Hand-book of the Temne Language.* Government Printing Office, Freetown, Sierra Leone.

Swanton, John R.

1928a Aboriginal Culture of the Southeast, pp. 673–726. Bureau of American Ethnology Annual Report, Vol. 42, Washington.

1928b List of Trails. In *Indian Trails of the Southeast*, edited by W. E. Myer, pp. 746–748. *Vol. Annual Report 42.* Bureau of American Ethnology Annual Report, Vol. 42, Washington.

1928c Social Organization and Social Usages of the Indians of the Creek Confederacy, pp. 23–472. Annual Report, Vol. 42. Bureau of American Ethnology Annual Report, Vol. 42, Washington.

1953 *The Indian Tribes of North America.* Bureau of American Ethnology Bulletin 145. Smithsonian Institution, Washington.

Sylvester, Herbert M.

1909 *Maine Coast Romance: The Land of St. Castin.* W. B. Clarke, Boston.

Taylor, E. G. R.

1930 More Light on Drake. *Mariner's Mirror* 16 (2): 134–151.

Thoreau, Henry David

1966 *The Maine Woods.* Thomas Y. Crowell, New York.

Tooker, Elisabeth

1971 Clans and Moieties in North America. *Current Anthropology* 12 (3): 357–376.

Trigger, Bruce G. (editor)

1978 *Northeast.* 15. Smithsonian Institution, Washington.

Turgeon, Laurier

1986 Les Français en Nouvelle-Angleterre avant Champlain. In *Champlain: La naissance de l'Amérique française*, edited by L. Raymonde and D. Vaugeois, pp. 98–112. Septention, Québec.

Ubelaker, Douglas H.

1988 North American Indian Population Size, A.D. 1500 to 1985. *American Journal of Physical Anthropology* 77 (3): 289–294.

Unwin, Rayner

1960 *The Defeat of John Hawkins.* Ballantine Books, New York.

Varner, John Grier and Jeannette Johnson Varner (editors)

1962 *The Florida of the Inca.* University of Texas Press, Austin.

Vaughn, Alden T.

2006 *Transatlantic Encounters: American Indians in Britain, 1500–1776.* Cambridge University Press, New York.

Vega, Garcilaso de la

1956 *La Florida del Inca.* Fondo de Cultura Económica, Mexico City.

Verner, Coolie

1950   The First Maps of Virginia, 1590–1673. *Virginia Magazine of History and Biography* 58 (1): 3–15.

Wallace, Paul A. W.

1952   Historic Indian Paths of Pennsylvania. *Pennsylvania Magazine of History and Biography* 76 (4): 411–439.

Wang, Limei, Birgit Waltenberger, Eva-Maria Pferschy-Wenzig, Martina Blunder, Xin Liu, Clemens Malainer, Tina Blazevic, Stefan Schwaiger, Judith M. Rollinger, Elke H. Heiss, Daniela Schuster, Brigitte Kopp, Rudolf Bauer, Hermann Stuppner, Verena M. Dirsch, and Atanas G. Atanasov

2014   Natural Product Agonists of Peroxisome Proliferator-Activated Receptor Gamma (PPARγ): A Review. *Biochemical Pharmacology* 92 (1): 73–89.

Whalen, Michael E.

2013   Wealth, Status, Ritual, and Marine Shell at Casas Grandes, Chihuahua, Mexico. *American Antiquity* 78 (4): 624–639.

White, John

1906   The Fourth Voyage made to Virginia, in the Yere 1587, by Governor John White. In *Early English and French Voyages, Chiefly from Hakluyt*, edited by H. S. Burrage, pp. 279–300. Barnes and Noble, New York.

Williams, David

1949   John Evans' Strange Journey: Part I. The Welsh Indians. *American Historical Review* 54 (2): 277–295.

Williams, Gwyn A.

1979   *Madoc: The Making of a Myth.* Eyre Methuen, London.

Winship, George Parker

1905   *Sailors Narratives of Voyages along the New England Coast, 1524–1624.* Burt Franklin, New York.

Wood, Peter H.

2018   Missing the Boat: Ancient Dugout Canoes in the Mississippi-Missouri Watershed. *Early American Studies* (Spring): 197–254.

Woodbury, Hanni

2003   *Onondaga-English / English-Onondaga Dictionary.* University of Toronto Press, Toronto.

Worth, John E.

2014   *Discovering Florida: First-Contact Narratives from Spanish Expeditions along the Lower Gulf Coast.* University Press of Florida, Gainesville.

Wroth, Lawrence C.

1970   *The Voyages of Giovanni da Verrazzano 1524–1528.* Yale University Press, New Haven.

Wurtzburg, Susan and Lyle Campbell

1995   North American Indian Sign Language: Evidence of Its Existence before European Contact. *International Journal of American Linguistics* 61 (2): 153–167.

Index

Ship names and foreign terms are Italicized. Proper nouns of foreign origin are not Italicized